PROGRESS ON FAMILY PROBLEMS

PROGRESS ON FAMILY PROBLEMS

*A NATIONWIDE STUDY
OF CLIENTS' AND COUNSELORS' VIEWS
ON FAMILY AGENCY SERVICES*

by DOROTHY FAHS BECK
and MARY ANN JONES

FAMILY SERVICE ASSOCIATION OF AMERICA/NEW YORK

HU
43
.B36

8

Dedicated to
further improvement
in service to families

The following foundations have contributed
toward the support of this research:

Prospect Hill Foundation

Ittleson Family Foundation

New York Community Trust
(Mildred Anna Williams Fund)

van Ameringen Foundation

Shell Companies Foundation

Acknowledgments

This report is the product of the cooperation of many. The willingness of four-fifths of the membership to report their services under a common plan made possible the collection of the large and rich pool of data that provides the foundation of this report. The contribution of each participating agency included the local launching and administration of the study, the submission of extensive staff reports on all cases applying during the sample week, and the carrying out of the time-consuming follow-up of their clients. These complex and demanding tasks were accomplished largely at their own expense and with the help of countless staff members and volunteers. Project funds covered at best only the basic minimum of out-of-pocket extras and sometimes even these were contributed by the agencies involved. Without this level of commitment and the willingness of agencies to invest their own time and funds in this joint effort, this type of nationwide study would never have been achieved.

A major contributor to the idea phase of the project was the FSAA Research Advisory Committee. Under the able chairmanship of Professor David Fanshel, of the Columbia University School of Social Work, this committee provided useful guidance and support in the planning and implementing of the study. Agency representatives on this committee also helped with the pretesting of the schedules and proposed important refinements. In addition to his role as committee chairman, Professor Fanshel gave valuable counsel and warm support at critical points throughout the project and helped in arranging needed computer and technical resources. The authors are deeply grateful for his help and leadership in support of the project.

Many others, who can not be mentioned individually, also contributed ideas that helped to enrich the end product. Those who shared their ideas generously with staff in the planning stage, including members of the Research Advisory Committee, represented a wide range of professional experience. Among them were academic and community council researchers, agency executives and professional service directors, the staff of FSAA and other national organizations, and minority group representatives. Special acknowledgment is due the Black Caucus of FSAA for the many suggestions made by their research committee and their leaders generally about schedule content and data collection procedures. Their contributions served to broaden the perspective of the project.

The authors are also greatly indebted to Professor Eugene B. Shinn, of the Columbia University School of Social Work, who served as consultant throughout the analysis phase of the project. Professor Shinn introduced project staff to the complexities of computer programming, provided continuing consultation in this area, and made a number of helpful suggestions in regard to the statistical analysis in general.

Additional help in solving feasibility problems encountered in the computer processing was provided by Carlos Stecher, of the staff of the Columbia University Child Welfare Research Program. The authors wish to express appreciation for his help in facilitating this phase of the analysis. The authors are also indebted to the Child Welfare League of America for access, as needed throughout the project, to their card-counting sorter.

Another type of contribution was made by faculty and students in two schools of social work, who prepared two supplementary reports. Dr. Edmund A. Sherman, of the Child Welfare League of America and the Hunter College School of Social Work, supervised the analysis of the phone study returns by twelve graduate students as a group research project. Charlotte Tileston, while a student at George Warren Brown School of Social Work of Washington University, analyzed the returns from the family life education meetings during the sample week, with the help and guidance of Professor William Gordon. Without this added volunteer investment, these two reports would not have been possible.

Charlotte Tileston, along with Alvin Wasserman, also served on the project staff over a prolonged period. Both helped with coding, analysis of computer returns, and checking of the final text and charts. Charlotte Tileston also assisted with the programming of the computer runs. Their thoughtful, conscientious attention to details and their many helpful suggestions contributed substantially to the quality of the final product. Dena Domenicali also provided coding assistance during much of the project, including work in several specialized areas. Many others who can not be acknowledged individually also assisted for shorter periods with essential coding and clerical tasks. The authors wish to express their appreciation for the energy, enthusiasm, care, and competence that all of these staff members invested in the processing of the enormous amount of data involved.

Other FSAA staff have also carried important functions related to the project. Colleagues and administration have provided an atmosphere of consistent support and encouragement. Bonnee Waldstein and Joyce V. Hansen deserve special mention for the many essential secretarial services they performed willingly and competently and for their responsible monitoring of the follow-up process. Bonnee Waldstein also assisted with the statistical analysis and prepared most of the preliminary sketches of the charts for the artist. Edith H. Nolder and Jennifer Villiger carried responsibility for the editorial and production aspects of the final report and facilitated in every way possible its early release. The final artwork was produced under the direction of F. W. Taylor, of Northport, New York.

The mounting of a study of this magnitude was made feasible by generous contributions over three years from four foundations—the Prospect Hill Foundation, the Ittleson Family Foundation, the New York Community Trust (from the Mildred Anna Williams Fund), and the van Ameringen Foundation. Publication of the final report was supported in part by the Shell Companies Foundation of Houston, Texas.

The support of all contributors is warmly acknowledged not only by the authors, but also by FSAA as a whole. Without the combined contribution of these five foundations, a study of the scope, magnitude, and complexity of the present project would not have been financially feasible.

CONTENTS

PROGRESS ON FAMILY PROBLEMS

INTRODUCTION

THE FINDINGS IN PERSPECTIVE

For family agencies, the period since 1960 has been one of stimulus, challenge, and innovation. New community concerns and needs, a new awareness of old problems, and new sources of funding together provided the stimulus. Widespread questioning of program relevance and effectiveness presented the challenge.[1] Innovation—many-sided and fast-moving—was the response. Agencies in substantial numbers shifted their focus, their target populations, the location of their offices, their methods of case-finding, the settings in which they work, the nature and timing of their contacts with clients —even their goals. Outreach to the disadvantaged, concern for minorities, and advocacy for institutional change all received new emphasis. The atmosphere of experimentation also extended to include new patterns of staffing, decision-making, interagency collaboration, and funding.[2]

As this dynamic decade approached an end, agency staffs and boards, both local and national, became increasingly eager for some broad assessment of their progress. How far had they come in meeting the challenge? Had their brave experiments actually resulted in reaching a higher proportion of the disadvantaged? Were their services more relevant? Were their clients actually achieving progress on family problems? Where should agencies be moving in the years ahead?

Stimulated by this climate of concern, the Family Service Association of America initiated in 1970 a major stock-taking effort.

The present study is the result. To an unusual degree it represents a joint product. Its successful completion has required a sustained cooperative investment by both FSAA and four-fifths of its Member Agencies. In the present report, the findings are returned to the contributors for utilization in a continuing process of renewal, growth, and change.

The study plan

A central goal throughout has been to achieve a broad perspective. By intent, the study's dimensions are three-directional. It looks back on what was, inward and around to what is, and forward to what should be. An earlier study in 1960[3] provided a baseline for trends. A dual perspective on the present was obtained from counselors and clients. Placement of the findings in the context of the country as a whole was facilitated by the timing of the initial data collection to coincide with the 1970 federal census.

Although the feasibility of a nationwide study of agency caseloads had been demonstrated in the 1960 study, the changed circumstances of 1970 required an enlarged and modified approach. Planning for outreach in relation to the needs of inner city families required a larger sample, revised problem categories, a broader program coverage, more attention to environmental problems, modification of data-gathering methods to accommodate to new types of services, maximum use of the new computer technology, and most of all some direct feedback from those served. To this end, the sampling period was expanded from the one-day pattern of 1960 to an entire week. All types of agency programs were included,

provided they involved direct, in-person contact with an identified client. All Member Agencies in both the United States and Canada were invited to participate. Actually, 273, or 81 percent of the total membership, did report their intake for one week in the late spring of 1970. This excellent participation rate yielded a United States sample of 3,596 cases from 266 agencies, which provides the data for this report, plus a Canadian sample of 150 cases from seven Canadian agencies, which was reported on separately.[4] To the maximum extent feasible, these cases were followed to closing or for two years. Closing reports were obtained on 94 percent of the sample and follow-up reports either by interview or mail questionnaire for 53 percent of the total. The result is by far the largest pool of client responses ever available on family agency service.

This exceptionally large and diverse sample represents the merging of a wide range of types of clients, agencies, programs, and communities. Naturally, therefore, the results reflect average practice by an unselected group of practitioners and agencies—not practice limited to the most skilled practitioners in the most adequately administered and funded agencies. This large-scale, unselected sample contributed by many agencies has four major advantages: It provides a national perspective. It permits comparisons with the general population. It facilitates the assessment of trends. And finally, it can be subdivided in many ways by type of client and type of service without eroding the sample size to the point where conclusions become meaningless.

Necessarily, this type of design also entails constraints. Reporting requirements had to

be limited to easily identifiable categories. Consideration of intangible aspects of diagnosis and treatment had to be foregone. Monitoring of data collection had to be by mail only. Agencies could not be asked to modify their normal service patterns to accommodate to random assignment of cases either to different treatment approaches or to a no-service control group. (Fortunately, with the help of advanced computer facilities, it was possible to minimize some of these handicaps by heavy use of statistical controls, plus several composite indices.) Moreover, certain agency functions had to be omitted because they did not fit the study reporting format. Services not covered include consultation to and training of other professional persons in the community, help with community planning and with community and neighborhood development, encouragement of institutional change, and research.

The report format

While the results necessarily leave some key questions unanswered, they do provide data on a wide range of questions: Who are the users of family service? What problems do they bring? What services do they ask for and receive? Why do they terminate? What are their views about the services provided? To what extent do they make progress in coping with their problems as a result of service? How do outcomes differ in relation to client characteristics? In relation to service input? A series of eleven sections, illustrated by more than one hundred charts, sheds light on these issues. Each chart is accompanied by an explanation, plus some brief commentary on the implications. Each chart with its comments is sufficiently independent of the others to permit the reader to browse among them at will, guided by his own interests.

This overview does not attempt a simple summary. Rather, it presents from among the many findings those with clear implications for agency policy. Findings of this type are presented in relation to six central issues: Whom should agencies serve? How should current programs be modified to maximize their relevance and effectiveness? To what extent does family agency service actually help families achieve progress in coping with their problems? What are the implications of the findings for practice? What are the implications of the findings for local agency evaluation efforts? And finally, how do the outcome findings compare with those of other studies, and how can the differences be explained? The following sections review the clues from the findings on each of these issues.

Clientele served

Viewed in the perspective of the decade, young families with an above-average number of children continued in 1970 as in 1960 to be the major users of family service. Within this group, the number of families broken by divorce or separation not only was disproportionately high, but also showed a clear increase over 1960, particularly in single-parent families headed by a woman. The consequence was a correspondingly high proportion of children in the client group who were living with only one parent or with none. For families disrupted by marital conflict, family service agencies are clearly an important part of the network of family supports available to them.

Another major change in the decade has involved a shift in clientele away from families with preadolescent children toward those with adolescent children. Secondary shifts include further concentration of agency clients in the major metropolitan areas and an increase in the proportion of Catholic clients, resulting in a more representative clientele from the point of view of religious preference.

In racial and ethnic origin, the clientele of agencies changed little between 1960 and 1970. Black clients continued to be represented in nearly twice their proportion in the general population. At the same time, such other minorities as persons of Spanish origin and American Indians and Orientals continued to be grossly underrepresented.

With regard to the indicators of socioeconomic status, agency clients were substantially below the general population with respect to family income and also below the income levels that would normally be expected in relation to their educational and occupational characteristics. Consistent with this pattern, clients were high in the percentage of unemployed, in the proportion below the federally defined poverty level, and in the proportion receiving public assistance—principally Aid for Families with Dependent Children. On the other hand, agency clients were approximately similar to the general population in average occupational status and even slightly above the general population in educational level. In combination, these facts suggest that status discrepancy may be one source of strain for agency families.

Assessed in relation to a 1960 baseline, there has been a noticeable downward shift in the socioeconomic characteristics of the client group relative to the general population. This was evident both on the composite socioeconomic index and also on two of the three separate components of this index (education and income). Although agency clients and the general population both gained in income and education levels, agency clients lagged in their *rate* of gain, thus shifting their relative status downward. These findings undoubtedly reflect the results of agency outreach efforts and the extensive program innovations during the decade. They run counter to the trends that would have been anticipated from the comments of certain critics of the field. For example, Professor Richard Cloward asserted in the early 1960s that there had been "a general disengagement from the poor by private social agencies" and that the "private agency . . . now exists chiefly to serve middle-class people."[5] Similarly, Herman Levin predicted in 1963 that "the voluntary family and children's service agency is heading for a future of progressive specialization and that this specialization will lead to an increasingly refined casework service offered to people of increasingly higher income levels."[6] This prediction is definitely not borne out by the trends in family agency service in the decade of the sixties. The movement has been clearly in the opposite direction.

On the other hand, the major gaps in services noted in 1960 have persisted with only minimal change. These gaps include gross underrepresentation of persons aged fifty-five and over, persons of Spanish origin, nonwhite groups other than black, and families living in small towns and rural areas. Persons not living in family units are even more underrepresented than in 1960. Included among the nonfamily persons being missed are young people in the premarital stage, single and widowed of all ages living apart from their families, and those choosing to experiment with new life-styles that bypass marriage.[7] Faced with this great range of unmet needs, agencies face difficult issues of priorities in the use of their chronically limited resources.

The clientele of agencies can also be identified in terms of the problems they bring. In the main, clients come with multiple and relatively severe problems. These tend to be concentrated in the area of internal family relationship and individual personality problems. Marital problems were consistently the highest category, followed closely by children's problems. About one problem in four involved the interaction of family members with the wider world of work, school, money, housing, or leisure. In 5 percent of the cases, some major social or behavioral problem was primary, such as delinquency, alcoholism, mental illness, or drug abuse. Most clients, particularly those at the lower socioeconomic status levels, also reported multiple environmental problems that were seriously affecting the welfare of their families.

A major focus on marital and children's problems is another characteristic of agency caseloads that has remained stable over the decade of the sixties. The major increase was in the problems of adolescents—problems related to their personality adjustment, their educational or vocational activities, or their use of leisure time. These increases suggest a growing parental concern with intergenerational problems—no doubt stimulated by parent-child conflict over a whole new range of life-style issues—hair, music, dress, sex, drugs, work, religion, and authority. The major declines were of quite a different order. These mainly involved fewer applications related to mental illness and economic and employment problems—shifts that probably mirror the development of alternative community resources, such as community mental health centers, vocational services, and expanded income support programs.

Analysis of presenting problems by socioeconomic status and stage of the family life cycle revealed major variations. Family relationship and individual adjustment problems declined by socioeconomic status but remained dominant at all levels except the lowest. In contrast, problems related to income, housing, unemployment, and other environmental problems increased markedly, overtaking family and personal problems at the lowest level. By stages of the family life cycle, marital problems peaked early; children's problems, when the children reached adolescence; and practical problems, in the final stages of the family life cycle.

The decision of agencies about whom they will serve determines the types of problems with which they must wrestle and what practical services they will need to provide or arrange. The need for tangible services tends to be characteristic of the economically disadvantaged and the aged; thus, outreach to these groups requires corresponding program adaptations. On the other hand, the need for help with relationship problems appears to be essentially universal. Moreover, there is also little evidence of major socioeconomic differences in outcomes that might help an agency make the hard decisions about which population group should receive priority.

Probably agencies are currently best prepared to serve the groups they are now serving—principally young parents with children. However, they do not appear to be fully utilizing the preventive potential that is theirs by reason of their in-depth understanding of the sources of marital conflict. For example, they are not reaching young people in any substantial numbers at the point when they are choosing their future partners, or when they are struggling with the early marital adjustment process. There are few requests for premarital counseling, and the average number of years married for the present sample was twelve. Agencies apparently are not thought of as a resource at these critical early transition points.

While the need for some increased investment in preventive services seems clear, certain issues of feasibility remain unclear. For example, how can agencies reach the small towns and rural areas? How can they help the larger communities cope with the increase in such major social and behavioral problems as delinquency, drug abuse, crime, and alcoholism? Mounting of major programs either in the rural areas or in the inner city would seem to require much greater resources than are now available to agencies. In the case of the central city, a cooperative approach to the renewal and revitalization of total neighborhoods would also be needed. The optimum role for family agencies in such efforts remains unclear. Certainly advocacy is one component—including the documentation through case illustrations of the concrete human needs and problems of those involved.

Program patterns

Closely related to the issue of who should be served is that of what services should be provided. Currently, agency services concentrate heavily on counseling related to family relationship and individual personality problems, particularly marital and children's problems. In terms of interview time, about three-fourths of agency time is concentrated on therapeutic efforts with cases having these problems as their major focus. A second important function is referral. In this area, agencies serve a social brokerage role. They provide referral both through direct contacts and by phone, often in conjunction with other consultation and the provision of information about community resources. These services are supplemented by a variety of other services and tangible aids designed to help clients cope with financial, legal, and environmental problems and to meet their needs for homemaker service, day care, other caretaking services, adoption, mental health services, family life education, and advocacy.

Since clients tend to seek out those agencies that can help them with their most urgent problems, an agency can in large measure select its clientele by the types of services it offers and by how it interprets these services to the community. Lower-status clients and minorities faced with multiple environmental problems are unlikely to come in substantial numbers to an agency that provides few practical services, no caretaking, and little assistance with financial, legal, housing, and environmental problems. On the other hand, multiservice centers and other special projects, specialized services for the aging, and Travelers Aid and legal aid departments tend to focus on service to clients from the lower socioeconomic levels. Adoption services and family life education are utilized mainly by families from the upper- and middle-status groups. Provision of service to the aging requires a special program repertoire that includes a variety of caretaking and protective services, plus friendly visiting and escort services.

Agencies can also influence whom they serve by the sources of referral they cultivate. Families coming on referral from churches and those reached through the mass media and telephone directory tended on the average to be upper- and middle-status clients, whereas those reached through referral from business, industry, and labor unions and through public and private social agencies were in the main from the lower socioeconomic levels. Even the place of the first interview has implications for the clientele that will be served. Agencies seeking to reach the disadvantaged should be in a position to see clients who drop in without appointments and those who need to be seen in their homes. They must also be prepared to take the initiative in recruitment. In fact, every agency program or policy decision influences who will or will not be served. Clarity in regard to agency goals is therefore essential.

Service trends since 1960 reflect the same shift toward a greater investment in service to the disadvantaged that was noted earlier in relation to the type of clients served. Particularly noteworthy was the virtual elimination within a decade of the differential in number of interviews by socioeconomic status and the great reduction in racial differences in interview counts. Comparison of 1960 and 1970 data indicate that this change was accomplished by a marked reduction in long-term service for upper- and upper-middle-status clients and by a sharp increase in the number of interviews provided at the lower socioeconomic status levels. Trends of benefit to the disadvantaged were also evident in the increase in the number of interviews provided in relation to all practical types of problems for which trend data could be secured. Outcome findings further confirmed that lower socioeconomic status is not in itself predictive of outcomes when other factors are held constant. Clients at all levels showed a positive response to counseling and to family agency service in general. These findings run counter to the assertion that counseling and family agency service generally are primarily suitable for middle- and upper-status clients.[8]

Other documented gains since 1960 include: (1) a decrease in the proportion of one-interview cases; (2) involvement of more family members in treatment; (3) more frequent involvement of the husband in the first interview and in treatment generally; (4) a substantial decrease in the length of time clients are kept on the waiting list; (5) a reduction in applications for financial assistance that agencies can not provide; (6) a decline in referrals elsewhere because the service needed was not available at the agency, and (7) an increase in the use of group treatment. Internal evidence from the present study indicates that changes of these types were in the best interest of clients.

Other modifications of service to accommodate to the problems of the urban poor and minorities were too new to be assessed on a trend basis, but their existence at the end of the decade is documented in the present study. These include multiservice centers, a wide variety of special projects, agency initiative in the recruitment of clients in hard-to-reach neighborhoods, and the inclusion of advocacy as part of the services available to clients.[9] These many modifications of agency service programs attest to the desire of agency leaders to adjust their programs to the needs of the disadvantaged and their flexibility in doing so. On the other hand, the findings on the influence of environmental problems and external factors on outcomes underscore the relevance to the needs of clients of additional agency initiatives at the neighborhood, community, and national level. Expansion of services directed to modifying the environment is a necessary complement to the service provided by agencies at the individual and family level.

That further changes in agency programs are needed is also evident from the fact that about half the complaints reported by clients related to agency procedures such as fees, waiting time, office hours, office location, and the like or to unmet needs or gaps in the availability of service. Several indicators also pointed to problems in the provision of service to lower-middle-class black families and to some unidentified strains reflected in a disproportionate number of early closings and closings on counselor initiative at the lowest socioeconomic level. Nevertheless, in spite of these evidences of problems in selected areas, about four out of five clients reported that the services of agencies were "helpful" or "very helpful."

In regard to type of service, direct services received the most positive evaluations, and referral services the fewest, while counseling services took an intermediate position. The fact that about one-third of the clients referred did not follow through on their referral also indicates problems in this area. Advance contact by the counselor with the resource to which a client is referred was found to increase significantly the proportion of clients who follow through on a referral. This is an area in which agencies, by a simple modification of procedure, can greatly increase their effectiveness.

Overall outcomes

In addition to looking at the clientele and services of family agencies, some examination of outcomes seemed essential. Two criterion measures were used. The first was the traditional global rating. The second involved a new approach developed especially for the project—a change score based on a composite of ratings by counselors or clients in several component areas. Only the second approach requires further explanation.

The change score was designed to provide a simple but highly sensitive measure that would be usable in a nationwide study. In this modestly financed project involving widely scattered and numerous participating agencies, it was manifestly impractical to employ special research interviewers or trained raters or to conduct psychological tests at the beginning and end of treatment. Likewise, it was not practical to seek verification of changes from outside observers or from official records. The change score, therefore, represents change as perceived by those closest to the treatment process—the client and the counselor. Its components cover changes in four areas: in the problems specific to the case, in problem-coping generally, in aspects of family relationships that presented problems, and in individual family members.

These components were selected on the premise that the principal function of casework counseling is helping clients cope more adequately with their problems.[10] Since most treatment in family agency settings involves a time-limited and partialized approach to problems, it did not seem realistic to define the goals more broadly in terms of improvement in total family functioning or enduring personality change. Instead, multiple, small, interrelated changes specific to the particular problems that receive attention were considered the essence of change in casework.[11] This, therefore, is what the change score was designed to capture.

To obtain this type of score, participants were asked for a series of simple judgments of improvement, no change, or deterioration in multiple areas. They were expected to use all evidence available to them, both tangible and intangible, and to rate the direction of change on the basis of their own value judgments. The total score which summarizes these ratings reflects scope rather than amount of change. Areas or types of problems that were not a problem for a particular client were not included in the final score for that client. Neither was credit given for prevention of deterioration, although maintenance of current levels is sometimes the most that service can accomplish and is of definite benefit.

In actual practice, counselors' scores turned out to be based on an average of sixteen evaluations; clients' scores, on seventeen. The validity of the score rests on a combination of the face validity of the component items, plus the internal consistency of the total scores with the separate global ratings of the same respondents and with other factors normally assumed to be related to outcomes. Final scores showed a relatively high correlation with global evaluations by the same party,[12] but were considerably more revealing than the global evaluations in the analysis of specific treatment issues.

In the main, these two outcome measures, the global evaluation and the change score, yielded a balance of evaluations strongly on the positive side. Clients in the follow-up sample reported global ratings of "much better" considerably more often than did their counselors (32 versus 17 percent). Counselors tended to select the more modest evaluation of "somewhat better." When the two improvement levels were combined, about seven in ten of both counselors' and clients' global evaluations for this group reflected improvement. "No change" reports were also about equally frequent from both parties—25 percent from counselors and 24 percent from clients. Reports of deterioration were infrequent, but were higher from clients than from counselors—6 percent versus 4 percent. Agreement between counselors and clients was high on the overall percentage of cases improved, but much lower when comparisons were made on a case-by-case basis.

The change scores provided further confirming evidence of the prevailingly positive direction of change during treatment. For counselors' scores, positive scores outnumbered negative ones in the ratio of twenty-nine to one; for clients' scores, the ratio was eleven to one. Viewed in terms of averages,

clients' scores were again higher than those from counselors—+5.0 versus +4.8 for the same cases. Again, clients were more extreme in their ratings than were counselors, both on the positive side and on the negative. Again, there was considerably more disagreement between counselors and clients on the scores for individual clients than on the general averages.

The component evaluations that entered into the computation of the scores likewise were strongly positive in direction. The highest proportion of positive ratings was found for changes in specific problems and changes in problem-coping—findings consistent with the problem focus of most counseling in family agency settings. Differences between counselors and clients were greatest for changes in family relationships and for improvement in individual family members. In both areas, improvement ratings were more frequent from clients than from counselors, probably because clients were better informed about what was going on within the family on a day-to-day basis.

To what extent can these positive outcome findings be attributed to the services provided by the agency? To what extent do they reflect merely a bias in the follow-up sample, the influence of external circumstances, or spontaneous recovery from crises? Since agencies were not asked to deny service in order to provide a control group, it is not possible to be sure. Nevertheless, various internal analyses of the data provide considerable clarification on these issues.

To begin with, could limitation of the reported outcomes to the follow-up sample explain the strong positive balance in the evaluations cited? To answer this question,

client change scores missing because of the lack of a follow-up report were estimated from the relationship between counselors' and clients' change scores, when both did exist. When these estimates were substituted for missing clients' scores, clients' ratings for all cases having a counselor's score averaged +4.8 (instead of the +5.0 figure for the follow-up group only); corresponding counselors' scores averaged +4.3 (instead of the +4.8 figure for the follow-up group). Thus, although there was a distinct upward bias in the follow-up sample, the average was still strongly positive when this bias was corrected.

To clarify further the sources of the gains reported, at the time of follow-up, clients were asked directly for their opinion about the helpfulness of agency service, the principal reason for the changes they reported, and the influence of external factors on these changes. Eighty percent of the clients contacted reported that agency service was "helpful" or "very helpful." The main reasons clients cited for the changes noted were also consistent with the interpretation that agency service was the primary source of the gains reported.

In assessing the influence of external factors, it was fortunate that a substantial group of clients—943 cases in all—indicated no external factors influencing the changes reported. When the analysis was limited to this group, 35 percent reported their total situation as "much better" following agency service and another 39 percent of the same group reported that it was "somewhat better." In combination, a total of 74 percent of those for whom no external influences were reported saw their total problem situation as improved. This same group showed average change scores of +5.1 for clients' reports and +4.9 for counselors' reports. Thus, when the analysis was limited to cases reporting no external influences affecting the outcomes reported, the overall positive findings remained essentially unchanged. External factors, therefore, were not perceived by at least half the clients as accounting even partially for the positive changes reported.

Finally, what about spontaneous recovery from crises as the explanation of the highly positive outcomes? This interpretation was tested by comparing cases receiving extensive service with those receiving only minimum service, the thought being that minimum service cases would provide the nearest available approximation of the results to be expected from spontaneous recovery. These comparisons represent an imperfect test since even these minimum groups received some service such as referral, legal advice, temporary financial assistance, or at least an opportunity to be heard, plus some review and assessment of their problems. Nevertheless, these minimal service groups provide the best test available under the circumstances of what would have happened without treatment.

Fortunately, it proved feasible to identify six types of minimum service comparison groups: (1) cases receiving only one interview; (2) cases receiving other services but not counseling; (3) cases receiving counseling in only one problem area; (4) cases in which only one family member was seen; (5) cases involving married couples in which only one spouse was seen; and (6) cases terminated by referral because the service they needed was not available at the agency.

(See section 9 for details.)[13] Because these minimum service groups were not based on random assignment, a correction process was devised to discount for the differences in the types of cases in the various subgroups. This relatively new procedure involved computing for each case an individual "predicted score" that would reflect the average outcomes for all cases with similar characteristics in the follow-up sample. Outcomes for each subgroup were then assessed on the basis of whether actual scores were significantly above or below these predicted scores.[14]

In combination, these six comparison groups provide convincing evidence that outcomes vary consistently, substantially, and significantly in relation to the amount and type of service input. For counselors' scores, the difference from the predicted scores on all these dimensions varied in the expected direction and at a statistically significant level in relation to the amount of service input. In addition, counselors' scores for all minimum service comparison groups were significantly below their corresponding predicted levels. In contrast, cases in the maximum service category for each dimension were significantly above predicted levels. Clients' change scores also showed similar patterns on these same dimensions, but here differences did not always reach statistical significance, usually because clients receiving only brief service tended to give surprisingly favorable reports of change.

Although this pattern of favorable changes following short contact suggests that normal recovery processes probably were also a factor, neither these explanations nor chance can account for the consistent association of outcomes with the *amount* of service provided. If spontaneous recovery were the principal explanation, outcome levels should be approximately equal for all subgroups rather than markedly associated with service input. Moreover, use of deviations from predicted outcomes in making these assessments essentially rules out the explanation that the differences by amount of service could be accounted for by the types of cases involved. Therefore, the only logical explanation for the consistent variation in the change scores in relation to the level of service investment made by the agency is that, in the main, the improvement reflected the results of agency service.[15]

Findings with implications for practice

Although the issue of effectiveness that has been dealt with thus far is of overriding importance for the field as a whole, for practitioners, knowledge of the factors associated with good and poor outcomes can contribute infinitely more to the improvement of service. Of the findings with specific implications for practice, probably the most important in the present study is that of the marked association of the counselor-client relationship with outcomes. With minor exceptions for clients' scores, this factor was found to be twice as powerful as a predictor of outcomes as any other client or service characteristic covered by the study and more *powerful* than all client characteristics combined. An unsatisfactory relationship was found to be highly associated with client-initiated disengagement and with negative explanations by the client of his reason for terminating.

Fortunately, clients were usually satisfied with the relationship with their counselor. In fact, 57 percent reported that they were "very satisfied" with this relationship; another 27 percent, that they were "satisfied"; and only 8 percent that they were "dissatisfied." Outcomes for this last group were among the least satisfactory for any subgroup in the entire study.

Although this intangible relationship is not easy to study, it nevertheless deserves much more attention in casework research than it has yet received.[16] Questions which need to be pursued in depth include: What specific aspects of this relationship are crucial and why? How can practitioners be helped to improve their relationships with their clients? What are the implications of these findings for recruitment to the profession?

Counselor-client disagreement is a second factor closely related to outcomes. Since study schedules posed many questions in parallel form to both counselors and clients, it was possible to compare the perceptions of the two parties on many dimensions and to use the findings to construct a disagreement index. The resulting scores reflected not active arguments, but simply how the two parties to the relationship reported the same items. Defined in these comprehensive terms, disagreement was surprisingly pervasive—in the definition of what the problem was, the kind of help needed, the treatment approach that was appropriate, the level of satisfaction in the counselor-client relationship, the reason for termination, and the evaluation of outcomes.

On the average, counselors and clients differed on four out of eleven items included in the index. Although many of these differences considered separately were probably of little importance, on a cumulative basis, disagreement proved to have a significant association with counselors' outcome scores second only in predictive power to the counselor-client relationship itself. High disagreement scores were also significantly associated with clients' outcome scores, with an unsatisfactory counselor-client relationship, and with a high rate of client-initiated disengagement, but were only minimally associated with socioeconomic status. Although disagreement is not primarily a matter of sociocultural differences between counselors and clients, its true sources remain elusive.[17] Casework would benefit from an intensive exploration of these sociocultural differences and how they can best be handled.

Confirmation of the value of a family approach to treatment was another major finding of significance for practice. Change scores increased when both marital partners or more family members generally were seen. Improvement was higher for husbands when either family interviews or husband-wife interviews were used as the primary modality rather than individual interviews. In general, persons seen improved more frequently than persons not seen. These patterns prevailed not only for husbands and wives but also for children. Findings in all these areas were stronger on counselors' than on clients' reports. Clients' reports, although also slightly favoring husband-wife or family interviews as opposed to an individual interview approach, gave particularly strong support to group treatment.

Clients' reports also gave modest support to planned, short-term treatment. On many dimensions their ratings showed a consistent but slight and usually not statistically significant differential in favor of a planned, time-limited approach, particularly for husbands. Counselors' scores, on the other hand, showed no appreciable overall differential in favor of either planned short-term or long-term service. Thus, when the savings in terms of interview time (nine versus thirteen interviews on the average) are taken into account, the planned, short-term approach appears to be the more cost-effective whenever it is feasible. Findings on scores by number of interviews also suggest a similar conclusion since the increment added to the average scores lessened as number of interviews increased, particularly beyond fifteen interviews. These findings are not to be understood as favoring an automatic cut-off point for service. Exceptionally good results were reported for cases that began on a planned, short-term basis but were later continued beyond fifteen interviews. Likewise, much higher change scores were reported for clients who persisted until service was completed than for clients who for any reason terminated prematurely.

Analysis of client characteristics in relation to outcomes indicated that individualized information about clients and their problems was more closely related to outcomes than were clients' objective characteristics. For counselors' change scores, the indicators most closely associated with outcomes were the counselor's initial estimate of outcomes, the severity of the client's total problem situation, the relative difficulty of the type of principal problem involved, and the extent of the client's involvement in seeking help. Clients' change scores were also associated with these factors, but yielded an additional set of prognostic clues that included the direction of influence of external factors during the treatment period, the total number of environmental problems affecting the family, and the age of the family head. When other factors were statistically controlled, socioeconomic status, race, and family size were not predictive of outcomes.

When the principal concern was a marital or children's problem or an adult personality problem, the client's definition of the locus of the problem also provided a clue to outcomes. Clients who defined the locus of the problem as either within themselves or in a relationship in which they were personally involved achieved the highest outcome scores. The lowest scores for any problem group were reported for those who denied that they had any problem. Nevertheless, no category of clients or problems was identified for which change scores showed, on the average, no improvement or actual deterioration. This finding, coupled with the difficulty counselors had in making correct predictions of outcomes, suggests that use of presenting client and problem characteristics or intake judgments of probable outcomes to screen out cases not likely to benefit from agency service will result in denying service to many that can be helped.

Other findings of significance relate to the negative effects of delay in service. One clear finding in this area was that the longer the delay in recall from the waiting list, the less likely the client was to return when recalled. The findings on results also confirm the negative effects of delay in seeking help. Better outcomes were achieved, for example, with fewer interviews when the total problem situation was rated mild. When the

most important problem was a marital one, the amount of progress achieved declined with the duration of the marriage, particularly in the case of husbands. Progress on marital problems was also less, and the rate of client-initiated disengagement higher, when the application for help was delayed until after the couple had separated. These findings all point to the need to encourage the early and prompt use of agency service for emerging problems before they become chronic. They argue for reaching clients with problems at the earliest point that their motivation is sufficient for effective work.

Only limited data were available on the practice implications of the objective characteristics of the counselor. When the information on the sex and race of the counselor was analyzed in relation to outcomes, number of interviews, and client-initiated disengagement, the data were found to favor assignment to male counselors when the principal client was a man and to black counselors when the client was black.

Finally, comparison of counselors' and clients' reports on parallel items showed major differences in perspective. Counselors were less aware than clients of changes in the early interviews and of changes in family relationships generally, including changes in sexual relationships, and changes in family members not seen by the counselor. In addition, counselors tended to give higher outcome ratings than clients to changes in problems related to income, housing, employment, use of leisure time, and problem situations of the elderly. They were also less aware of environmental problems in general. These findings suggest that in the presence of heavy reality stresses, clients are

less likely than counselors to give positive reports on small, instrumental gains. On the other hand, clients appeared to be less aware than counselors of problems related to personality adjustment, mental illness, and child-rearing practices. They were also less likely to report perceptual gains related to the concept of the problem and possible solutions. In general, whenever either party held an extreme view, either positive or negative, about outcomes, the other tended toward a considerably more moderate position—a fact that suggests that the closest feasible approximation of the truth may be provided by some merging of the two perspectives. In any case, in spite of these many differences, there were relatively few areas in which the overall views of the two participants yielded different recommendations for practice.[18] These findings suggest that continued study of the opinions of both parties on the same situations and mutual in-person exploration of the sources of these differences would be a productive area for future research.[19]

Findings with implications for local agency evaluation

Experience with the present study supports the utility of the change score as a general measure of the outcomes of counseling service. It proved to be considerably more sensitive to the nuances of change than the global score, yielded a higher degree of agreement between counselors and clients, and gave seemingly appropriate answers to a wide variety of practice issues. Fortunately, given written instructions, it can be readily hand-computed. Although the length of the form and response time required has seemed to some to present a problem, clients proved willing to invest the time needed. For agencies, the potential gains seem to more than outweigh the additional investment required. For agencies wishing to focus on special subgroups, some additional outcome measures to take account of specific goals and problems for the group involved would increase the utility of the inquiry.

The findings of the present study also suggest that clients are an indispensable resource for the assessment of service outcomes. Not only do they know considerably more than their counselors about the total range of changes that have occurred, but they also evaluate these changes from their own rather than the agency's perspective. Moreover, since counselors receive little, if any, feedback about changes in brief service cases, client evaluation is particularly important in such instances. In the present study, clients reported considerably more change after one, two, or three interviews than did counselors, while counselors described their ratings for the majority of such cases as based on "very little evidence." In view of the fact that 56 percent of all clients receive three interviews or less, loss of adequate information on such cases would leave agency service evaluations grossly incomplete.

Clients also have other assets as reporters of change. Clearly, they are a better resource than counselors for information on changes in family members not seen by the counselor, changes in problems or family relationships not directly discussed, and the influence of factors other than agency service. They are also the best reporters of their

decisions, actions, response to referrals, use of community resources, and internal feelings about their problems. They are the only ones who can report on their expectations, their reactions to service and agency policy, their unmet needs, and their relationship with the counselor. In addition, clients can provide a useful correction for bias stemming from the counselor's personal self-interest and his professional preferences.

There are also negatives involved in the use of clients as informants. Some do not respond or can not be located. Some are handicapped as reporters by education, language, or emotional barriers. Their diagnostic understanding is limited. Their classification of problems and their reports of service received are imprecise. They are often unaware of subtle perceptual changes or tend to forget them. They may not give due credit for gains in the intermediate steps in problem-solving. Their ratings are probably affected by day-to-day fluctuations in their moods and circumstances. Nevertheless, they remain the consumers of agency service. It is the progress that they make on their family problems that gives meaning to the entire service program of the agency. Therefore, if one had to choose between clients and counselors as reporters of change, present findings would favor reliance on clients.

Fortunately, client follow-up proved not only productive but feasible. In the main, clients were interested and cooperative and seldom complained about the follow-up process or refused to be seen. The major problem was in locating them. Agencies were ingenious about reducing costs. Students, agency staff, volunteers, and board members

all were recruited as interviewers and all proved interested in, and equal to, the task. Agencies also learned to use a flexible mix of interviews in the home, in the office, and by phone, combined with mail questionnaires for those who had left the area. All approaches proved reasonably satisfactory. (For additional details, see the Appendix account of the follow-up experience.)

In the present study, national staff provided the forms and procedures, helped with the monitoring, analyzed the returns, and reported the findings. If client follow-up is to become feasible locally, most of these functions will have to be carried by local staff, preferably with some guidance from the national office. The task on this basis will become more difficult and more expensive. Nevertheless, the return can be great, not only for the interpretation of the agency to the community and funding bodies, but also in the stimulation of improvements in practice and agency decision-making.

For agencies that wish to move in this direction, four major cautions are in order: (1) The sample should be large enough to support sound conclusions; (2) the percentage of nonresponse should be minimized in every possible way and the remaining bias acknowledged and evaluated; (3) delay in follow-up should be avoided, since forgetting and extraneous developments may soon blur the role of agency service; and (4) costs should be realistically budgeted—including the preparation of an adequate report on the findings.

Further development of the approach requires exploration of the following topics, probably with the help of national leadership and outside funding: (1) the extent to which client responses can be validated against more complex and costly measures of outcomes[20]; (2) the degree to which reported gains are maintained over extended time periods; (3) the amount and nature of disagreement on outcomes between different family members; (4) the kinds of changes that occur in a comparable no-service control group, if one can be found[21]; (5) the sources of difference between counselors and clients on specific ratings; (6) the revisions needed to adapt the questionnaire to the various concrete services; and (7) whether the same clients report different evaluations when approached by mail and by personal interview. If questions of these types can be answered, and if client follow-up can be made operational locally, client follow-up studies undoubtedly can play an important part in the improvement of service.

The outcome findings in the perspective of other studies

In general, this report has not attempted to place the findings in the perspective of other studies. To have done so would have involved a major expansion of the text and a different format. In a few situations, brief reference has been made to findings of other studies. However, in the light of the prevailing controversy over the effectiveness of casework and the marked difference between the findings reported here and some that are commonly cited, comment on the sources of this discrepancy from the perspective of current findings seems indicated.

This discussion utilizes the two-category classification suggested by Steven Paul Segal for outcome research in social work:[22] research with populations of clients with psychologically based problems, usually involving clients motivated for treatment, and research on social problem populations, usually involving clients who are not motivated for treatment, at least initially. The former are characterized by absence of control groups and use of "soft data" criterion measures, principally ratings by the therapist. The latter usually involve control groups and behavioral criterion measures. Both the population and the research approach of the present study more nearly approximate the former, although many of the problems of the clients studied could not be said to be psychologically based.

For the studies of psychologically based problems, Segal reports an average overall improvement rate of 72 percent, with a range for specific studies from 47 to 92 percent.[23] These figures compare closely with the global ratings by counselors in the present study—66 percent improved when the total sample is taken into account, and 72 percent improved when ratings are limited to cases with a follow-up report.

Relatively few published studies provide client ratings, but those that do also reflect a generally positive client response.[24] Studies that permit close comparisons between counselors' and clients' views differ on whether clients' ratings on an overall basis are higher, lower, or about the same as those of counselors, and on the extent of case-by-case agreement. Ludwig L. Geismar, in his study, reported that client-worker pairs agreed on the direction of change in overall functioning in 86 percent and also showed relatively high levels of agreement in component areas.[25] The difference between his experience in this respect and the relatively low agreement found in the present study probably reflects the close and continuous contact that workers in his project had with their clients and their many visits to the home. The contrast suggests that the extent of counselor-client agreement is partly a function of the amount of information available to the counselor.

Segal, in presenting his summary of the literature, defines the 72 percent average improvement in these studies as no better than the "base line" figure reported by Hans J. Eysenck for the spontaneous remission rate for neurotics in the absence of treatment.[26] However, there is considerable reason to challenge this conclusion. Eysenck's reviews of psychiatric literature on which this assertion is based have been extensively criticized as "averaging of clusters of poor data to arrive at a nonexistent baseline."[27]

In a much more comprehensive review of 101 controlled-outcome studies in psychotherapy not involving institutional populations, Julian Meltzoff and Melvin Kornreich report that of the fifty-seven studies considered adequate enough for valid conclusions, "84 percent showed positive effects of psychotherapy that were statistically significant."[28] They summarized their conclusions as follows: "We have encountered no comprehensive review of controlled research on the effects of psychotherapy that has led convincingly to a conclusion in support of the null hypothesis [no change]. On the contrary, controlled research has been notably successful in demonstrating significantly more behavioral change in treated patients than in untreated controls. In general, the better the quality of the research, the more positive the results obtained."[29]

Thus, although the present study reports

nearly the same percentage of improvement as the average for other social work studies of the treatment of motivated clients with psychologically based problems, the grounds for assuming that this rate of improvement is no better than the normal spontaneous remission rate for the types of clients involved appear to be totally inadequate. The fact that this type of deduction finds little support in the findings of Metzoff and Kornreich is particularly convincing. However, in the absence of a classical type of control group, it is impossible to be sure.

When comparisons are made with the second group of studies—those involving formal control groups[30]—the contrast is marked. Not only are the present findings considerably more positive than those usually cited, but the ratio of positive to negative findings is much higher. In combination, the data give little support to Joel Fischer's reports of frequent deterioration as a result of casework.[31]

From present findings, it is clear that one factor contributing to the lack of positive findings in these controlled studies is the type of population involved. With several exceptions, the studies quoted in these reviews have been limited to one or more of the following types of subjects—delinquents or potential delinquents, public assistance recipients, or multiproblem families living in adverse inner city environments and facing deficits in essential basic supports. Each of these characteristics has been shown in the present study to be significantly associated with relatively low change scores.[32]

A second adverse influence on the results in these other studies stems from the use of cases that did not seek counseling on their own initiative. In the effort to secure equiva-lent control groups without denial of service, researchers have utilized the total population of a school, housing project, group work project, or public assistance caseload and only later have attempted to involve those selected for the treated group in the use of service. The result is inevitably a sample with low average motivation. Again, the present study has demonstrated that low client involvement in seeking service is significantly associated with low change scores.[33]

A third difficulty with some of the controlled studies commonly cited is their overriding concern to use "hard data" outcome measures. Their emphasis in this respect seems to ignore the nature of casework gains already cited, namely that they tend to be small, multiple, diverse, often intangible, and relevant to the problem receiving attention. To achieve their goal of objective criterion measures, some of the investigators selected types of outcomes possibly not achievable and in any case probably of greater concern to the wider community than to those receiving the service, as for example, a shift from public assistance to self-support or a reduction in delinquent behavior. Such goals often originate outside the client and may never be accepted by him as in his interest.[34] Other criterion measures involve items only marginally related to the services received except for a small proportion of the sample.

Another source of low outcomes is the selection of measures that assume goals that are unrealistic in relation to the service provided. The wide use in such studies of Geismar's scale for rating total family functioning is a case in point. Yet, Geismar himself, after completing a major study using his own scale, acknowledged its unrealistic aspects. In a concluding section, he commented: "Significant improvement in total social functioning and prevention of economic dependency not only strain the imagination of man but also make demands on many systems."[35] The present study has endeavored to define goals in a more circumscribed way—in terms of progress on the specific problems identified at intake, plus related effects involving spread to other family members.

Another problem about the outcome measures used in other studies is their insensitivity to small changes of the type to be expected from casework counseling. For example, the top item in Geismar's rating scale was "adequate." However, nearly half of the ratings of component areas (47 percent) for the families in his Family Life Improvement Project were already adequate-level ratings at the beginning of the experiment and, hence, had no chance to show improvement.[36] Moreover, on certain of the scales used in these studies, the typical change associated with treatment is less than one point.[37]

Also contributing to the insensitivity of rating procedures is the tendency of some investigators to rate all cases on the same items regardless of whether these items were germane to the problems that received attention. For problems infrequently encountered, this practice inevitably reduces almost to the vanishing point the possibility of demonstrating change. The present study purposefully avoided merging in total scores ratings of changes on nonexistent problems.

Two other findings of the present study suggest yet another aspect of these controlled studies that may have blurred the identification of the effects of treatment, namely the typically long period between the intake and the outcome assessments. In the present study, external factors were found to have a strong influence on clients' scores, even in the relatively short time spans involved. When the final assessment of outcomes is delayed for three years or more, as in some studies, the cumulative effect of external factors may well overwhelm and submerge the effects of treatment. This risk is further accentuated by the fact, also documented in the present study, that the incremental value of additional interviews tends to decline after the early interviews and reaches a peak, apparently in the thirty-to-fifty-interview range, beyond which point group averages do not increase, at least on the criterion measure used in this study. While this may result to some extent from the nature of the change score itself, the pattern is probably also inherent in the dynamics of crisis intervention. If the major gains from casework occur mainly in the first four months but are assessed only after thirty-six months or longer, much that is extraneous could have happened in the meantime to erase the gains or the memory of the gains.[38]

Present findings also throw into question the conclusions of studies of casework effectiveness based on comparisons of outcomes achieved by trained versus untrained workers. Given random case assignments, this procedure can test differences in outcomes utilizing staff with two levels of training—on-job training and academic training. It does not test the effectiveness of casework per se since casework can not be defined, as some have suggested, as "the service of professional caseworkers."[39] The fallacy involved is dramatically highlighted by present findings

showing the counselor-client relationship and counselor-client disagreement to be the two factors most predictive of outcomes—both aspects of the treatment interaction in which trained caseworkers clearly have no monopoly.

Still another reason for these repetitive no-difference findings of many controlled studies is their small sample size. It is a well-known statistical reality that unless true differences are very large, they can not be proved statistically significant with small samples. This constraint is especially limiting when the differences tested involve percentages rather than measurement data. Many of the findings reported in other studies would have been significantly in favor of casework if they had merely persisted at the same level in moderately larger samples. For this reason, the large sample available in the present study has been a major asset.

Two characteristics of the reviews of research on casework effectiveness also warrant comment. One of these involves the stringent requirements imposed on which studies qualify for inclusion. The requirements selected tend to reduce the pool of available evidence[40] and to confine it mainly to atypical client groups. Another characteristic is the tendency of reviewers to simplify their task by reducing complex studies to simple yes-no answers about casework effectiveness and, in so doing, to overlook many significant gains reported in selected areas.

Finally, few studies have addressed the issue that is central to the improvement of service: How much of what type of service, provided to what type of clients, results in what type of gains? It was the struggle with this issue and its implications for practice that revealed in the present study the close association between outcomes and the

amount of service provided. Further struggle with this issue represents the most fruitful approach available to the improvement of service effectiveness.

In summary, then, casework has been judged ineffective because of its inability to demonstrate statistically significant gains with types of cases unusually resistant to change and atypical of agency caseloads, using in many instances small-sample control group comparisons, inappropriate concepts of the nature of casework, and unrealistic and insensitive outcome measures. In spite of the obvious need to limit conclusions to the type of universe sampled, at least one reviewer concludes that professional casework "not only has . . . failed to demonstrate that it is effective, but lack of effectiveness appears to be the rule rather than the exception."[41] The present study not only demonstrates a consistent positive association between amount of service and improvement, but also cites evidence for alternative explanations for the findings of other studies. In so doing, it calls into question the inference that casework as a whole is "ineffective" and suggests that this is probably a wrong conclusion. Given the human needs that, as a result, may be left unserved, this may well be a tragic error. It is hoped that the present study will lend support to a more balanced view. If it has also provided useful clues for the further improvement of agency service, it will indeed have contributed in a double sense to *Progress on Family Problems*.

1
WHO COMES TO FAMILY AGENCIES?

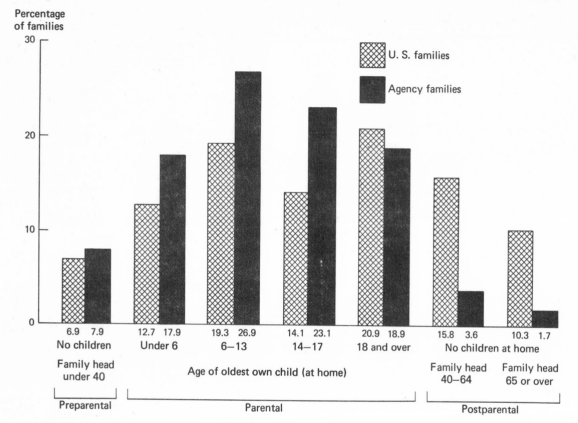

Characteristics of families

	Average				Percentage	
	Agency clients	U.S. population			Agency clients	U.S. population
Family size	4.3	3.6	Families with one or more children			
			Under 6		39.4	26.1
Number of own children			Under 18		79.8	54.9
Under 6	.6	.4				
Under 18	2.1	1.3	Doubled-up families		3.9	2.5

Young families with children are the heaviest users of family service. Families at all stages, from the preparental to the time the oldest child reaches eighteen, were proportionately more frequent in the clientele of agencies than in the general population.[1] These are the stages when applications tend to focus on marital and children's problems (see chart 23). Beginning with the time the oldest child reaches eighteen, the relative position of agencies and the general population is reversed. This is followed by a sharp drop-off in agency families in the empty-nest and post-retirement years.

This pattern of service focused principally on young families has changed little since 1960. The median age of the heads of the families was still the same as in 1960—thirty-eight years. Similarly, the median age of family heads in the country as a whole remained at forty-five years.[2] During the same period, families headed by an adult sixty-five or over dropped from 5 to 3 percent of the clientele of agencies while in the general population they continued at close to 14 percent.[3] The elderly tend to overlook family agencies as potential resources. Likewise, family agencies are not equipped to cope with the needs of this group.

Whatever the reason, the heavy focus of agencies on young families enables them to reach and influence homes with a higher than average number of children. Their exceptional opportunities to exert a constructive preventive influence on the country's future citizens are highlighted both in the chart and in the table below it.[4] ■

Chart 2

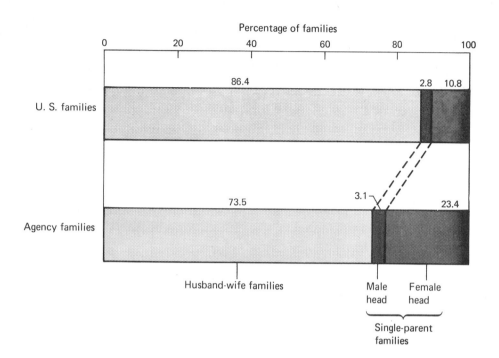

Percentage of families

U. S. families 86.4 2.8 10.8

Agency families 73.5 3.1 23.4

Husband-wife families

Male head | Female head

Single-parent families

Single-parent families are disproportionately heavy users of family service. Among sample families applying to agencies, 23 percent were headed by a woman as compared with only 11 percent of families in the general population.[5] Applicants from single-parent families headed by a man were much less frequent—3 percent for both agency and U.S. families. Only 74 percent of agency families were intact as compared with 86 percent of U.S. families.

During the 1960-70 decade, single-parent families increased out of proportion to other groups as users of family service. For agencies reporting in both years, the proportion of agency families headed by a woman increased from 19.4 to 23.4 percent, while the corresponding increase for the general population was only from 9.3 to 10.8. During the same decade, broken families headed by a man increased from 2.1 to 3.5 percent of agency families, whereas this group in the general population changed little (from 2.9 to 2.8 percent).[6]

During this same period there was a compensating downward shift in the proportion of intact families served by agencies (from 78.5 in 1960 to 73.0 in 1970), while for the general population, there was only a minor change (from 87.8 to 86.4 percent). Clearly, single-parent families are increasingly applying to family agencies for help with a wide range of family problems and crises.

Family agencies also serve persons living alone or with nonrelatives. These clients do not appear in this chart since it is limited to families. Thirteen applications out of 100 came from persons living alone or with nonrelatives. This proportion of nonfamily persons to families in agency caseloads is not only very low in relation to the general population but also has remained remarkably constant during the last decade—and this at a time when both the young and the elderly are increasingly living away from their families. If the applicant group had reflected the patterns of the general population, 27 percent instead of 13 percent of applicants in 1970 would have been from individuals not living in family units. Even in 1960 such applications would have totaled 23 percent instead of the actual figure, 13 percent.[7]

This contrast suggests that agency caseloads are reflecting the family focus of their core service rather than the growing public concern over the problems and new life-styles of persons not living in traditional family units, such as unmarried couples, homosexual couples, runaways, commune residents, isolated aged, transients, and migrants. Whether this gap in agency service should be reduced at the expense of service to families is a value issue that each agency must settle for itself. ■

MARITAL STATUS OF FAMILY HEAD

Chart 3

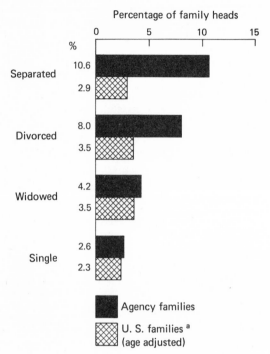

Percentage of family heads

| | 0 | 5 | 10 | 15 |

%

Separated — 10.6 / 2.9

Divorced — 8.0 / 3.5

Widowed — 4.2 / 3.5

Single — 2.6 / 2.3

■ Agency families

▨ U. S. families [a]
(age adjusted)

[a] U. S. percentages corrected for comparative purposes to give same representation to family heads under 45 as in the agency sample.

Most of the single-parent families shown in chart 2 lost their partners through marital conflict rather than death. Families served by agencies were more than three times as likely to be headed by someone who was separated due to marital conflict than was the case for families of similar ages in the general population.[8] Likewise, more than twice as many agency as U.S. families were headed by a divorced person, while only one-fifth more were headed by someone who had lost the spouse through death. The reverse side of this picture is, of course, that there were fewer intact families in agency caseloads than in the general population (see chart 2).

When the figures were expanded to include all persons fourteen years of age or over instead of family heads only, heavy use of agencies by families torn apart by marital conflict was again evident. Those in this age range served by agencies included three times the proportion of separated and a third more divorced than did the general population.[9]

These contrasts have increased considerably since 1960. Based on data limited to the same agencies in both years, the increase for divorced family heads was from 2.7 to 8.0—an increase of nearly two hundred percent. The increase for separated family heads was less striking (from 10.0 to 11.6 percent), while the trend for intact families served by agencies was the reverse (see page 17). In terms of percentile points, all these changes were considerably larger than were those for the country as a whole.[10]

The toll of marital conflict is also evident in figures on whom children were living with. In comparison with the general population, twice as many children per hundred served by agencies were growing up without both parents in the home (28 percent versus 14 percent).[11] Nonwhite clients were at a particular disadvantage in this respect. Nearly half (46 percent) of nonwhite children under eighteen in the agency sample lacked a two-parent home as compared with 23 percent of white children served by agencies. The parent missing in most of these cases was the father, as is clear from chart 2.

This heavy use of agencies by one-parent families stems directly from the particular needs and vulnerabilities of the separated and divorced. Many apply originally in the heat of the emotional crisis and trauma of separation or abandonment. Later when crises again arise, they again seek agency help with problems and emergencies that a two-parent family could perhaps weather without outside help. When there are two to share the load and provide emotional support, a couple can often manage by shifting roles and pooling resources, effort, and know-how. For the one-parent family, the family agency is an important substitute resource in times of trouble and crisis. ■

Chart 4

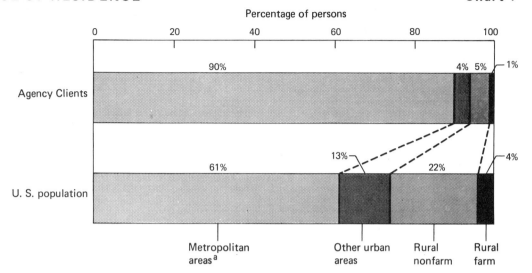

Percentage of persons

a Excluding rural residents in metropolitan areas.

wide areas. Community support is also not organized in units large enough to support an agency of minimum size. Community Chests and United Funds usually do not exist, and there are no alternate facilities for raising money. In most situations, a population of at least 50,000 is needed to support an agency of minimum size. In some areas, agencies have developed outposts through which small communities purchase service from central cities. Such arrangements will no doubt be expanded as the network of voluntary support expands. In many areas, however, only a broad statewide agency can provide the service needed. ∎

Family agency service is confined almost entirely to persons living in major metropolitan areas. At the time of the study, 90 percent of agency clients but only 61 percent of the general population lived in one of these major areas.[12] Other urban areas account for only 4 percent of agency clients but for 13 percent of the U.S. population. Rural nonfarm residents were more than four times as numerous proportionately in the country as a whole as in the clientele of agencies. Similarly, only one percent of agency clients lived on farms as contrasted with 4 percent of the general population.

This concentration of agency service in the larger urban centers is also evident when the sample is classified according to the size of the city where the agency that provided the service was located. On this basis, cities of 100,000 or over account for 68 percent of the clientele of agencies but only 43 percent of the general population.[13] This heavy proportion of users of family service in the larger cities was particularly marked for the nonwhite group. Sixty-nine percent of nonwhite agency clients utilized agencies located in cities of 250,000 or more as contrasted with only 45 percent of the white clients.[14] For both racial groups, the location of family agencies is such that large segments of the population living in small towns and rural areas have little or no access to family agency services.

Instead of declining, this gap in service has increased slightly since 1960.[15] Progress in filling this gap is difficult to achieve since serving these outlying areas presents major obstacles. Distances are great and those needing service are thinly distributed over

Who comes to family agencies?

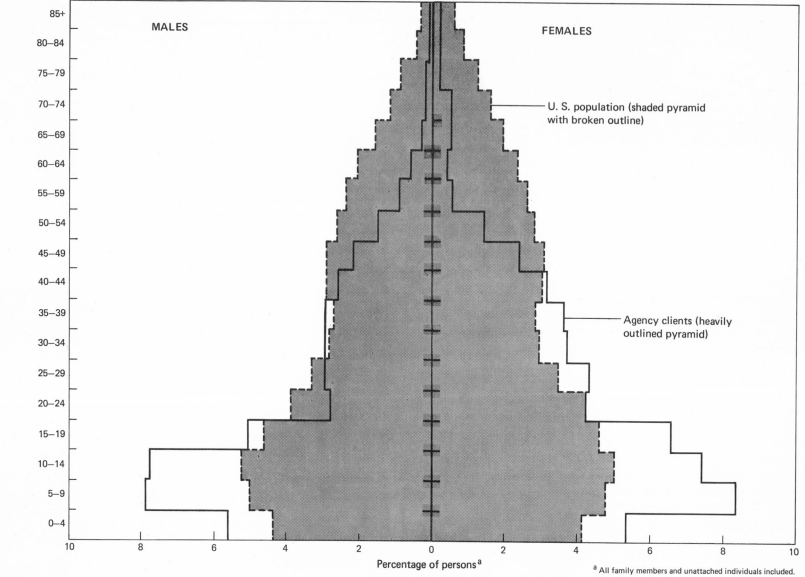

AGE

85+

80—84

75—79

70—74

65—69

60—64

55—59

50—54

45—49

40—44

35—39

30—34

25—29

20—24

15—19

10—14

5—9

0—4

MALES

FEMALES

U. S. population (shaded pyramid with broken outline)

Agency clients (heavily outlined pyramid)

10   8   6   4   2   0   2   4   6   8   10

Percentage of persons[a]

[a] All family members and unattached individuals included.

Chart 5 consists of two pyramids, one super-imposed on the other. The lightly shaded pyramid outlined with a broken line represents the age-sex distribution of the United States[16] and the area outlined with a heavy solid line, that of the clients of family agencies. Counts relate to persons, not cases, with all family members and unattached individuals included regardless of whether a particular family member was or was not seen by the agency.

A comparison of the overlapping pyramids leads to three conclusions:

1. Clients of family agencies consist predominantly of young families with school-age children. (Contrasts with the general population were greatest for persons aged five to nineteen.)

2. Persons forty-five and over (and particularly those fifty-five and over) are being missed. The latter group was only a little over one-fourth as large proportionately in the clientele of agencies as in the general population.

3. There is an excess of women in the agency group in the child-bearing years (fifteen to forty-four).

The explanations seem obvious: The predominance of younger persons reflects the concentration of agency service on marital and children's problems. The imbalance of women probably results from the relatively heavy use of agencies by divorced and separated women with children. The gap in service to persons at the older age levels is primarily the result of the focus of agencies on family relationship problems. Older persons are less likely to need counseling and more likely to require types of supportive services not normally available through family agency programs.

Comparisons with a decade earlier (see table) identify several major shifts in the client group:

1. The proportion of persons in the age group ten to twenty-four has increased by about a third. This rapid growth rate contrasts with an increase of only about a fifth for this same group in the general population.

2. A drop of about equal amount in the percentage of children under ten occurred in both the client group and the general population.

3. A major deficit in service to persons sixty-five and over continues to exist. This

Age distribution

Age group	Percentage of persons		Percent change
	1960	1970	
Agency clients[a]			
Under 10	32.4	26.5	−18.2
10 to 24	26.0	34.9	+34.2
25 to 64	39.0	35.8	−8.2
65 and over	2.6	2.7	+3.8
U.S. population			
Under 10	21.7	18.2	−16.1
10 to 24	22.8	27.7	+21.5
25 to 64	45.5	44.2	−4.9
65 and over	9.2	9.9	+7.6

[a]Same agencies both years.

group increased for agencies at only half the rate of increase for the same group in the population at large, even though it started far behind general population levels.

The ten-year trend is obvious: greater involvement of agencies with parents of adolescents and continued noninvolvement with persons at older age levels, at least as far as initial recruitment to the client group is concerned. The drop for children under ten for both groups probably is to be attributed in the main to the declining birthrate. The great increase for adolescents and young adults suggests that parents of teenage children are reaching out increasingly to agencies for help in coping with the new life-styles, problems, and stresses of the younger generation. This explanation is also suggested by the increase during the same period in the proportion of adolescent adjustment problems brought to agencies (see page 39). The data provide no explanation for the continued bypassing of persons in the retirement years.

These facts pose a value dilemma: Which age groups should receive priority in use of scarce agency resources? Is it more important to concentrate on the young and thus invest in the future? Or should this priority be modified to take greater account of the critical and often tragic needs of the aged who can no longer fend for themselves? ∎

RACIAL AND ETHNIC MINORITIES

Chart 6

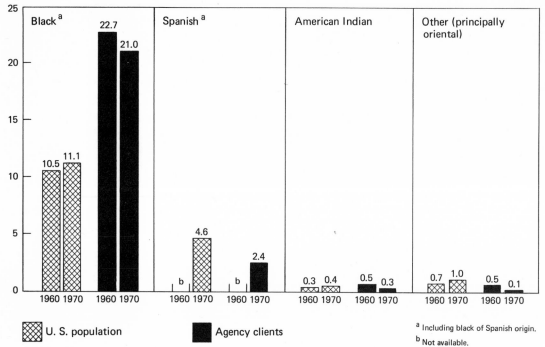

Percentage of total persons

U. S. population   Agency clients

a Including black of Spanish origin.
b Not available.

The most striking aspect of chart 6 is the evidence presented that black persons were served by agencies in nearly double their proportion in the general population.[17] These figures do not mean that black persons were receiving service disproportionate to their need. Counts do not and can not take into account relative need for service. On this there are no statistics. However, if the need for service is proportionate to relative disadvantage, as shown by socioeconomic indicators, perhaps all the minority groups shown in this

chart could be said to have above average needs.

In sharp contrast to the black group, persons of Spanish heritage were served by agencies in only about half their proportion in the general population.[18] Within this group Mexicans were the most underrepresented (see chart 7),[19] probably because they are often farm or migrant workers and are therefore less likely to live in the cities where family agencies are located. Other factors adding to the discrepancy for the Spanish group in

general include (1) the known underreporting of agency outreach programs for Spanish groups and (2) differences in definitions of the Spanish group. (The general population figures cover all persons of acknowledged Spanish origin whereas agency data classify all family members according to the country of birth or parentage of the family head or spouse, thus missing some third-generation Spanish.) However, the main explanations probably stem not from technical reasons but from reality factors. Because of major barriers, such as language, cultural differences, and residence in barrios, the provision of family service to this group requires special program adaptations, including the employment of Spanish-speaking counselors and the location of branch offices in convenient areas.

Even less in evidence in agency caseloads than the Spanish were American Indians and Oriental clients. Both were substantially below their proportions in the general population.[20] Counts were so low for both groups as to be almost nonexistent. There were only fifteen American Indian cases and six Oriental cases in the entire sample, representing a total of sixty persons. Reaching these minorities again requires special reaching-out efforts because of cultural and language barriers and the fact that they often live on Indian reservations or in Chinatowns.

Still another minority group deserves mention, namely, the foreign-born. Of all family heads in the agency sample, 5.6 percent were born abroad. This group was a diverse one, consisting mostly of white family heads born either in Europe or Canada. The active immigration service of some Jewish agencies probably accounts for a good number of this

Section one

group. Of the total foreign-born group, only about one in twelve was from a Spanish-speaking country. In the country as a whole, 4.7 percent of all persons were born abroad.[21] Conclusions about relative representation are not possible since the agency census asked the place of birth only for family heads and their spouses whereas the figure available for the United States covers all residents.

Trends since 1960 (for the same agencies) show a drop in the proportion of each of the minorities for which data are available. In the case of the Spanish group, changes in definitions eliminate the possibility of comparison. The significance of these declines is not clear. There was some acknowledged underreporting of outreach programs for black and Spanish clients in 1970. In addition, the minute samples for all minority groups except black clients make conclusions about trends hazardous.

It should also be noted that the slight drop in black persons as users of family service between 1960 and 1970 represents a drop only in the person count. The proportion of black cases moved from 18.8 percent in 1960 to 19.0 percent in 1970. This drop in the person count, but not in the case count, was found on further examination to result mainly from an increase for the same agencies from 4 to 15 percent within the decade in the proportion of black applicants not living in families, with no corresponding increase in white applicants not living in families. A secondary factor was a slight drop in the average size of black families being served by agencies. It should also be noted that families served by advocacy efforts on behalf of groups of people rather than specific identified families are not reflected in these counts.

Who comes to family agencies?

Chart 7

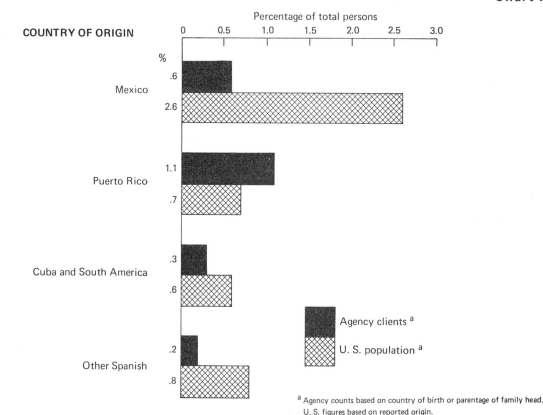

COUNTRY OF ORIGIN

Percentage of total persons

Mexico — %, .6, 2.6
Puerto Rico — 1.1, .7
Cuba and South America — .3, .6
Other Spanish — .2, .8

Agency clients [a]
U. S. population [a]

[a] Agency counts based on country of birth or parentage of family head. U. S. figures based on reported origin.

In spite of these qualifications, it is abundantly clear that, in the larger perspective, agencies have barely managed to maintain their minority clientele in spite of their many outreach efforts in the last decade. Further gains in the coming decade will require more widespread, persistent, and dedicated effort, plus the willingness to innovate in the establishment of agencies, outposts, and specialized services where minority clients actually live, whether on Indian reservations, in Chinatowns, in ghettoes or barrios, or in migrant labor camps. Also needed will be the employment of indigenous staff who can speak the languages involved and communicate with full awareness of cultural differences. ■

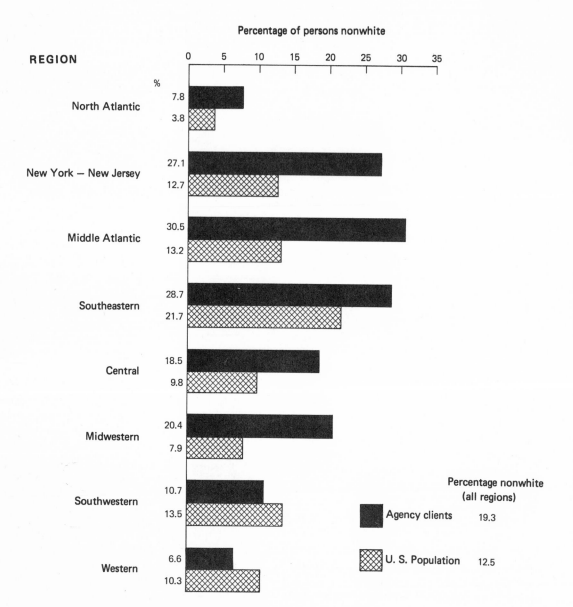

Percentage of persons nonwhite

REGION

	%		
North Atlantic	7.8		
	3.8		
New York — New Jersey	27.1		
	12.7		
Middle Atlantic	30.5		
	13.2		
Southeastern	28.7		
	21.7		
Central	18.5		
	9.8		
Midwestern	20.4		
	7.9		
Southwestern	10.7		
	13.5		
Western	6.6		
	10.3		

Percentage nonwhite
(all regions)

■ Agency clients   19.3

▨ U. S. Population   12.5

The extent to which nonwhite families utilize family agency service varies markedly by region. At the time of the study, agencies in all regions except the Southwestern and Western were serving nonwhite clients in greater numbers than their proportion in the general population.[22] Nevertheless, there were significant regional differences, as will be evident in the accompanying table. Black clients fell below their proportion in the general population in the Western and Southwestern regions. For the American Indians, the gap in services was largest in the Southwestern, Southeastern, and Western regions where the great majority of Indians are located. The Oriental group was not being served in significant numbers in any region, but again the gap was greatest in the Western region, the home of many Chinese and Japanese.

Shifts in the 1960-70 decade in the clientele of the same agencies showed increases in the proportion of nonwhite clients in four regions (New York-New Jersey, Middle Atlantic, Southeastern, and Western) and decreases in the other regions.[23] None of the changes was statistically significant except in the Southwestern region where the drop was from 30.7 to 10.3 percent (based on a very small 1960 sample).

In the country as a whole there was no perceptible change within the decade in the proportion of nonwhite cases served by agencies (20.0 percent in 1960 versus 19.6 percent in 1970). The implications of these findings have already been discussed (see chart 6).

Agency clients	Black	American Indian	Other[a]
All regions	18.8	0.3	0.3
North Atlantic	7.6	0.2	—
N.Y.–N.J.	26.6	0.5	—
Middle Atlantic	30.2	0.4	—
Southeastern	28.7	—	—
Central	18.4	—	0.1
Midwestern	19.4	1.1	—
Southwestern	10.3	0.4	—
Western	4.4	—	2.2
U.S. population			
All regions	11.1	0.4	1.0
North Atlantic	3.3	0.1	0.5
N.Y.–N.J.	11.6	0.1	1.0
Middle Atlantic	12.8	0.1	0.4
Southeastern	21.3	0.2	0.2
Central	9.4	0.1	0.3
Midwestern	7.1	0.4	0.4
Southwestern	11.7	1.3	0.5
Western	5.2	0.7	4.4

[a] Mostly Oriental.

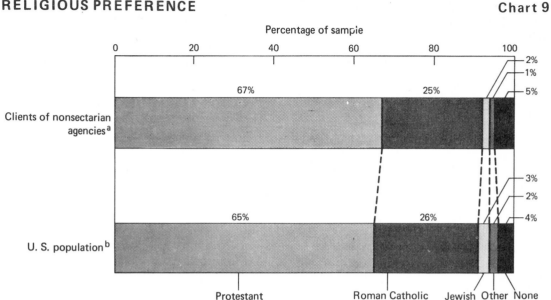

Percentage of sample

Clients of nonsectarian agencies[a] — 67% Protestant, 25% Roman Catholic, 2%, 1%, 5%

U. S. population[b] — 65% Protestant, 26% Roman Catholic, 3%, 2%, 4%

Protestant   Roman Catholic   Jewish Other None

[a] Cases classified by religious preference of family head (or applicant if not a family unit).
[b] Based on ten national Gallup surveys in 1970 covering 16,523 persons 21 and over.

The clients of nonsectarian family agencies appear surprisingly similar to the general population in their religious preferences.[24] About two-thirds identified themselves as Protestant, one-quarter as Roman Catholic, and 2 percent as Jewish. The one percent shown as "other" were mostly Eastern Orthodox. One in twenty disclaimed any formal religious ties or preference.

Trends in the decade of the 1960s for nonsectarian agencies showed modest declines in the proportion of Protestant and Jewish clients and an increase in the proportion of Catholic clients and in the proportion of those claiming no religion.[25] The meaning of these shifts is not clear.

These findings describe only the clientele of the nonsectarian agencies. Both the Catholic and the Jewish groups in many of the larger cities maintain separate agencies that serve principally persons of the same faith. If the clientele of these sectarian agencies had been added to those shown in the chart, the figures would have been 61 percent Protestant, 24 percent Catholic, and 9 percent Jewish. This brings the representation of the Jewish group to three times their proportion in the general population—an impressive record of support and utilization of family service by this group.

Who comes to family agencies?

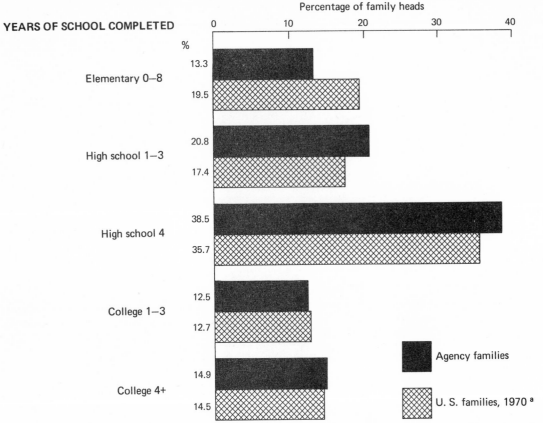

Percentage of family heads

YEARS OF SCHOOL COMPLETED

| | 0 | 10 | 20 | 30 | 40 |

%

13.3
Elementary 0–8
19.5

20.8
High school 1–3
17.4

38.5
High school 4
35.7

12.5
College 1–3
12.7

14.9
College 4+
14.5

■ Agency families

▦ U. S. families, 1970 [a]

[a] U. S. percentages corrected for comparative purposes to give same representation to family heads under 45 as in the agency sample.

The typical family applying to a family agency is headed by a high school graduate. The same is true of the typical U.S. family. In comparisons based on age-adjusted figures for the general population,[26] the proportion who had gone on to college or beyond was almost identical. The major difference was that a higher percentage of family heads in the general population had not gone beyond the eighth grade while somewhat more agency family heads had attended high school. Even this difference would have been reduced if comparisons could have been limited to metropolitan areas; however, currently available U.S. data for 1970 do not permit this refinement. This small difference is also reflected in the median years of school completed by agency family heads, namely 12.4 for agencies and 12.2 for the general population. In short, insofar as education of the family head is concerned, those applying for agency service are about on a par with their age counterparts in the population at large.

As would be expected from the general expansion in educational opportunities, trends in educational achievement since 1960 have been sharply upward for both groups.[27] Beginning with the completion of high school, the proportion for each group at the upper end of the educational ladder has increased and the proportion below this point has decreased. This upward thrust has been faster for the general population than for agency clients. For family heads in the general population, the median years of education shifted from 10.6 to 12.2, while that for agency family heads shifted only from 12.1 to 12.4. The net result has been a downward shift in the *relative* educational rank of the clientele of agencies in comparison with the population at large. This change is consistent with, and probably partly the direct result of, agencies' attempts to reach out to the disadvantaged and serve them more adequately. ■

The occupational profile of employed family heads served by agencies, with some exceptions, follows that for the country as a whole.[28] For agencies, the clerical and sales group showed the greatest excess over the general population. Agencies were also slightly higher at the two extremes—the professional and technical group and the unskilled group. The largest deficit for agencies was in the managerial group. Smaller deficits appeared for skilled and semiskilled blue-collar occupations and for service workers.

To facilitate comparisons, unemployed family heads and farmers were excluded from the figures shown. Unemployed family heads were more than twice as numerous in the agency sample as in the general population (7.7 percent versus 3.1 percent), while farm occupations were almost nonexistent (0.4 percent versus 4.4 percent).

In the perspective of the decade, agency trends accented the middle groups.[29] The skilled blue-collar group doubled, while the clerical and sales group increased by almost one-half. Professional and technical workers increased much faster in the general population than in the clientele of agencies while for agencies the managerial group actually declined. Except for service workers in the general population, the lesser skilled occupations dropped for both groups, but agency declines were larger. New ways being developed to reach these hourly wage workers who have difficulty with office appointments include extending office hours and contracting with industrial concerns and labor unions for on-site services. ▪

Who comes to family agencies?

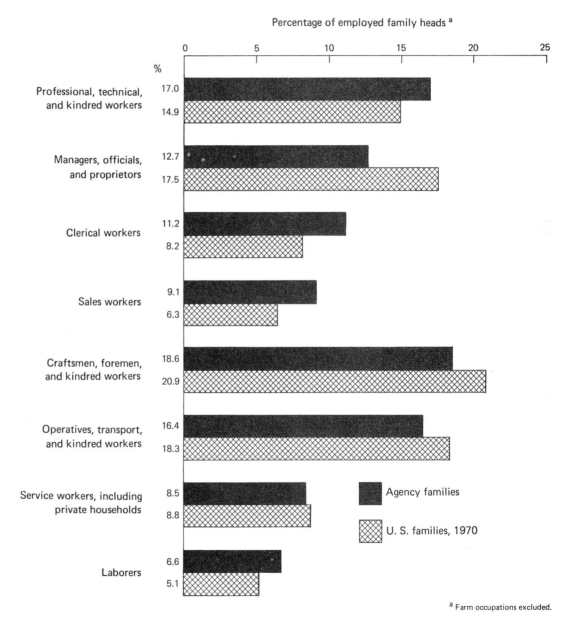

Percentage of employed family heads [a]

Occupation	%
Professional, technical, and kindred workers	17.0 / 14.9
Managers, officials, and proprietors	12.7 / 17.5
Clerical workers	11.2 / 8.2
Sales workers	9.1 / 6.3
Craftsmen, foremen, and kindred workers	18.6 / 20.9
Operatives, transport, and kindred workers	16.4 / 18.3
Service workers, including private households	8.5 / 8.8
Laborers	6.6 / 5.1

■ Agency families

▨ U. S. families, 1970

[a] Farm occupations excluded.

27

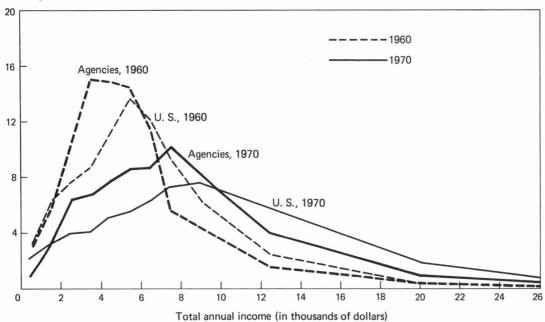

Percentage of families

Agencies, 1960

U. S., 1960

Agencies, 1970

U. S., 1970

- - - - - 1960
———— 1970

Total annual income (in thousands of dollars)

income for both groups during the decade. This shift reflects the combined influence of the rising productivity and affluence of the country as a whole and the effects of inflation.

These gains are even more clear when trends are stated in terms of median incomes. In the decade between 1959 and 1969, the median family income for U.S. metropolitan areas jumped from $5,956 to $10,474. In the same period the median income for agency families in these areas rose only from $5,063 to $7,822. In terms of real income corrected for cost-of-living changes,[31] the increases were not as great as they appear: The $10,474 median income for U.S. families in 1970 reduces to $8,327, and the $7,822 median for agency families, to $6,218.

Clearly, the *relative* position of agency clients in comparison with families in general shifted downward in income during the decade as it did in education even though the basic trend for both groups was upward for both indicators. This shift in relative position is probably the direct result of conscious agency efforts to reach out and extend service to the less privileged. ■

Agency families are clearly below the general population in total annual family income.[30] Comparison of the solid lines in the chart showing the distribution of income for both groups in 1969 reveals that agency families cluster more heavily in the lower third of the range than do families in general. At all income levels below $10,000, they are proportionately higher than families in the general population. At this point the lines cross. Above $10,000 the proportion of families at each income level is higher for the general population than for agency clients. Only 2 percent of

agency families had incomes of $25,000 or more in 1969 as compared with 6 percent of families in the general population. In both instances the income figures cover all reported income for the year for members from all sources, including public assistance. To avoid distorted comparisons resulting from differing proportions of rural and small-town residents, all comparisons have been limited to metropolitan areas.

The marked shift to the right in the solid lines as compared with the broken ones indicates a substantial upward trend in family

A substantially higher proportion of agency families have incomes below the poverty line than is true of U.S. families in general.[32] For both white and nonwhite groups, agency figures were at least 40 percent higher than U.S. figures. Racial contrasts were even more marked. Three and one-half times as many nonwhite as white clients were living below the poverty line at the time of the census. Similar racial differentials were evident in the general population. In addition, there were substantial differences in median income when the two groups were considered as a whole.

Another feature of chart 13 is the inclusion of special segments for persons receiving public assistance. In this respect, also, agency clients ranked higher than the general population, and nonwhite clients ranked higher than white clients by a considerable margin.

A third notable feature of this chart is the significant proportion of the poverty group that was not receiving public assistance. While some doubtless were students supported by parents or other resources, elderly living on savings, or rural residents with noncash income, a substantial number must have been denying themselves essentials, either to avoid applying for public assistance, or because they were not aware of this resource. Still others probably had their applications denied by reason of restrictive eligibility requirements. To the extent that the basic needs of this poverty group are unmet for whatever reason, local and national advocacy efforts are called for to fill the gap.

Finally, the reader may be puzzled by the fact that some persons above the poverty line are shown as receiving public assistance. Among the more obvious explanations are the following: Public assistance may have been

POVERTY STATUS OF FAMILIES
(Urban areas)

Chart 13

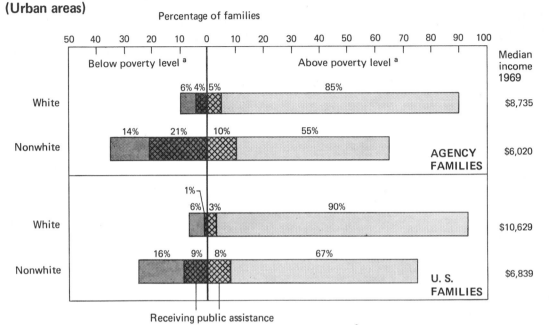

Percentage of families

a U. S. definition of poverty applied to 1969 income data.

granted to only one family member, as for example, an aged, blind, or disabled person, while the poverty definition is based on total family income. Again, a family may have been on public assistance only part of the year and self-supporting the rest of the year, a distinction which is lost when income is reported on a yearly basis. The most important explanation, however, is the very conservative definition of the poverty line used by the federal government. While it takes account of family size, whether the family head is sixty-five or over, and whether the family lives on a farm, it makes no adjustments for regional cost differentials or for special family circumstances. Each family member is given the poverty rating of his family as a whole. Actual dollar figures range from about $1,500 as the upper limit of poverty for a single person living on a farm to about $6,000 for a family of seven or more living in a city. In view of the high proportion of clients who are below the poverty line by this stringent definition, it is obvious that family agencies are serving the poor in substantial numbers. ∎

Who comes to family agencies?

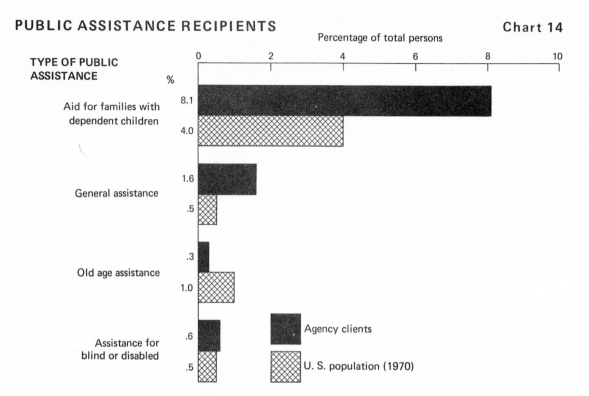

Chart 14

Percentage of total persons

TYPE OF PUBLIC
ASSISTANCE

%

Aid for families with
dependent children — 8.1 / 4.0

General assistance — 1.6 / .5

Old age assistance — .3 / 1.0

Assistance for
blind or disabled — .6 / .5

Agency clients

U. S. population (1970)

not keep pace with the growing numbers of public assistance recipients in the country. This may reflect the development in the 1960s of expanded provision for counseling and other services in addition to money by departments of public welfare.

Nonwhite families were overly represented in the welfare component of the clientele of agencies. Nearly a third (31 percent) of nonwhite agency families were receiving public assistance, in sharp contrast to 9 percent of white families. In the general population, 17 percent of the nonwhite families received public assistance as compared with 4 percent of the white families.[35] Once again the figures reflect the struggle for economic survival of a group in double jeopardy—that of being poor and that of being black. ∎

Agency efforts to reach out to the disadvantaged are also reflected in the findings on service to public assistance recipients. In comparison with the general population,[33] twice the proportion of agency clients were receiving aid to families with dependent children and about three times the proportion were on general assistance. Agencies were about on a par with the country as a whole on service to recipients of aid to the blind and disabled. Recipients of old age assistance were conspicuously absent. Only one-third as many proportionately were agency clients as were in the general popula-

tion. This finding once more confirms the tendency of agencies to concentrate on service to young families and to bypass the elderly.

Measured in terms of proportions of total caseload, agency service to public assistance clients expanded from 9.9 percent in 1960 to 11.7 in 1970 for those agencies that reported in both years. During the same period, the proportion of persons in the general population receiving public assistance increased from 3.7 to 5.9 percent.[34] While the agencies still serve public assistance clients in twice their proportion in the general population, the rate of increase over the decade did

The socioeconomic status scores

The following three charts present a general overview of the socioeconomic status of family agency clients. In contrast to previous charts, they utilize a composite score that merges three indicators of socioeconomic status: education, occupation, and income.

The actual scores for each case were computed as follows: Each case was separately rated for the education and occupation of the principal breadwinner and for the income of the family as a whole, using scores based on the relative position of the case (in percentile terms) in relation to the total adult population of the country. These scores were then added together and the total divided by three. The result was a single score having a potential range of 1–100. Actually, relatively few scores approached either extreme (because of the averaging process). These composite scores were grouped into six categories and given labels ranging from upper to lower socioeconomic status. The procedures and sources are explained further in the Appendix.

These labels are intended to help the reader visualize the various subgroups. In actuality, the various groups overlap and blend into each other with no sharp dividing lines to demarcate differences in ways of life and values. The accompanying table indicates the socioeconomic characteristics typical of families in each socioeconomic group.

Characteristics of the various socioeconomic groups

Socioeconomic group	Average years of school completed[a]	Percent of family heads employed full time	Modal occupations[a]	Average family income (1969)
Upper (SES 85-100)	16.6	90	Professional or technical (62%) Managerial (25%)	$19,060
Upper middle (SES 75-84)	14.6	88	Professional or technical (47%) Managerial (26%)	14,027
Middle middle (SES 65-74)	13.2	84	Professional or technical (25%) Managerial (24%)	10,795
Lower middle (SES 50-64)	12.1	77	Skilled craftsmen (27%) Clerical (24%)	8,831
Upper lower (SES 30-49)	11.0	62	Operatives, transport, and kindred workers (21%) Skilled craftsmen (19%)	6,217
Lower lower (SES 0-29)	8.2	29 (38% not in labor market)	Service workers (24%) Laborers (22%)	3,648

[a]Based on data for chief breadwinner.

SOCIOECONOMIC STATUS OF FAMILY AGENCY APPLICANTS[a]

Chart 15

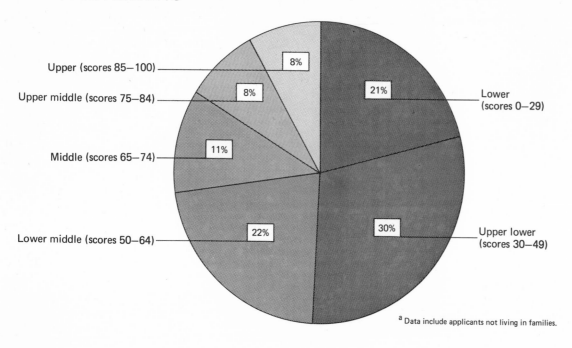

Upper (scores 85—100) — 8%

Upper middle (scores 75—84) — 8%

Middle (scores 65—74) — 11%

Lower middle (scores 50—64) — 22%

21% — Lower (scores 0—29)

30% — Upper lower (scores 30—49)

[a] Data include applicants not living in families.

the total group was 49.6. Subgroups differed markedly. White clients, for example, averaged 52.6 and nonwhite clients, 35.8. As will be shown later, both problems and services vary substantially by the socioeconomic and racial characteristics of the clients.

In chart 15, each case was counted once regardless of the number in the family. When each family member was counted separately, using the socioeconomic status score for the family as a whole, the distribution remained essentially unchanged.[36]

Because of the difficulty of securing basic data, this chart, like most of the others, excludes clients served only by phone, those served through family life education (unless they also received other services),[37] and those served indirectly through agency advocacy programs directed toward improving conditions for families generally. ■

Chart 15 is directed to the question: How middle class are the clients served by family agencies? Classifications are based on the scoring process described on the preceding page. The answer is fairly clear: Applicants with socioeconomic scores below 50 (the two sections on the right half of the circle) comprise slightly more than half the total. The education, occupation, and income characteristics that these sections represent are shown in the table on page 31. The largest single group is the one termed "upper lower," with scores ranging from 30 to 49. As one moves clockwise around and up the status scale, the groups

become progressively smaller. The top two categories are each under 10 percent.

In combination, the two lowest groups exceed by a considerable margin all three of the middle status groups. If the category described as "lower middle" is added to the two described as "lower," the total becomes nearly three-quarters, as contrasted with only 27 percent designated as "middle," "upper middle," and "upper." Perhaps the best single characterization would be to say that the consumer group served by family agencies is typically lower or lower middle in socioeconomic status. The average socioeconomic score for

Chart 16 places the findings on the socio-economic status of agency families in dual perspective: comparison with the general population and comparison with the previous decade. To improve comparability with the general population, all the figures have been limited to metropolitan areas. U.S. figures have also been adjusted to the age composition of the client group.[38] Unfortunately, 1970 data for the country as a whole are not available.

By simple addition, it will be apparent that 68 percent of families in the general population in metropolitan areas in 1960 had socioeconomic scores at or above the midpoint score of 50, whereas only 53 percent of agency families were in the same range. In contrast, 47 percent of the clientele of agencies in these areas fell below a score of 50 as compared with only 32 percent of the general population. For both groups, the major concentration was in the two middle categories, a natural consequence of averaging component scores.

Overall average scores also place agency families below general population levels. Their average score was 54.3 in 1960 while that for U.S. families in these same areas was 59.6, after adjustment to the age composition of the sample.

In the perspective of the decade, the largest drop for agency clients occurred at the highest status level, while the only increase came at the lowest level. Here the percentage nearly trebled—from 3.8 to 9.1 percent. This increase is statistically significant. During this same decade, the average socioeconomic status score for agency families in metropoli-

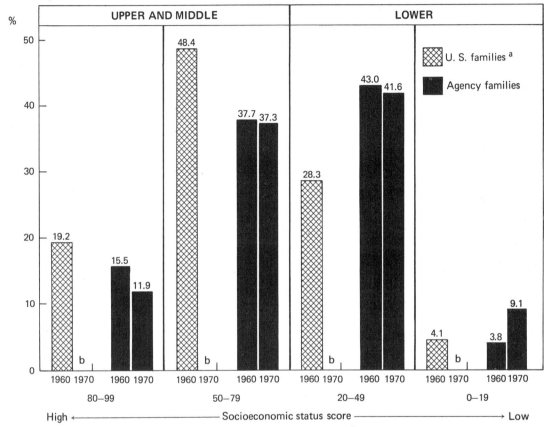

Percentage of family heads

a Corrected to age distribution of 1960 agency sample.
b Data not available.

tan areas dropped from 54.3 in 1960 to 50.6 in 1970.[39]

These findings confirm the conclusions from the earlier charts on education and income, indicating that the clientele of agencies shifted moderately during the 1960-70 decade toward the lower half of the socioeconomic status scale. This shift is consistent with agency efforts to reach out and expand service to the disadvantaged and to minority groups and to adapt their service programs more closely to the special needs of these groups. ■

Who comes to family agencies?

RELATIVE POSITION OF AGENCY AND U. S. FAMILIES ON SOCIOECONOMIC INDICATORS: 1960 and 1970

Chart 17

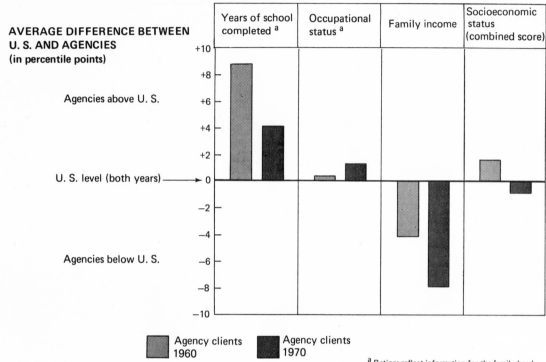

AVERAGE DIFFERENCE BETWEEN U. S. AND AGENCIES
(in percentile points)

Agencies above U. S.

U. S. level (both years) ➞

Agencies below U. S.

Agency clients 1960

Agency clients 1970

[a] Ratings reflect information for the family head. Occupational data apply to employed family heads.

Chart 17, the final chart on client characteristics, shows in summary form the shifts during the decade of the 1960s in the relative position of agency clients in relation to the general population on socioeconomic status.[40] Each bar represents the difference between the average rank of agency families and the average rank of the general population on the same characteristic for the same year. The first three sections of the chart show the component indicators of socioeconomic sta-tus—education, occupation, and income. The final section combines education, occupation, and income into a single composite figure.

From the results, it is evident that both in 1960 and again in 1970 heads of agency families were somewhat above those in the general population in education, very slightly above them in occupational status, and well below them in income. When the three indicators are combined, the above-average scores for education are counterbalanced by below-average scores for income, leaving the summary score only a little above the general population in 1960 and a little below it in 1970.[41]

In the decade from 1960 to 1970, the average position of agency clients moved downward on all of the indicators except occupation. The drop was over four percentile points for education, nearly four points for income, and two-and-one-half points for the total socioeconomic score. These findings again confirm earlier conclusions that during the decade of the 1960s a downward shift occurred relative to the general population in the socioeconomic status of family agency clients. In other words, by 1970 agency outreach programs were beginning to modify the composition of their total caseload.

This chart also highlights in a new perspective a source of stress for heads of agency families: In spite of the fact that they had more than the usual number of children to support, their incomes were well below those of their counterparts in the general population of similar occupational and educational background. These facts suggest questions they do not answer. To what extent did the problems of these families contribute to this discrepancy? To what extent did the discrepancy contribute to the problems? ∎

2
WHAT PROBLEMS DO CLIENTS BRING?

PROBLEMS OF FAMILY AGENCY CLIENTS Chart 18

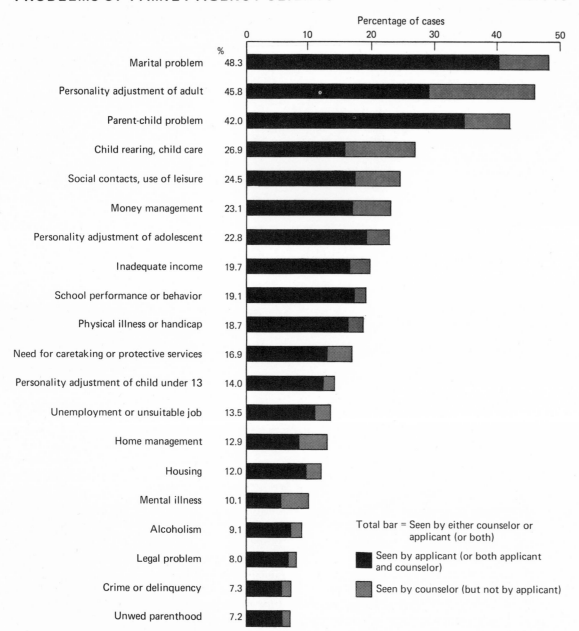

Percentage of cases

	%	
Marital problem	48.3	
Personality adjustment of adult	45.8	
Parent-child problem	42.0	
Child rearing, child care	26.9	
Social contacts, use of leisure	24.5	
Money management	23.1	
Personality adjustment of adolescent	22.8	
Inadequate income	19.7	
School performance or behavior	19.1	
Physical illness or handicap	18.7	
Need for caretaking or protective services	16.9	
Personality adjustment of child under 13	14.0	
Unemployment or unsuitable job	13.5	
Home management	12.9	
Housing	12.0	
Mental illness	10.1	
Alcoholism	9.1	
Legal problem	8.0	
Crime or delinquency	7.3	
Unwed parenthood	7.2	

Total bar = Seen by either counselor or applicant (or both)

Seen by applicant (or both applicant and counselor)

Seen by counselor (but not by applicant)

Family relationship and personal adjustment problems clearly predominate among problems brought to family agencies. In the opinion of both the counselor and the client, marital difficulties take top place. Parent-child problems ranked second among the reported concerns of applicants while counselors' views gave second rank to adult personality adjustment problems and third rank to parent-child problems. All showed frequencies above 40 percent. Three new problem categories introduced in 1970—child-rearing and child care practices, problems in social contacts and use of leisure time, and money management—took fourth, fifth, and sixth place, in that order. Personality adjustment problems of adolescents were reported much more often than were the adjustment problems of children under thirteen (23 versus 14 percent). School problems and inadequate income were each reported for one applicant in five, unemployment for one in seven, and housing problems for one in eight. Major social and behavior problems of wide community concern, such as alcoholism, unwed parenthood, and crime and delinquency, were each noted for 7 to 9 percent. Among the problems cited too seldom to be included on the chart were work performance (5.3 percent), drug abuse (4.2 percent), and mental retardation (2.9 percent).

Also apparent from the chart are substantial differences between the counselors' view of clients' problems and the way they report that clients see them. The bars showing the heaviest disagreement include personality adjustment problems of an adult, mental illness, social contacts and use of leisure time, and problems related to child rearing or home and money management. In general, the tendency was for counselors more often to define problems in terms of the personality adjustment or relationship problems of the applicant and for applicants to describe their problems in terms of difficulties with other family members or situations outside the family.

Counselors identified a total of 4.0 problems per case at intake, with little variation in this average by socioeconomic status and race. However, they reported applicants as seeing only 3.3 problems. When queried at follow-up, clients themselves actually reported an average of 4.4 problems as present when they first came to the agency—a third again as many as counselors thought these clients saw at intake.

In addition to reporting more problems, clients also identified their problems different-ly. Only 36 percent of the problems they were reported by the counselor to have seen at in-take were confirmed by the client at follow-up.[1] In the main, this difference probably should be attributed to differences in label-ing of problems, to inaccuracies in reporting, to forgetting, and to change resulting from treatment and the passage of time in clients' perceptions of their problems. Nevertheless, this discrepancy should serve as a warning to counselors that the picture they obtain at in-take is necessarily a very partial one.

While the total number of problems varied little by socioeconomic status, the types of problems reported changed dramatically (see chart 19). Clients reported relationship and personality adjustment problems more fre-quently at upper than at lower socioeconomic levels and problems related to lack of essen-tial economic supports and caretaking prob-lems more often at lower than at upper lev-els. Family and home management problems appeared with about equal frequency through-

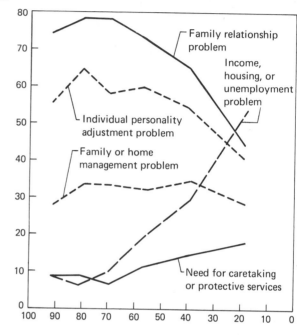

Percentage of cases

High ← Socioeconomic status score → Low

out the range. At all levels except the lowest, family and individual relationship problems ex-ceeded all other categories shown and never dropped below 40 percent.

These figures reflect the client's view as re-ported by the counselor at intake. Addition of the counselor's diagnostic perspective to that of the client moderates the declines shown in the chart, accentuates the increases, and intro-duces some upturn at the lowest socioeco-nomic level for family and home management problems. In general, clients' problem as-sessments tended to be conservative and to understate rather than exaggerate the pic-ture of problems as assessed by a trained professional. ■

What problems do clients bring?

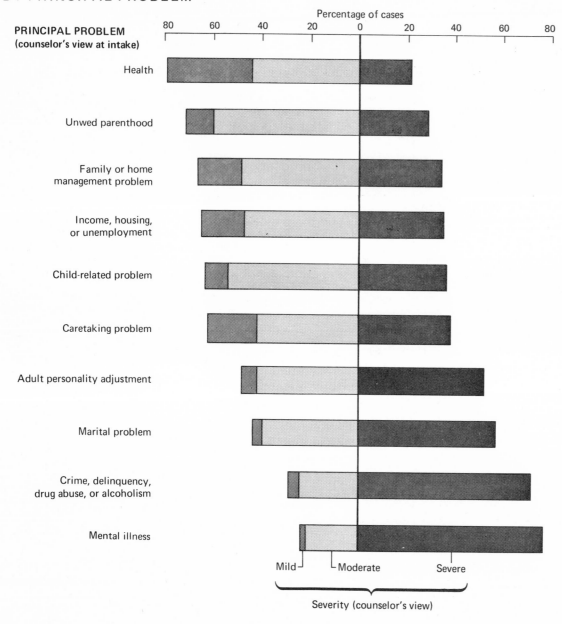

PRINCIPAL PROBLEM
(counselor's view at intake)

Percentage of cases

Health

Unwed parenthood

Family or home
management problem

Income, housing,
or unemployment

Child-related problem

Caretaking problem

Adult personality adjustment

Marital problem

Crime, delinquency,
drug abuse, or alcoholism

Mental illness

Mild — Moderate — Severe

Severity (counselor's view)

Nearly half of the clients who come to family agencies face severe problem situations. In the judgment of the intake counselor, the total problem situation was severe for 46 percent of the applicants, moderately severe for 44 percent, and mild for only 10 percent. A higher proportion of white than nonwhite clients were rated as having severe problem situations.[2]

Severity levels also differed markedly by principal problem. The highest proportion of severe situations was reported when the counselor identified mental illness as the principal problem. Problems of crime, delinquency, drug abuse, and alcoholism were close competitors. The total problem situations of at least seven cases in ten in both these groups were rated severe. Both also showed an almost total absence of mild cases.

More surprising than the high severity ratings for these two groups was the high proportion rated severe among those applying because of marital problems. Almost three out of five marital cases were rated severe, while only about 3 percent were mild. Almost equal severity levels were reported for adult personality adjustment problems. In sharp contrast, more than half of the unwed parenthood cases were rated as having only moderately severe problems. The highest proportion of mild situations was found among those whose principal problem was in the health area. These variations in severity help to explain the differences in outcomes by principal problem reported in chart 79. ■

Percentage of clients
with problem

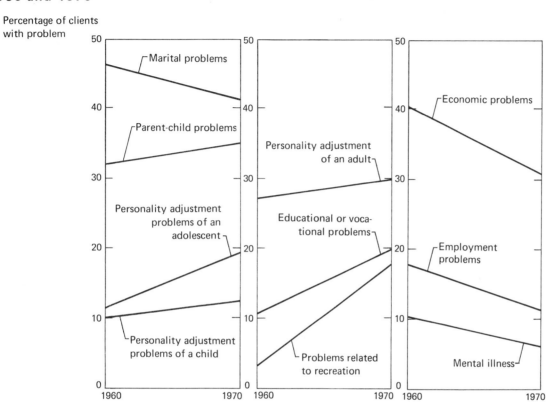

Chart 21 illustrates certain major shifts that have occurred in the last decade in the problems clients bring to agencies.[3] The major increases were all directly or indirectly related to the problems of adolescents or young adults and were statistically significant. Once again they suggest the increased use of family agencies by parents concerned about their adolescent children—their new life-styles, their problems in growing up in congested urban areas, their school and vocational adjustment, and

their differing views on recreation and morals.[4]

These increases were counterbalanced by declines in four areas. One of these, the downward trend for mental illness, probably stems in part from the shift of such cases to the newly developing community mental health centers. It may also reflect an increasing reluctance of both counselors and clients to refer to someone as mentally ill.

Two other major decreases—those for economic and for employment problems—may be

related to the proliferation of public job training, employment, and public assistance programs. Increases in governmental assistance for such programs have no doubt encouraged a narrowing of the public image of the functions of the family agency.

The other decline, that for marital problems, is probably the result of the shift toward adolescent problems since marital problems are more characteristic of earlier periods in the family cycle when the children are younger (see chart 23).

Whatever the reason, all these declines were statistically significant. In addition, changes in similar directions for the same problems were evident in counselors' reports of presenting problems and in the views of both counselor and client on the principal problem. This consistency further confirms the conclusion that the changes noted do, in fact, represent real trends rather than chance fluctuations. The actual figures were as follows:

	Percentage of clients with problem	
	1960	1970
Marital problem	46.2	41.2[a]
Parent-child problem	32.0	35.2
Personality adjustment of		
An adolescent	11.3	19.2[a]
A child	9.9	12.3
An adult	27.2	29.9
Educational, vocational problem	10.7	19.9[a]
Recreational problem[b]	3.1	17.5[a]
Economic problem	40.4	30.9[a]
Employment problem	17.9	11.5[a]
Mental illness	10.5	6.3[a]

[a]Difference is statistically significant.
[b]Change may have been accentuated by changes in problem list.

What problems do clients bring?

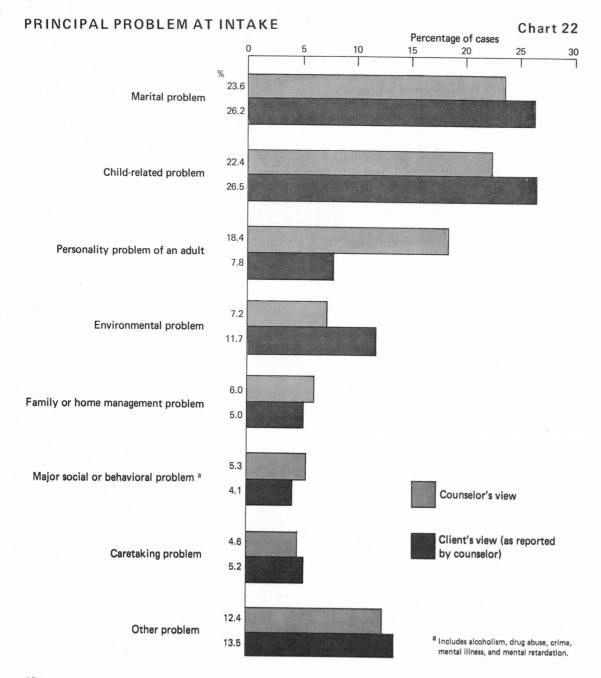

Chart 22

Percentage of cases

	Counselor's view	Client's view (as reported by counselor)
Marital problem	23.6	26.2
Child-related problem	22.4	26.5
Personality problem of an adult	18.4	7.8
Environmental problem	7.2	11.7
Family or home management problem	6.0	5.0
Major social or behavioral problem [a]	5.3	4.1
Caretaking problem	4.6	5.2
Other problem	12.4	13.5

[a] Includes alcoholism, drug abuse, crime, mental illness, and mental retardation.

Marital and children's problems were the two most frequent principal problems seen at intake. Counselors ranked marital problems slightly ahead whereas clients mentioned children's problems somewhat more often.[5] In both instances, clients were more likely than counselors to see one of these two areas as their primary concern. Personality adjustment problems of adults (including work performance) ranked third and problems of income, housing, and unemployment, fourth in counselors' ratings. Clients' views reversed this order. In selecting the primary problem clients gave greater weight than counselors to inadequate income, housing problems, and unemployment. A similar but much smaller reversal occurred in the relative rank of family or home management problems and caretaking problems. Major social or behavioral problems (alcoholism, drug abuse, crime and delinquency, mental illness, and mental retardation) were seen as primary in one case in twenty by counselors and in one case in twenty-five by clients. The largest component of the "other problem" category was unwed parenthood for both counselor and client. This category also included health problems, family problems other than marital or parent-child, legal problems, and problems of travelers and migrants.

The clients' views of the principal problem cited here were the clients' opinions as reported by the intake counselors. These views differed from the counselors' own views in about four out of ten cases (42 percent). Based on counselors' reports, clients appear to have described their principal problem in terms that placed the problem outside themselves. For example, clients tended to bypass the category of personality adjustment of an adult and also reported fewer child-rearing

Type of principal problem[a]	Percentage of cases			
	Upper or middle SES		Lower SES	
	White	Nonwhite	White	Nonwhite
Marital problem	35.3	33.6	19.1	15.4
Child-related problem	31.0	27.3	23.0	22.0
Personality problem of an adult	8.9	5.6	7.9	3.0
Family or home management problem	3.6	9.8	6.2	5.1
Environmental problem	3.6	6.3	16.2	26.7
Major social or behavioral problem	3.4	2.8	5.3	3.6
Caretaking problem	4.2	3.5	5.9	6.4
Other problem[b]	10.1	11.2	16.3	17.9

[a]Client's view as reported by counselor at intake.
[b]Includes other family relationship problems, unwed parenthood, legal problems, health problems, and other problems.

and parent-child problems and less mental illness and mental retardation than did their counselors. They reported more personality adjustment problems of children or adolescents, problems of social contacts and use of leisure time, and problems related to income, housing, and unemployment. Agreement was high on such easily recognizable problems as caretaking needs and unwed parenthood.

Client follow-up reports provided an opportunity to check the counselor's view of what the client thought was the principal problem against what the client himself reported as the principal problem. On this basis, the percentage of disagreement on the principal problem

increased from 42 to 47 percent. Both percentages undoubtedly overstate the true level of disagreement since there is no way in a national study of this scope to train both counselors and clients in the consistent use of problem labels, especially when the list is a long one. In many instances, the apparent disagreement may reflect no more than a client's calling his child's problem a school behavior problem and the counselor's calling it a problem involving the personality adjustment of a child. The figures therefore serve mainly as an alert to counselors that counselor-client differences in problem definition may be greater than they are aware of at intake.

A look at variations in principal problem by socioeconomic status reveals in general the same patterns by socioeconomic status as for problems in general (see chart 19). Details appear in the table at left.

Within the same socioeconomic levels, nonwhite clients were more likely than white clients to report practical types of problems as primary and less likely to define their principal problem as related to family and personal adjustment. These patterns were evident regardless of whether counselors' or clients' views were used as the source.

Changes in the relative frequency of various principal problems between 1960 and 1970 in the same agencies also repeated the patterns reported in chart 21 for all problems. Based on the counselors' views of the principal problem, only two changes—both decreases—reached statistical significance, namely: mental illness, which dropped from 7.8 percent in 1960 to 3.1 in 1970; and personality adjustment of an adult, which dropped from 22.7 percent in 1960 to 17.6 in 1970. Both are consistent with the shift in

the delivery of mental health services to community mental health centers.

Switching focus to the clients' views of the principal problem as reported by the intake counselor, one finds the following six trends to be statistically significant:

	Percentage of cases	
Decreases:	1960	1970
Marital problems	30.1	25.7
Economic problems	16.7	8.4
Mental illness	2.9	1.1
Increases:		
Personality adjustment of an adolescent	3.7	6.7
Educational and vocational problems	1.4	4.1
Housing	1.4	3.6

Again these changes point to shifts in community service delivery patterns toward less use of family agencies for economic problems and for mental illness. They also highlight once more the increased use of family agencies for help with the problems of adolescents. Since marital problems are highest in the early years of marriage, the downward drift in these problems is probably another result of the greater use of agencies by parents of adolescents. ∎

TYPE OF PROBLEMS BY FAMILY STAGE
(Families only)

Chart 23

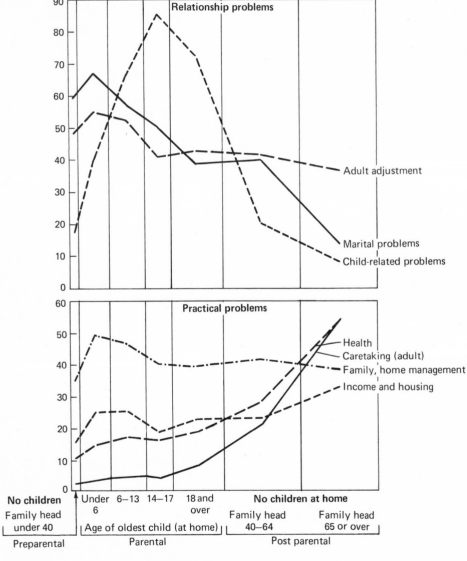

Percentage of families

Relationship problems

Adult adjustment

Marital problems

Child-related problems

Practical problems

Health
Caretaking (adult)
Family, home management
Income and housing

No children
Family head under 40

Under 6   6–13   14–17   18 and over

Age of oldest child (at home)

No children at home
Family head 40–64   Family head 65 or over

Preparental   Parental   Post parental

Family stage

The types of problems for which agency families need help differ markedly by the position of the family in the family life cycle. In chart 23 the sections show the stages of this cycle; the width of each section represents the length of time the typical family remains in that stage; and the lines indicate the problems that families bring.[6]

What story do these lines tell? In the brief period before the children are born, marital problems exceed all others as the focus of requests to agencies. Adult personality problems rank second, reflecting the difficulties inherent in the mutual accommodation process. Family and home management problems come third, suggesting the special stresses of establishing a home and allocating role functions.

As the family circle expands with the arrival of children, a variety of new relationship and practical problems come to the fore. By the time the oldest child enters school, children's problems begin to overtake marital and adult adjustment problems. They peak at the 90 percent level by the time the oldest child reaches adolescence.

The advent of the empty nest coincides with age-related increases in health and caretaking problems. With the coming of the retirement years, relationship problems decline, only to be replaced by an ever-increasing load of practical problems. As the end of the family life cycle approaches, caretaking, health, and family and home management problems all approximate or exceed the 40 percent level—and this at a point when the capacity to cope with such problems is rapidly eroding.[7] ■

42

Section two

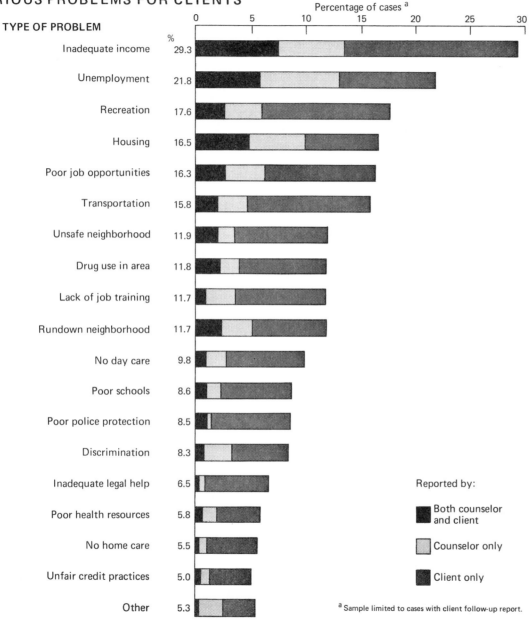

Percentage of cases [a]

TYPE OF PROBLEM

	%
Inadequate income	29.3
Unemployment	21.8
Recreation	17.6
Housing	16.5
Poor job opportunities	16.3
Transportation	15.8
Unsafe neighborhood	11.9
Drug use in area	11.8
Lack of job training	11.7
Rundown neighborhood	11.7
No day care	9.8
Poor schools	8.6
Poor police protection	8.5
Discrimination	8.3
Inadequate legal help	6.5
Poor health resources	5.8
No home care	5.5
Unfair credit practices	5.0
Other	5.3

Reported by:

■ Both counselor and client

▨ Counselor only

▨ Client only

[a] Sample limited to cases with client follow-up report.

In addition to internal family problems, clients and counselors also reported numerous situations stemming from lack of needed family supports or conditions in neighborhood or community that were causing serious difficulty.[8] Of these, inadequate income was by far the most frequent. It was cited as a problem for three out of ten users of family service. Unemployment, which was reported by one in five, ranked next. It was followed closely by recreation, housing, and poor job opportunities, which were reported for one client in six.

The returns brought some surprises. Lack of recreational opportunities and transportation facilities ranked higher than anticipated, and poor schools, poor health resources, unfair credit practices, and absence of home and day-care facilities ranked lower than anticipated. The relatively high rates of concern over rundown or unsafe neighborhoods and drug use in the area, although no surprise, highlight the urgent need for large-scale governmental action to arrest the deterioration of urban living environments.

In a high proportion of cases, only the client reported the problem. Counselors tended to be more aware of problems with an immediate, direct, and identifiable impact on the applicant, such as inadequate income, unemployment, and housing. They seldom reported adverse neighborhood conditions. To become more effective advocates for families, agency staff need to become much more alert to external problems generally and their impact on families and more involved in community efforts to correct them. ■

Chart 25

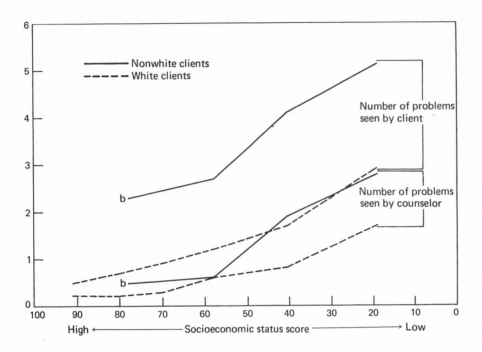

Average number of
environmental
problems

Nonwhite clients
White clients

Number of problems
seen by client

Number of problems
seen by counselor

High ← Socioeconomic status score → Low

[a] Cases with follow-up report.

[b] Nonwhite cases for the top three socioeconomic categories
are combined because of small samples.

The second equally striking feature of this chart is the substantial and consistent differential between counselors and clients in their reporting of environmental situations. On the average, counselors reported less than half as many such problems as did their clients (0.8 versus 1.8). Contrasts in some instances were considerably greater.

In addition to the marked association of neighborhood, community, and support problems with socioeconomic status and race, high counts for these problems were also found associated[10] with number of family and personal problems at intake, large family size, low self-involvement in seeking help, principal problems resistant to improvement, and predictions of little improvement by counselors. Clearly, families attempting to cope with more than their share of such problems are often the same ones that must carry an above-average load of family and personal problems.

Within agency programs, clients with high counts for neighborhood problems tended to cluster in certain special programs, such as legal aid departments, special projects, travelers aid programs, mental health units, and multiservice centers.[11]

Problems of these types will yield only to large-scale action by total communities, states, and the nation as a whole. Armed with direct knowledge of their tragic toll, family agencies, with the help of clients, are increasingly taking leadership in advocacy to correct these conditions. ■

The unequal impact of adverse external conditions is strikingly evident in chart 25. White clients at the lowest socioeconomic level reported six times as many environmental problems per family·as did white clients at the highest level (2.9 versus 0.5). For nonwhite clients, the average for the lowest level was more than two-and-one-half times that for the highest (5.1 versus 2.0). Within each status level, nonwhite clients usually

reported two to four times as many environmental problems as did white clients. For the total nonwhite group the general average was 4.0, or almost triple the 1.4 figure for the total white group.[9] Variations in specific environmental problems followed similar patterns by socioeconomic status and race, the only exception being discrimination, which was more often mentioned by upper and middle than lower status nonwhite clients.

3

HOW DOES
SERVICE BEGIN?

SOURCE OF REFERRAL

Chart 26

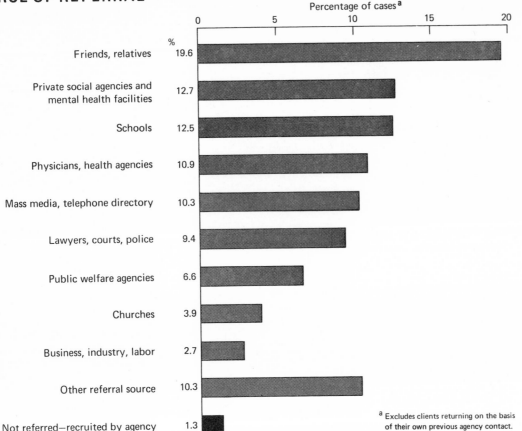

Percentage of cases^a

	%	
Friends, relatives	19.6	
Private social agencies and mental health facilities	12.7	
Schools	12.5	
Physicians, health agencies	10.9	
Mass media, telephone directory	10.3	
Lawyers, courts, police	9.4	
Public welfare agencies	6.6	
Churches	3.9	
Business, industry, labor	2.7	
Other referral source	10.3	
Not referred—recruited by agency	1.3	

^a Excludes clients returning on the basis of their own previous agency contact.

The decision to seek help from a family agency usually begins with a referral. As families become aware of and concerned about their problems, they begin to explore cautiously and confidentially for solutions. In the process they often turn to trusted friends or professional persons and ask what to do. The answers they receive may start them on one of the many paths to the family agency. Something of this process is reflected in chart 26 on referral source.

Two out of ten applicants reported that they had come to the family agency at the suggestion of friends, relatives, or neighbors—in other words, on the advice of someone in their informal social network. An additional one in ten found their way to the agency using clues from more impersonal sources—a magazine article, a newspaper reference, a radio or television program, a local lecture, or a telephone book listing. Most of the rest were referred or steered to the agency by a professional person. Schools, private social agencies, and mental health facilities took the lead among such referrals, followed by medical, legal, and public welfare referrals. Only slightly more than one percent were recruited by family agencies themselves, and only about 3 percent were referred by a business or industrial firm or labor union.[1]

The same referral sources headed the list in 1960 as in 1970. The only statistically significant change during the decade was a drop in self-referrals from 28.5 percent in 1960 to 20.7 in 1970 (excluding those from telephone book leads). Referral patterns for family agencies are clearly fairly stable.[2] ■

Chart 27 shifts the focus to the socioeconomic status of clients who come from each referral source. In order, from high to low on the proportion in the upper half of the range, referrals by ministers and rabbis came first. Next highest were those who found their way to the agency on their own, using clues from public information sources, such as radio, TV, magazine articles, lectures, and telephone book listings—all channels that avoid any need to confide in outsiders. The more personal route—that of seeking the advice of close relatives, friends, and neighbors—was more characteristic of clients with somewhat lower status ratings. Those coming on referral from such professionals as teachers, physicians, and psychiatrists were almost equally balanced between the two halves of the range. A slight shift toward the lower half began with referrals with a more authoritarian flavor—those from lawyers, courts, and police officers. The shift increased for persons referred by industrial firms and labor unions and by social service agencies, such as public welfare offices. Lower status applicants in this last group exceeded the upper and middle in the ratio of seven to three. Among those recruited on agency initiative through such activities as case-finding in depressed neighborhoods and location of services in housing projects, storefronts, and outreach centers, the lower status group exceeded the middle and upper by more than four to one. These sharp contrasts suggest that agencies can influence whom they serve by how and where they interpret their services and invite referrals. ■

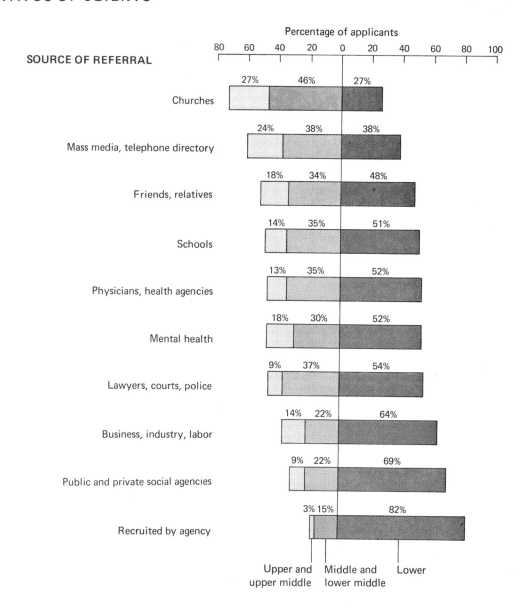

How does service begin?

SERVICES PROVIDED BY PHONE ONLY
(At point of intake [a])

Chart 28

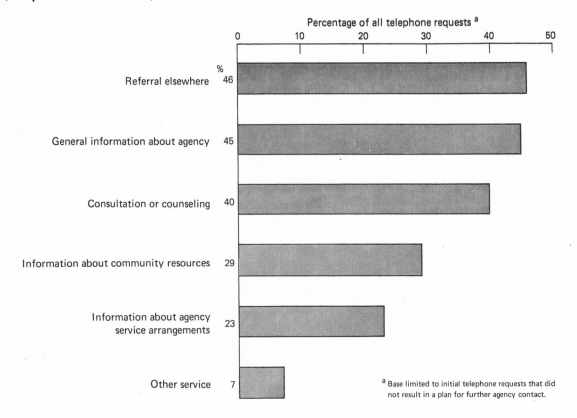

Percentage of all telephone requests [a]

| | 0 | 10 | 20 | 30 | 40 | 50 |

%
Referral elsewhere — 46

General information about agency — 45

Consultation or counseling — 40

Information about community resources — 29

Information about agency service arrangements — 23

Other service — 7

[a] Base limited to initial telephone requests that did not result in a plan for further agency contact.

Actual contact with a family agency usually begins with a phone call. This first phone contact is often the most critical point in the whole help-seeking process. The response may well determine whether an anxious applicant musters enough courage to come in for a face-to-face interview, or whether he succeeds in reaching another community resource that can help him with his problem.

To provide some picture of this critical initial phase of agency service, 139 agencies, or approximately half of all participating agencies, volunteered to report all initial phone calls during their census week. Together these agencies submitted 2,935 reports of initial phone contacts.[3] These reports divided, in the ratio of three to two, into two groups: those who made arrangements for further agency service and those who did not.

Of the three-fifths who made an appointment for further service, three-quarters actually came in for a face-to-face interview. The services received by this group prior to the first interview are not covered in the chart. Nearly three in ten received some advance counseling; one in twenty was given information on other community resources; and a similar proportion was helped with a related referral. In addition, almost all had a chance to learn about the agency, assess whether the services were right for them, express any fears or concerns they had about using help, and make arrangements for a first appointment.

The rest of the callers (two out of five) made no plans for further service by the agency. This is the group shown in chart 28. Nearly half of this group were referred or steered elsewhere, four in ten received consultation by phone, and three in ten were given information about other community resources. Similar services were also provided to persons making an appointment but not keeping it.[4] These elusive, intangible, but essential services are often lost track of in agency reports.

On the average, agencies serve by phone seven additional families or unattached individuals that they do not see for every ten that they see in person. Although little noticed and seldom reported, these services of information, referral, and phone consultation are essential ones, both for those directly involved and for the total community, which must cope with the wider consequences of these problems if they are left without attention. ■

For most clients, the first face-to-face contact with the counselor takes places in the office. In the present sample nearly four out of five made an advance appointment. One in ten arrived on a drop-in basis. Another one in fourteen was seen in the client's own home. This was most likely to happen when the problem involved home management, caretaking, health, housing, or lack of social contacts. Three percent were seen in such places as a clinic, school, or housing project. The average number of interviews before closing was lowest for drop-ins (3.2 interviews) and highest for home interviews (11.1).

The location of the first interview varied markedly by socioeconomic status. First interviews in the office were most characteristic of upper and middle-status clients while office drop-ins and home interviews increased in the lower range. Within each status group, nonwhite clients were less likely than white clients to be seen by appointment in the office (58 versus 82 percent); they were much more often seen on a drop-in basis or in the home. These findings leave little doubt that if the lower socioeconomic groups are to be reached, service can not be restricted to the office or to advance appointments. Agencies must be prepared to see clients in their own homes or neighborhoods whenever and wherever they can be reached.

A further question: Was agency service actively sought out by the applicants or was it urged on them by some outside authority? The answer is that most agency contacts were client-initiated, usually by a family member.

Chart 29

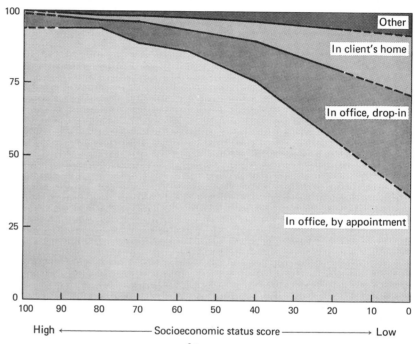

Percentage of cases [a]

Other

In client's home

In office, drop-in

In office, by appointment

High ←——————— Socioeconomic status score ———————→ Low

[a] Percentages at lower and upper extremes of socioeconomic status represent projections of trends prevailing at midpoints of top and bottom intervals.

In over half (54 percent), the wife alone took the initiative; in 17 percent, it was the husband (or both wife and husband). Three percent were inititated by a person under twenty-one and 7 percent by other adult relatives. The initiative came from an outside professional person—a physician, psychiatrist, minister, lawyer, or teacher—for only 12 percent. In 2.5 percent the first contact was initiated by the agency itself. Proportionately more nonwhite than white clients were agency-recruited (7 versus 2 percent), while fewer nonwhite clients came on the initiative of the wife (48 versus 55 percent). As will be documented later, client involvement in the help-seeking process is associated with improved outcomes. ∎

How does service begin?

PERSONS SEEN IN FIRST INTERVIEW: 1960 and 1970 (Husband-wife families)

Chart 30

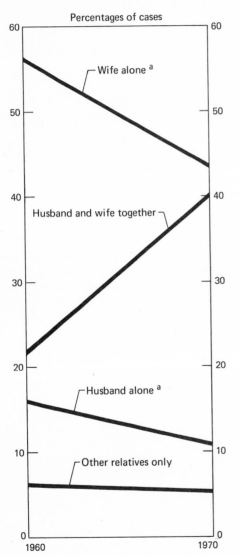

Percentages of cases

Wife alone [a]

Husband and wife together

Husband alone [a]

Other relatives only

1960   1970

[a] Or with relative other than spouse.

Face-to-face contact with a family agency usually begins with an initial interview with a professional counselor. In this interview, the applicant explains his situation and problems, the counselor makes an initial diagnostic assessment, and together they plan for next steps. Agencies have been making an increasing effort to involve both husband and wife in this critical initial encounter. The returns indicate that they have made dramatic progress toward this goal.

There was a highly statistically significant increase, in the decade of the 1960s, in husbands and wives coming in together for their first interview—for the same agencies, from 21.6 to 40.1 percent. This sharp increase is combined with a major decrease in wives being seen without their husbands and a lesser decrease in husbands coming in without their wives. This marked shift toward early involvement of both spouses probably reflects not only a greater agency effort to include both spouses but also an increasing readiness of husbands to share the responsibility for seeking help for home and family problems.

Husbands and wives coming in together proved to be particularly characteristic of intact families at the upper socioeconomic levels. The proportion of partners who came in together declined as status levels declined. For white couples the decline was from 43 percent to 27 percent; for nonwhite couples, the decline was from 30 percent to 14 percent. The absence of the spouse was compensated for by an increase in mothers or fathers coming in alone or with their children.

These figures apply to intact families where there was both a husband and a wife available for the intake interview. In single-parent families with a male head, it was usually the separated husband or father who came in. In families headed by a woman, it was the wife or mother who came in, often bringing one or more children. The individual not living in a family unit usually came in alone.

When broken families and unattached individuals were added to the counts for intact families, nearly six clients in ten were found to come in alone for their first interview. About one-fourth (24 percent) came in with the spouse. One in ten were mothers bringing other family members but not the spouse. Three or more family members were seen together for the first interview in only one case in twenty. Apparently total family involvement at the point of intake is still unusual despite the diagnostic and treatment values that many practitioners see in this approach.

Four out of five of these first interviews were with new cases. The other one in five involved reapplications. In reopened cases, the principal problem was more often a problem of adult personality adjustment, whereas marital cases were more likely to be first-time contacts. This pattern suggests a possible reason for the statistically significant drop (from 27 to 21 percent) between 1960 and 1970 in reopened cases: namely, the reduced use of family agencies for problems of mental illness or adult personality adjustment. ■

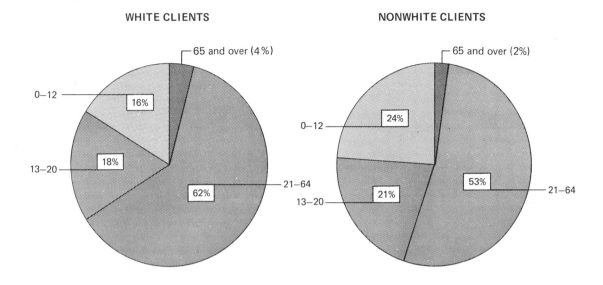

WHITE CLIENTS   NONWHITE CLIENTS

The needs of adult family members dominate clients' requests at intake. Nearly two-thirds of all initial requests were for service for someone aged twenty-one to sixty-four. This was by far the largest target group for both white and nonwhite clients. The needs of young people aged thirteen through twenty ranked next as the cause of requests from white clients. Those from nonwhite clients tended to focus more often on the needs of children under thirteen. The needs of family members sixty-five and over were seldom the focus of requests from either group, mostly because there were few from this group in the sample.

In general, requests from nonwhite clients tended to concentrate at somewhat younger age levels than did those from white clients. Nearly half of the requests from nonwhite clients were for service for persons under twenty-one as compared with only a third of those from white clients. This same focus on the needs of the young was also reflected in the relatively low requests from the nonwhite group on behalf of family members aged sixty-five and over. At the senior age level, requests from nonwhite clients were only about half as frequent as were those from white clients. The reasons for these differences in request patterns are not clear.

Another perspective on requests by age levels can be obtained by considering the proportion of all persons at each age level for whom service was requested.[5] On this revised basis, service was requested for 62 percent of adults twenty-one to sixty-four; for 58 percent of persons sixty-five and over; for 42 percent of adolescents and young adults aged thirteen to twenty; and for 22 percent of children under thirteen. Again, adults ranked at the top as the focus of requests, but persons sixty-five and over came out second instead of being a small segment at the bottom. This major shift is the result of taking account of the low number of persons sixty-five and over in the sample. Actually, this is a group with very high needs in proportion to their numbers. Viewed in this way, white-nonwhite differences were minor.[6] The major difference between them was that services were requested for a lower proportion of nonwhite persons sixty-five and over than for white persons in the same age group. ■

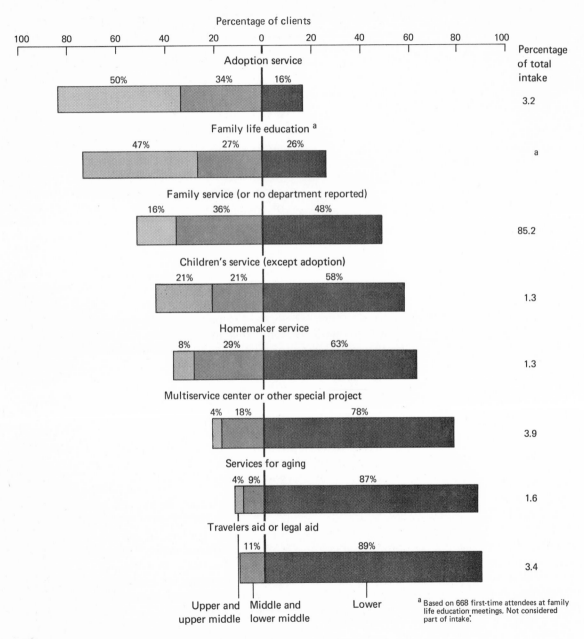

Percentage of clients

100 80 60 40 20 0 20 40 60 80 100

Percentage of total intake

Adoption service
50%   34%   16%
3.2

Family life education [a]
47%   27%   26%
a

Family service (or no department reported)
16%   36%   48%
85.2

Children's service (except adoption)
21%   21%   58%
1.3

Homemaker service
8%   29%   63%
1.3

Multiservice center or other special project
4%   18%   78%
3.9

Services for aging
4%   9%   87%
1.6

Travelers aid or legal aid
11%   89%
3.4

Upper and upper middle | Middle and lower middle | Lower

[a] Based on 668 first-time attendees at family life education meetings. Not considered part of intake.

The various departments and special programs of agencies vary greatly in the socioeconomic status of their clientele. Eighty-four percent of applicants for adoption services came from the upper and middle socioeconomic groups. Perhaps this was predictable in view of the added financial load involved in adopting a child. Similarly, nearly three quarters of those attending family life education meetings were from the upper half of the range. Information for these clients was obtained through a special supplementary study. They were not included in either the basic intake sample or in any other charts.[7] The relatively high status of those utilizing this service was unexpected, especially in view of the pioneer efforts of Project ENABLE to extend the benefits of family life education to ghetto neighborhoods and to the disadvantaged generally.[8]

Applicants for family service presented a relatively even balance between upper and lower socioeconomic groups. From that point on, the balance tipped strongly toward the lower half. About two-thirds of applicants for homemaker service were from the lower half of the range, as were four-fifths of those utilizing multiservice centers and special projects and nearly nine-tenths of those applying for services for the aging, travelers aid, or legal aid. The proportion of nonwhite clients applying to the various units followed a similar sequence, ranging from 8 percent for adoption services to 45 percent for special projects or multiservice centers.

The implications are clear. The type of program that an agency elects to provide has great influence on the types of clients it will succeed in reaching and serving. ■

The first interview involves a mutual exploratory process in which the applicant learns about the agency and the counseling process and the counselor explores the client's needs and problems, assesses whether the agency can help, and works with him on a plan for next steps. What types of decisions result from this process?

In the total sample, 72 percent of applicants were offered immediate service, 8 percent were placed on waiting lists, 6 percent of the applications were closed by referral, and 6 percent were terminated without referral either because the community lacked the service needed or because the client preferred to handle his problems on his own. Decision on 8 percent was deferred.

One-interview closings were more frequent at the lower than at the upper and middle-status levels and with nonwhite than with white clients. These differences appeared to stem mainly from higher needs among the disadvantaged for brief practical services. Thirty-two percent of nonwhite clients who terminated in one interview received financial assistance as compared with only 8 percent of the white group; 8 percent as compared with 3 percent received legal service; and 6 percent as compared with 3 percent received advocacy help. Nonwhite clients closing in one interview received an average of 1.1 services other than counseling; white clients, an average of 0.8. Reasons for closing in one interview were also consistent with this explanation of the white-nonwhite differential in one-interview closings.[9]

The relatively high proportion of upper and middle-status nonwhite as compared with white clients placed on waiting lists (18 ver

How does service begin?

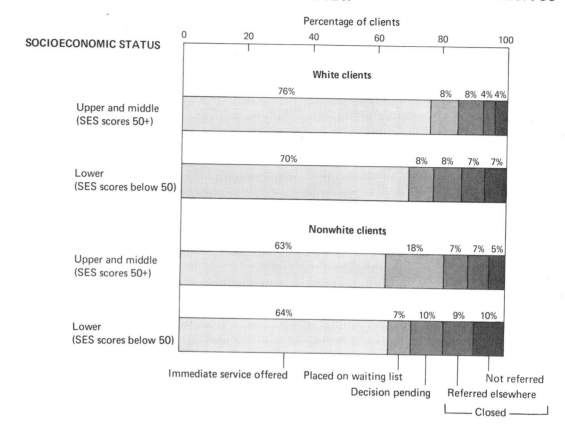

sus 8 percent) was both unexpected and statistically significant. Three explanations have been suggested: (1) Nonwhite clients are concentrated in the larger cities where waiting lists are more frequent;[10] (2) nonwhite upper and middle-class clients are more likely to need scarce evening and Saturday appointments since the wives are often working;[11] and (3) to the extent that matching of counselor and client by race is attempted, nonwhite clients would have to wait for openings with nonwhite counselors who comprised, at that time, only 16 percent of the total number of family service counselors.[12] Whatever the reason, this is a differential that should receive close monitoring at the local level lest service to upper and middle-class nonwhite clients be unfairly delayed. ■

LENGTH OF TIME KEPT ON WAITING LIST: 1960 and 1970

Chart 34

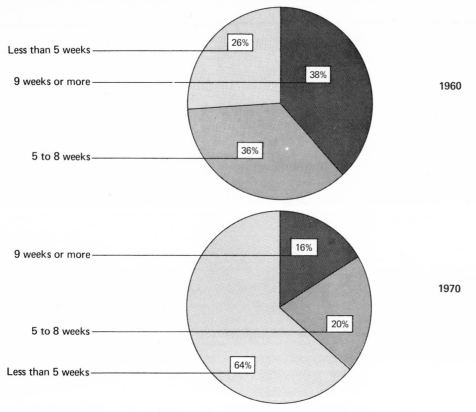

1960 pie chart:
- Less than 5 weeks — 26%
- 9 weeks or more — 38%
- 5 to 8 weeks — 36%

1960

1970 pie chart:
- 9 weeks or more — 16%
- 5 to 8 weeks — 20%
- Less than 5 weeks — 64%

1970

In 1970, one client in seven had to be asked to wait after the intake interview before further service could be provided. Of these, slightly more than a third had to wait five or more weeks before being recalled. Has there been any progress since 1960 in reducing these unfortunate delays? Chart 34 provides the answer.

Substantial delays are clearly much less frequent than formerly. Between 1960 and 1970 the proportion of clients kept waiting more than five weeks dropped from 74 to 37 percent; those kept waiting for nine weeks or more dropped from 38 to 17 percent. Both decreases are statistically highly significant. Both also represent important gains for clients.

Two benefits for clients resulting from this change can be directly documented from this study. The first is reduced drop-out from the waiting list. In 1970 the proportion who failed to return when recalled was only 21 percent as contrasted with 34 percent in 1960. This statistically significant reduction is the logical result of shortened waiting time.[13] The second benefit is that a higher proportion of cases are carried through to completion of service. In both 1960 and 1970, agencies without waiting lists had more terminations with service completed and fewer premature terminations because the client decided not to continue than did agencies with waiting lists.[14]

The negative consequences of waiting lists prompt a second question: Was there any reduction in the 1960-70 decade in the proportion of clients kept waiting? The answer unfortunately is no. For all agencies, the movement was in the reverse direction (12 to 14 percent), but the increase was not statistically significant.[15]

A more unexpected change was the virtual elimination of the socioeconomic differential in the clients asked to wait for service. In 1960, more than three times as many from the upper as from the lower end of the socioeconomic scale were placed on waiting lists.[16] By 1970 these same agencies showed considerably less difference—although it was still statistically significant.

Probably the great equalizer here was the movement toward planned short-term treatment. The long periods of service on parent-child problems formerly provided to the economically advantaged have largely been eliminated (see chart 41). Since most types of service are now brief, agencies try to provide this service to all applicants at the point of crisis when motivation is high. Unfortunately, intake pressures are such that many still have to wait for service. ■

4

WHAT SERVICES
DO CLIENTS
RECEIVE?

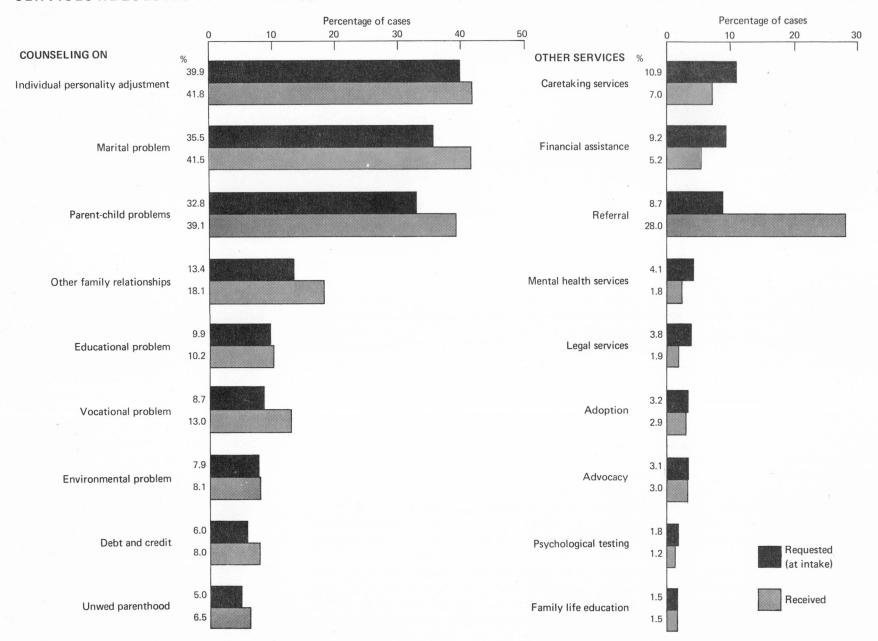

Percentage of cases

COUNSELING ON

	%
Individual personality adjustment	39.9 / 41.8
Marital problem	35.5 / 41.5
Parent-child problems	32.8 / 39.1
Other family relationships	13.4 / 18.1
Educational problem	9.9 / 10.2
Vocational problem	8.7 / 13.0
Environmental problem	7.9 / 8.1
Debt and credit	6.0 / 8.0
Unwed parenthood	5.0 / 6.5

Percentage of cases

OTHER SERVICES

	%
Caretaking services	10.9 / 7.0
Financial assistance	9.2 / 5.2
Referral	8.7 / 28.0
Mental health services	4.1 / 1.8
Legal services	3.8 / 1.9
Adoption	3.2 / 2.9
Advocacy	3.1 / 3.0
Psychological testing	1.8 / 1.2
Family life education	1.5 / 1.5

Requested (at intake)

Received

Family agency services are heavily concentrated in the counseling area. Some form of counseling was requested by 86 percent of applicants and provided to 91 percent. The frequency of counseling on various themes mirrors the problems presented at intake. In general, counseling about family relationships and individual adjustment problems exceeded by a considerable margin counseling about difficulties in the world of school, work, and money.

Counseling themes omitted because of low frequencies include health problems, alcoholism, child care, and use of leisure time. Premarital counseling was requested and received by fewer than one applicant in 100. Apparently, family agencies are not regarded as a resource for this important preventive service.

In the other service categories, referral ranked highest in frequency. Help with referrals was provided to three applicants in ten.[1] When this service was combined with counseling, 80 percent were found to have received counseling or referral only; 5 percent, some other service only; and 15 percent, both counseling and other services.

Caretaking services ranked next to referral in frequency among other services. Some service from this composite group was requested by one applicant in nine and received by one in fourteen. Home care or homemaker service was the largest single component of this group. The occasion for this type of service was usually the physical illness of the family caretaker or the need for care for a child or elderly person. Foster care or group home care, usually in relation to children of unwed parents, was extended to 1.5 percent of the sample. About one family in

100 received help with day care, mostly for children under six. Likewise, about one case in 100 received help related to provision of institutional care. Usually the need here was for care for an aged person, but some adults who were physically or mentally ill also received help of this type. One in 100 also received protective services. Of these, 60 percent were concerned with protection for children; 16 percent, with protection for adults with such problems as mental illness or alcoholism; and 24 percent, with protection for the aged in relation to management of their affairs. Visiting and escort service was provided to 1.5 percent, usually for the elderly, but secondarily for younger adults who were physically or mentally ill.

Other services provided by agencies were a miscellaneous group. One in eleven requested financial assistance, but only one in nineteen actually received any financial aid. Adoption, advocacy, psychological testing, and family life education[2] all were around the 3 percent level or below. Not shown are screening for other community services, public housing, camp, and the like.

In general, counseling and referral were provided more often than they were requested and other services less often. Many requests for homemaker service, day care, other caretaking services, and financial assistance went unmet, usually because the service was not one the agency could provide.

Comparisons of the same agencies in 1960 and 1970 indicate a trend in this ten-year period toward further agency specialization in counseling and a lesser investment in financial assistance and referrals. While data on services for 1960 are incomplete, the following shifts for cases receiving two or more

| Service | Percentage of cases | | | |
| | Requesting | | Receiving | |
	1960	1970	1960	1970
Counseling	67.6	88.1[b]	92.5	96.8[b]
Referral	19.6	9.3[b]	31.8	31.0
Financial assistance	17.1	10.2[b]	7.9	4.6[b]
Homemaker service[a]	3.9	3.6	4.2	3.0

[a]1970 figures include all home care services.
[b]Change from 1960 is statistically significant.

interviews are documented in the table above. Paralleling this trend toward concentration on counseling, there was also an increase from 42 to 55 percent in the proportion of cases in which fees were charged. This increase was also statistically significant.

Apparently, both agencies and the general public are increasingly seeing counseling as the cental function of a family agency. In 1960, many persons in the community still thought of family service agencies as a potential source for financial assistance. By 1970, this was less true. Even in 1970, however, only half of those who requested financial assistance actually received some minimum aid, usually a small sum to tide a family over in an emergency until public assistance or other support could be arranged. This drop in requests for financial help that agencies can not possibly provide reflects a gain in community knowledge of available resources. The result is a real saving in time and stress both for the applicants who formerly had to try again elsewhere and for the counselors who not only had to refer them but also had to cope with their disappointment or anger. ∎

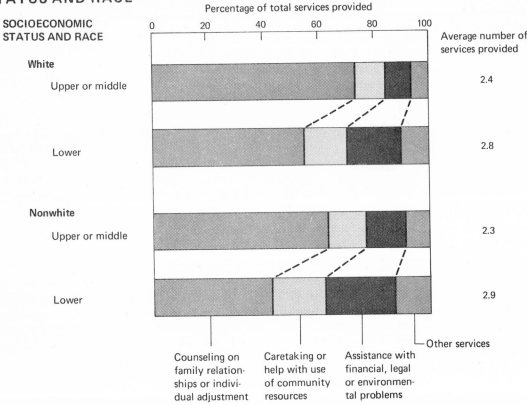

SOCIOECONOMIC STATUS AND RACE

Percentage of total services provided

0   20   40   60   80   100

Average number of services provided

White

Upper or middle — 2.4

Lower — 2.8

Nonwhite

Upper or middle — 2.3

Lower — 2.9

Counseling on family relationships or individual adjustment

Caretaking or help with use of community resources

Assistance with financial, legal or environmental problems

Other services

The types of service utilized varied markedly by socioeconomic status.[3] For white clients, the proportion of services that focused on relationship or individual adjustment problems dropped from 73 percent for upper and middle socioeconomic groups to 55 percent for the lower. Nonwhite clients showed a similar drop (from 63 to 43 percent).

Utilization of all other services was greater at the lower than at the middle and upper levels of the socioeconomic scale. Differentials were largest for services related to financial, employment, legal, or environmental problems. For white clients, the proportion of such services to the total at the lower level was more than double that at the middle and upper level (19 versus 9 percent). For nonwhite clients, the percentage was also nearly double (25 versus 13 percent). Similarly, caretaking services and referrals for white clients were nearly half again as high for the lower as for the middle and upper groups (16 versus 11 percent). Contrasts were only slightly less for nonwhite clients (20 versus 14 percent). Similar patterns were also evident for the "other services" category. Averages for the total number of different services utilized also showed some increase at the lower end of the socioeconomic scale, but this increase was less than for the major service categories.

Reports of services needed but not arranged by the agency followed, to some extent, similar patterns. For example, needs related to basic maintenance, medical care, housing, and employment were reported more frequently by clients from lower than from upper and middle socioeconomic groups. On the other hand, certain needs were common to all groups, among them the need for caretaking and protective services. Surprisingly, the unmet need most often identified by clients was that for mental health services. This need was reported by clients from upper and middle groups more often than by the lower, perhaps because of their greater general awareness of psychological problems. On the whole, counselors reported considerably fewer unmet needs than did clients. This is still another area where clients are an important source of information about the services needed by the community. ∎

AVERAGE NUMBER OF INTERVIEWS BY SOCIOECONOMIC STATUS AND RACE: 1960 and 1970

Chart 37

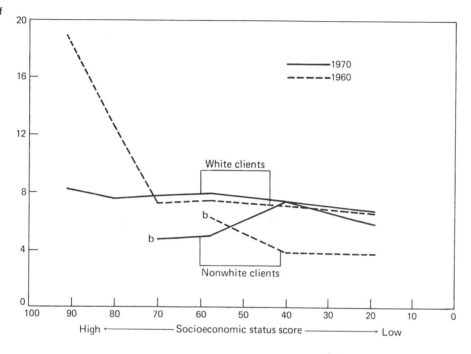

Average number of interviews (in two years) [a]

White clients

Nonwhite clients

1970
1960

High ← ————— Socioeconomic status score ————— → Low

[a] Including collateral interviews.
[b] Nonwhite cases not plotted beyond this point because of small samples.

problems with arrangements are a contributing factor.

This marked shift within a decade toward a more egalitarian pattern of service probably stems from at least three major sources: (1) the expansion of agency outreach programs, plus a generally greater emphasis on provision of practical services, (2) the increasing use of planned short-term service for clients at all socioeconomic levels, and (3) the reduced use of long-term individualized counseling with well-educated parents around parent-child problems.

For comparative purposes, the averages charted were restricted to the same agencies participating in both 1960 and 1970. Averages for all agencies included in the 1970 census were as follows:

Socioeconomic status	White clients	Nonwhite clients
Upper, upper middle, and middle	8.0[a]	4.9[a]
Lower middle	7.8	5.2
Upper lower	7.7	7.2
Lower lower	7.0	5.8

[a] Categories combined because of small nonwhite samples.

In the 1960-70 decade a striking reduction occurred in socioeconomic and racial differentials in the number of interviews provided to clients. In 1960 white clients in the top socioeconomic group were receiving, within two years, three times as many interviews on the average as were white clients at the lowest status level. By 1970 they were receiving less than one-quarter more. Similarly, in 1960, nonwhite clients in the two lowest socio-

economic groups were receiving only about 55 percent as many interviews as were white clients of similar status. By 1970, the averages for these two groups in the same agencies had become almost identical. The only noteworthy racial differences remaining were found in the average number of interviews received by clients in the middle and lower-middle socioeconomic groups. The reasons for this exception are not clear. Apparently,

This shift to the total 1970 sample increases the white-nonwhite differential but continues the pattern of minimal status differentiation. These 1970 differences in interview counts were statistically significant for race but not for socioeconomic status. ■

What services do clients receive?

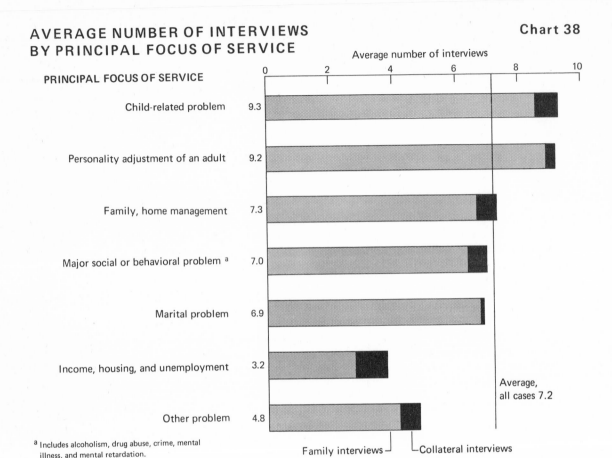

AVERAGE NUMBER OF INTERVIEWS BY PRINCIPAL FOCUS OF SERVICE

Chart 38

Average number of interviews

PRINCIPAL FOCUS OF SERVICE

	Average number of interviews
Child-related problem	9.3
Personality adjustment of an adult	9.2
Family, home management	7.3
Major social or behavioral problem [a]	7.0
Marital problem	6.9
Income, housing, and unemployment	3.2
Other problem	4.8

Average, all cases 7.2

Family interviews — Collateral interviews

[a] Includes alcoholism, drug abuse, crime, mental illness, and mental retardation.

agency's larger role in influencing public policy in these areas is not reflected in any of the census data. The "other problem" category also showed a relatively low average here because the principal service often involved making arrangements for such practical supportive services as homemaker service, day care, or other caretaking services. These variations need to be taken into account in program planning and budgeting, especially for new programs.

In addition to interviewing the family, it is often important for the counselor to talk to others who have known the client—teachers, physicians, psychiatrists, social workers, lawyers, ministers, employers, or probation and parole officers—in the hope that they can shed further light on the problem or help with its solution. Such collateral interviews were relatively frequent for children's problems, family and home management problems, and major social and behavioral problems but were infrequent for marital and adult adjustment problems, many of which involve confidential matters.

As would be expected, the average number of interviews with family members per case also varied by agency department. Legal aid departments, for example, averaged only 1.6 interviews; multiservice centers, 2.3; travelers aid, 3.0; homemaker service, 3.2; and services for the aging, 5.5 interviews. Other departments providing relatively complicated services showed above-average counts. Children's service departments, for example, averaged 9.3 interviews; special projects, 9.7; and mental health clinics operated by family agencies, 10.9 interviews. Family service departments were about in the middle, with an average of 7.0 interviews. ■

While the average case received 7.2 interviews, this figure varied markedly in relation to the principal focus of service.[4] Both children's problems and adult personality adjustment problems were well above average in this respect. Family and home management problems came close to the general average. Marital problems fell slightly below, as did major social and behavioral problems, such as alcoholism, drug abuse, crime and delin-quency, and mental illness. An important factor here is the difficulty of holding these cases in treatment. Income, housing, and unemployment problems also fell below the average on number of interviews but for a different reason. In many such cases, the most that the family agency can do for clients as individuals is to refer them to some specialized community resource and, if necessary, to serve as the client's advocate with this resource. The

Chart 39 presents an overview of how agencies allocate their most basic resource—interview time with a professionally trained counselor. The functional distribution shown was estimated by assigning to each major focus of service shown in chart 38 the number of interviews reported at closing for each client whose service centered on this problem. Cases with a relatively large number of interviews therefore contributed substantially more per case to the total for a given problem than did cases receiving brief service only.

When viewed in terms of time allocation instead of case frequency (see chart 22), children's problems shifted from second to first place, since they received more interviews than did marital cases. There was no change in the relative position of adult personality adjustment problems. Income, housing, and unemployment problems, on the other hand, shrank in importance, since brief service usually exhausted the help a family agency could offer. Major social and behavioral problems involving crime and delinquency, drug abuse, alcoholism, and so on received only 3 percent of the agencies' time, not because they were ignored but because of the tendency of such clients to drop out after a few interviews. This small percentage is noteworthy in light of the fact that a substantial proportion of the controlled studies of casework effectiveness[5] have limited their samples to delinquents, predelinquents, and parolees. Together, this group constituted only 7 percent of the intake sample for the present study, even disregarding service focus. Clearly, the major components of family agency services have not been covered by these evaluation studies.

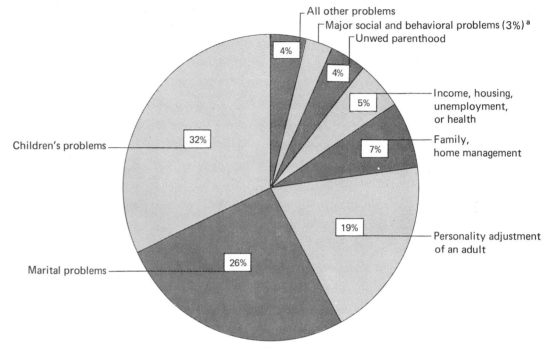

All other problems
Major social and behavioral problems (3%)[a]
Unwed parenthood
Income, housing, unemployment, or health
Family, home management
Personality adjustment of an adult
Marital problems
Children's problems

4%
4%
5%
7%
19%
26%
32%

[a] Includes alcoholism, drug abuse, crime, mental illness, and mental retardation.

Viewed in overall functional terms, about three-quarters of the interview time made available to this sample was allocated to family relationship and personal adjustment problems. The other quarter was invested in work on a variety of practical problems through supportive services combined with limited help with relationship problems. In terms of the age-group focus, about two-thirds of agency interview time invested in this sample went to helping adults with problems in their own lives and about one-third to helping parents cope with problems they were having with their children.

In viewing this chart, it is important to remember that the census did not undertake to cover all agency functions. Omitted because of lack of identifying information on the families served were consultation services to other professionals, community organization services, research, family life education through the mass media, and advocacy on behalf of neighborhoods, communities, and the nation as a whole.   ■

NUMBER OF INTERVIEWS: 1960 and 1970

Chart 40

Percentage of cases

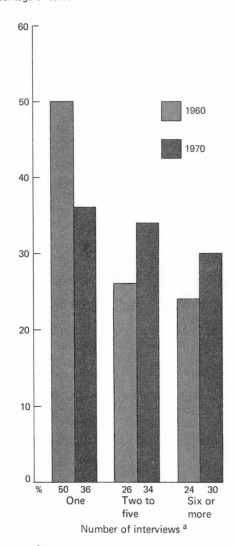

Number of interviews [a]

a Counts include only interviews with family members.

One of the most conspicuous changes in service patterns between 1960 and 1970 was the substantial drop in the proportion of one-interview cases. This drop (from 51 to 36 percent) was highly significant statistically. During the same period the proportion receiving two to five interviews increased significantly, as did the proportion receiving six or more interviews. These figures represent the number of interviews with family members within two years. All are limited to the same agencies in both 1960 and 1970.

The reason for the marked drop in one-interview cases is not immediately evident. Probably it is related in part to the drop in applications to agencies for financial assistance mentioned on page 57. In 1960 there were many applicants for financial help who had to be referred after one interview to the local public welfare program. By 1970 most clients had learned to apply directly to the public assistance office, thus avoiding this detour. The increased use of planned short-term service is probably a second major factor. Clients who are involved from the first in planning with their counselor for a specific, time-limited service are probably less likely to drop out after the first interview because of fear of involvement in an indefinitely prolonged treatment relationship. Whatever the reason, this major reduction in one-interview losses represents a real improvement in the ability of agencies to involve applicants in ongoing and presumably more productive service.

The reduction in drop-out after one interview was more than balanced by the increase in planned short-term service; the result was a slight net reduction in the average number of interviews for the same agencies as follows:

Type of interview	Average number of interviews	
	1960	1970
Interviews with family members	7.7	6.8
Collateral interviews	0.5	0.4
Total interviews	8.2	7.2

Little further detail is available for 1960 on type of interview. There was a minor and not statistically significant drop in the proportion of clients receiving a home interview (from 20.6 to 20.0 percent) and also a slight but statistically significant drop in the proportion receiving collateral interviews (from 16.1 to 13.9). In addition to service involving in-person contact, 46 percent of the cases in 1970 received some treatment by phone.

No data are available on planned short-term service for 1960. In 1970, 35 percent of the cases accepted in the first interview were assigned to planned short-term service. About three out of four of this group were told in the first interview that this was to be the plan. Proposed interview limits ranged upward to over sixteen interviews. For over half, the proposed limit was two to five interviews; for another fourth, six to nine interviews; 8 percent actually continued beyond fifteen interviews. Clearly, there are major differences in the concepts and practice of the field with regard to planned short-term service. ■

In addition to changes in total interview counts, comparisons over the 1960–70 decade indicate a marked shift in the problem areas in which agencies invest their interview time.[6] The most dramatic change and the only drop shown occurred in the investment in counseling on child-related problems.[7] For this group, the average number of interviews in 1970 was hardly more than half that in 1960 (8.7 instead of 16.7). Probably a major factor in this decline was the shift away from long-term service for relationship problems toward a planned short-term approach.

All major increases related to situations requiring caretaking or help with economic problems. The three largest increases were in services to the aged (1.3 to 5.6), substitute care for children (5.2 to 11.3), and services to unmarried parents (5.7 to 9.7). A number of other categories related to caretaking and support problems also showed increases. All were of the type that usually require multiple services or referrals, such as illness problems and economic and employment problems. Increases were minimal in marital problems and the personality adjustment of an adult.[8] Perhaps these increases in the caretaking and economic area were influenced by agencies' efforts to expand the range and amount of service to minorities, the poor, and the aged through special programs. ■

What services do clients receive?

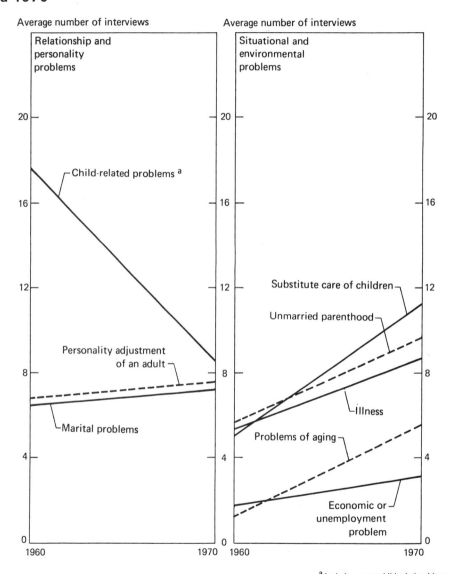

Average number of interviews

Relationship and
personality
problems

Child-related problems [a]

Personality adjustment
of an adult

Marital problems

Average number of interviews

Situational and
environmental
problems

Substitute care of children

Unmarried parenthood

Illness

Problems of aging

Economic or
unemployment
problem

[a] Includes parent-child relationships and the personality adjustment of a child or adolescent.

PRIMARY TREATMENT MODALITY [a]
(Husband-wife families)

Chart 42

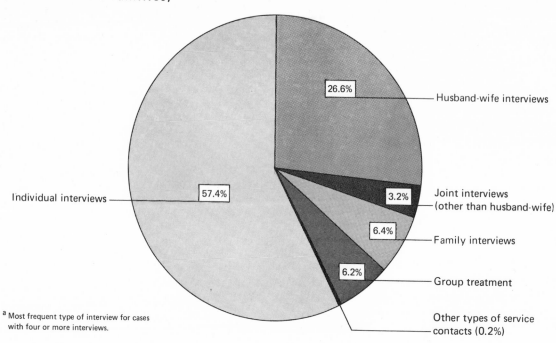

26.6% — Husband-wife interviews

Individual interviews — 57.4%

3.2% — Joint interviews (other than husband-wife)

6.4% — Family interviews

6.2% — Group treatment

Other types of service contacts (0.2%)

[a] Most frequent type of interview for cases with four or more interviews.

This chart shows the relative frequencies with which various modalities were used. In spite of the field's growing conviction about the value of a total family approach, individual interviews with one family member at a time was still the primary approach at the time of the census. This was true even when counts were limited to intact families continuing at least to the fourth interview. Husbands and wives were seen together more frequently than separately in only about one case in four. Family interviews (those involving three or more family members) were the primary modality for only one family in sixteen. Other combinations of two at a time, such as parent

Section four

and child or grandparent and child, were even less frequent. Treatment in groups that included unrelated persons was the primary approach for only one family in sixteen. Rarely were service contacts of other types, such as family life education, primary. These figures are not to be taken as a reflection of a diagnostic orientation to the individual rather than to the total family, since a family perspective often prevails even in individual interviews. The various modalities differed markedly in total number of interviews per case. Excluding collateral interviews, group treatment cases received an average of 22.9 interviews; individual interview cases, 7.2; family interviews, 5.5; husband-wife interviews, 5.3; and other joint interviews, 3.7.

Choice of treatment modality is greatly influenced by family composition. Husband-wife interviews, for example, can seldom be arranged when the marriage has already broken up. More common for one-parent families are interviews involving one parent and a child or individual interviews with the parent. For these and other practical reasons, individual interviews are increasingly the primary modality as one moves away from the intact family unit. This approach was primary for 56 percent of husband-wife families in the sample; 74 percent of families with a female head; 79 percent of families with another male head;

and 90 percent of individuals living alone or with nonrelatives.

Treatment modality also varied with the principal focus of service. For marital cases, husband-wife interviews were primary for nearly half (44 percent). Most of the rest of the marital cases were served mainly through individual interviews (51 percent). Family interviews and other joint interviews were rarely primary (one percent each), while group treatment was used with only two cases in 100. When children's problems were the principal focus, husband-wife interviews dropped to 18 percent and individual interviews to 47 percent, while family interviews rose to 17 percent, other joint interviews to 13 percent, and group treatment to 5 percent. Adult personality adjustment problems showed still a third pattern, being high on individual interviews (81 percent) and low on all other approaches except group treatment, which reached 3 percent.

Throughout, the term *primary treatment modality* refers to the type of interview most frequently employed for a given case.[9] When all interviews received by all cases in the sample were pooled without regard to primary modality, individual interviews increased to 62 percent of total interviews with a family member; husband-wife interviews dropped to 17 percent; and family interviews decreased to 5 per-

cent (because these were usually combined with some individual interviews). On the other hand, group treatment interviews rose to 10 percent of the total, owing to the high average number of interviews per case for those served primarily through group treatment.

Trend data on modality, insofar as they are available for the 1960-70 decade, are given in the table below:

	1960	1970
Percentage of husband-wife families receiving two or more interviews in which both partners were seen	56.8	68.6[a]
Percentage of all two-or-more-interview cases in which two or more family members were seen	61.9	73.6[a]
Percentage of all families in which two or more family members were seen	38.6	58.3[a]
Percentage of cases receiving group treatment	2.1	7.1[a]
Average number of family members seen	1.7	2.0[b]

[a]Difference is statistically significant.
[b]Significance of difference was not tested.

Significant progress toward involvement of more family members in treatment is evident. While these gains are substantial and impressive, the family service field still has some distance to go to achieve a truly family-centered approach to the solution of family problems. ■

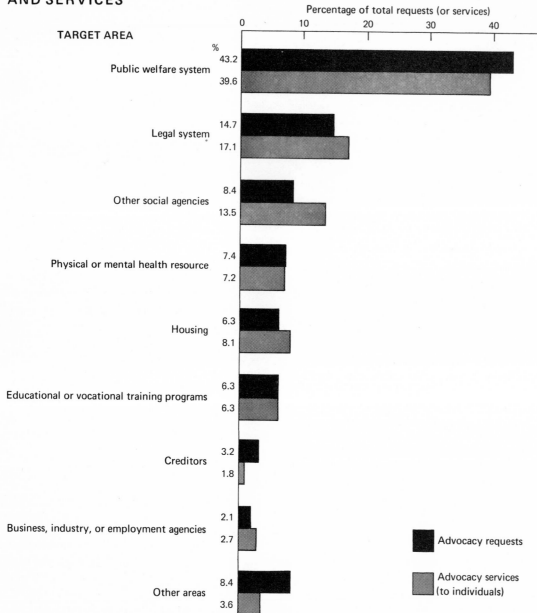

Percentage of total requests (or services)

TARGET AREA

Target Area	Advocacy requests	Advocacy services
Public welfare system	43.2	39.6
Legal system	14.7	17.1
Other social agencies	8.4	13.5
Physical or mental health resource	7.4	7.2
Housing	6.3	8.1
Educational or vocational training programs	6.3	6.3
Creditors	3.2	1.8
Business, industry, or employment agencies	2.1	2.7
Other areas	8.4	3.6

■ Advocacy requests

▨ Advocacy services (to individuals)

Increasingly, family agencies are taking the initiative in helping clients cope with their problems with other institutions. For the census sample, the public welfare system proved to be the major target of such efforts. Welfare institutions stimulated more than twice as many advocacy requests and services as any other institutional area. The legal system ranked second and other social agencies were third, with each of the other systems falling around or below 8 percent of the total. About eleven advocacy services were provided for every ten requested.

The lower socioeconomic groups and non-white clients were by far the most frequent users of advocacy service. Services of this type were also associated primarily with certain specialized departments, such as legal aid departments, multiservice center, programs for aging, and special projects.[10]

Evaluations of the helpfulness of advocacy services were asked for only when the agency had intervened in a problem relating to neighborhood or community conditions. For this small sample, clients evaluated three out of four of such interventions as helpful, while counselors reported four out of five as helpful to the client.

Since counselors, clients, and agencies differ in their concept of what advocacy service is, all statistics in this area must be considered rough approximations only. In addition, it is important to note that advocacy efforts on behalf of groups of families, neighborhoods, whole communities, or the nation were omitted by definition, not only from this chart but from the census as a whole. ■

Helping clients find and utilize other community resources is another important service of the family agency—one closely related to the advocacy function. In the present study about one referral in five was for mental health services. Slightly fewer (one in six) were for financial assistance. One in ten was for legal services and one in thirteen for each of the following: medical and dental care, help with employment or vocational problems, and caretaking services. Referrals related to housing, specialized education, alcoholism, and financial counseling were less frequent. Only a small number (about one in seventy) were for family planning help.[11]

The types of agencies to which clients were referred divided almost equally into fourths: one-fourth to public social agencies, one-fourth to private social agencies, one-fourth to physical or mental health facilities, and one-fourth to such other resources as private practitioners, vocational guidance agencies, group work centers, schools, courts, and churches. Access to the counselor's knowledge of these resources is an important component of agency service.

In about three cases in five (59 percent) the counselor paved the way for the client by advance contact with the agency to which the referral was made. This advance contact was more frequent when the client was from the lower socioeconomic group than when he was not (66 versus 49 percent; see chart 44). It also made a statistically significant difference in whether clients in general followed through on the referral. This difference was most marked with the lower socioeconomic group. With advance contact, only 13 percent of the lower

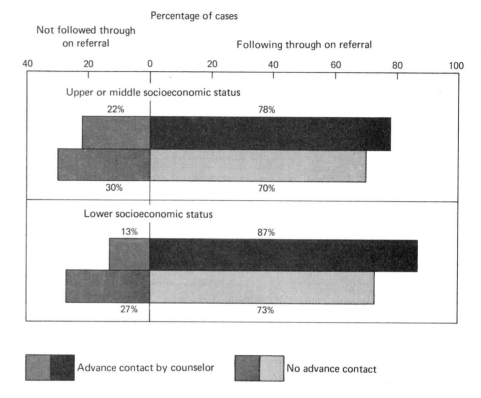

group failed to follow through as compared with 22 percent of the upper and middle group.[12] Since many of the referrals for upper and middle-status clients were to mental health resources, perhaps a reluctance to seek help with psychological problems was a factor in this contrast. Whatever the reason, advance contact by the counselor clearly helps assure that clients will actually reach the agency to which they have been referred. ■

What services do clients receive?

COMPLAINTS ABOUT

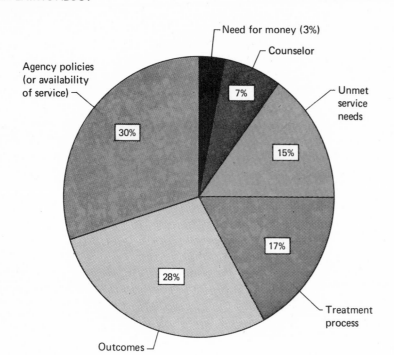

Need for money (3%)

Counselor

7%

Unmet service needs

15%

Agency policies (or availability of service)

30%

28%

17%

Outcomes

Treatment process

POSITIVE REMARKS ABOUT

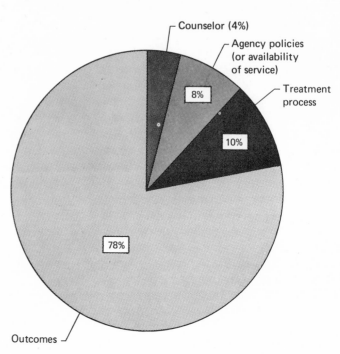

Counselor (4%)

Agency policies (or availability of service)

8%

Treatment process

10%

78%

Outcomes

What clients complained about and what they particularly liked about agency service are shown in the two adjoining circles—one showing complaints and the other positive remarks. In general, more clients offered positive comments than reported complaints (60 versus 49 percent)—in spite of the absence of any question about what clients liked about the agency or the service.

Complaints averaged about one per follow-up report. The most common complaint concerned agency policy or the unavailability of some needed service. Included here were remarks about not getting the services requested, the high fees, the inconvenience of office hours or office location, and having to wait too long for service. There were also more general complaints about red tape, bu-

reaucracy, lack of privacy, or agency atmosphere—too cold, clinical, and so on. Clients added suggestions for changes—for example, the establishment of a supervised playroom where children could wait while mothers were being seen. Others stressed the need for such additional services as emergency aid, money for basic maintenance, better housing, educational or vocational training, and the like.

Section four

Three in ten of the complaints focused on the outcomes of service. Most common here was a report that some other family member was worse, or not better, than before. Others noted that external conditions had failed to improve or had deteriorated, or that specific problems, such as alcoholism or infidelity, were worse instead of better. Particularly poignant were the expressions of disappointment and bitterness by the spouse who was left behind when the effort to save a marriage through counseling did not succeed. Some recognized that the agency had done all that it could, but that it had been too late. Others blamed the agency: "We followed the advice and it blew up in our face."

About one complaint in seven related to the treatment process. Most frequently the dissatisfaction was over the amount of advice given. Without exception, clients wanted more, not less, advice: "The counselor listened but did not give us the benefit of her thinking". . . "was too vague". . . "told us nothing". . . "answered all my questions with questions." While there were no complaints about too much advice, some did not like the advice they did receive or the solutions proposed by the counselor. Another frequent complaint was that the counselor would not make some other family member "behave." Still others reported disagreements with the counselor over what the problem was, what to do about it, or who should be seen. A number complained that counseling did not last long enough, but only one that it had lasted too long. A few complained about too many questions. Others recorded their objection to the interruption of treatment resulting from the counselor's unexpected departure from the agency. A few reported complaints of other family members, such as "my husband bitterly resents my going for therapy."

Another group of complaints related to the personal characteristics of the counselor. The most frequent objection was that the counselor did not seem to like them—did not care, seemed bored, pressured, impersonal, or even hostile. Another variation was to complain about the counselor's personality: "He was not warm"; "She needed help herself"; "She should go on a diet and take better care of herself." Others complained of the counselor's youth, inexperience, or manner: "He seemed like a teenage rebel"; "He was too groovy and hip." Some wanted a counselor of a different sex or marital status: "She was lovely but unmarried, without children, and unknowing on a gut level where I was at." No one complained about the race, ethnicity, or religion of the counselor.

There were nine positive comments for every ten complaints. In sharp contrast to three in ten of the complaints, nearly eight out of ten of these positive remarks related to outcomes. In this area positive comments outnumbered negative ones by almost two to one. Most frequently mentioned was satisfaction with the outcomes for the respondents personally—the change in their feelings about their problem, about themselves, and about their emotions generally: "I learned to like myself"; "I got more incentive to look for work"; "I gained insight." Comments on changes in the marriage included: "We came to a better understanding about our problem and why we are doing such harmful things"; "Now we're able to communicate. We're able to rule our emotions instead of them ruling us"; or, counseling "saved our marriage."

In commenting on the treatment process or the counselor, clients' positive remarks included expressions of appreciation for what it had meant to them to talk to an impartial and objective outsider, to "get a load off" their chest, or to renew their hope for the future. Others mentioned with appreciation the counselor's warmth, understanding, and professional competence. Still others recounted incidents when counselors had gone out of their way to help, such as visiting the client at home or in the hospital on their own time.

Positive comments on agency policies or the availability of service focused mainly on the value of certain direct, tangible services they had received. Others reported feeling welcome, feeling that the agency had tried, or feeling well treated. A number commented that they felt they could go back if the need should arise. Many comments were general: "Your agency is doing a great service."

A look at variations by subgroups indicates that clients from middle and upper socioeconomic groups volunteered both more complaints and more compliments than did those of lower status. Possibly they simply felt easier about communication in general. Nonwhite clients in the middle and upper socioeconomic groups were slightly higher in average number of complaints than white clients (1.3 versus 1.0 per case); in the lower-status groups they were slightly higher on positive comments (1.0 versus 0.9 per case).

In general, the comments clients volunteered on their mail questionnaires provided rich, colorful, and challenging feedback. This national experience suggests that use of client follow-up can provide an invaluable consumer perspective on local agency service. ∎

Chart 46

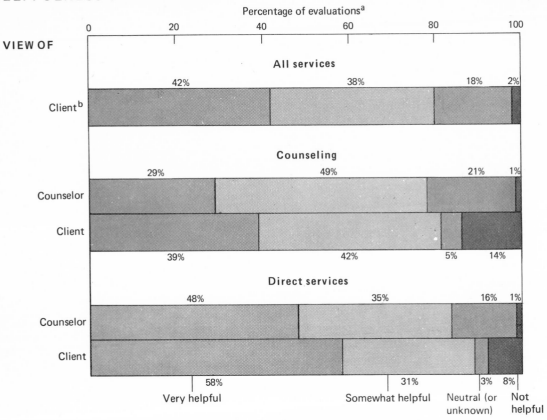

Percentage of evaluations[a]

VIEW OF

All services

Counseling

Direct services

Very helpful   Somewhat helpful   Neutral (or unknown)   Not helpful

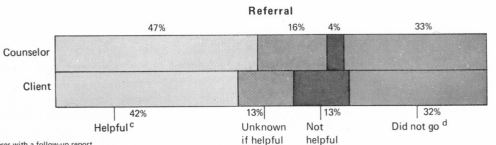

Referral

Helpful[c]   Unknown if helpful   Not helpful   Did not go[d]

[a] Based on cases with a follow-up report.

[b] No data were available on counselors' view of helpfulness of services as a whole.

[c] No detail on degree of helpfulness for client.

[d] Counselors' figure includes cases where it is unknown if client followed through.

In the follow-up process, both clients and counselors were asked about the helpfulness of services. Clients more often than counselors described specific agency services as "very helpful." Counselors preferred the more conservative rating of "somewhat helpful." Agency services as a whole were seen as "very helpful" by four in ten of the clients. Another four in ten saw them as "somewhat helpful." On the negative side, clients were more likely to report that the services were "not helpful," while counselors more frequently gave a neutral or "don't know" response. Obviously, counselors often lack information on whether agency services have helped.

Ratings of the helpfulness of referrals and of agency efforts at intervention in neighborhood and community situations provided two exceptions to this general pattern: 47 percent of counselors but only 42 percent of clients saw referrals as helpful;[13] 88 percent of counselors but only 79 percent of clients saw agency efforts at intervention in neighborhood or community conditions as helpful.[14]

Of particular interest were the many strongly positive comments from nonwhite clients about counseling.[15] A higher proportion of nonwhite than white clients reported this service as "very helpful." In contrast, counselors rated counseling as less helpful to nonwhite than to white clients. The source of this discrepancy is far from clear. Do counselors more readily undervalue the helpfulness of counseling when the client is nonwhite? Or do nonwhite clients, accustomed in many cases to greater deprivation, tend to be more appreciative when they do receive service? Or do they simply feel less free to report that service was not helpful? ■

5

WHO ARE THE COUNSELORS AND HOW SATISFACTORY IS THE RELATIONSHIP?

The counselors: some basic facts[1]

Sex of counselor:

75 percent of the cases had a woman as their counselor.

25 percent of the cases had a man as their counselor.

In 1967, 78 percent of all counselors in FSAA Member Agencies were women.[2]

Sex matching:

59 percent of the cases where a woman was most frequently seen had a woman counselor.

6 percent of the cases where a man was most frequently seen had a man counselor.

Extent of service by social work assistants or casework aides:

90 percent of the cases received no service from social work assistants.

5 percent of the cases received some but not all service from social work assistants.

5 percent of the cases received all service from social work assstants.

Position of counselor:

78 percent were caseworkers.

13 percent were casework supervisors.

7 percent were social work assistants.

2 percent were students.

While this study did not ask about the education of the counselor, as of January 1, 1971, 73 percent of all practitioners in Member Agencies had completed their graduate education.[3]

Number of different counselors:

78 percent of the cases had only one counselor throughout.

11 percent of the cases were transferred to a new counselor immediately after intake.

8 percent of the cases were transferred later in the course of service.

4 percent of the cases had two or more counselors simultaneously (usually for different family members).

Racial or ethnic group of counselor:

88 percent of the cases had a white counselor.

9 percent of the cases had a black counselor.

One percent of the cases had a Spanish counselor.

2 percent of the cases had a counselor of another racial or ethnic group.

In June 1971, 84 percent of the professional and paraprofessional staff of 261 Member Agencies were white; 13 percent were black; 3 percent were Oriental, American Indian, or other; and 2.1 percent were of Spanish origin.[4]

Racial matching:

92 percent of white clients had a white counselor.

28 percent of black clients had a black counselor.

15 percent of Spanish clients had a Spanish counselor. ■

PARTNER INCLUDED IN SERVICE CONTACT BY SEX OF COUNSELOR
(Husband-wife families)

Percentage of cases

Male counselor [a]

Husband seen	55.4
Wife seen	75.7

Female counselor [a]

Husband seen	45.8
Wife seen	69.3

Both husband and wife seen   Wife only seen   Husband only seen

[a] Based on sex of counselor closing the case (excluding students, social work assistants, and case aides).

Do the objective characteristics of the counselor make any difference in how treatment progresses? Or more specifically in the case of chart 47: Does the sex of the counselor make any difference in whether the husband and wife are both seen?

The answer is clearly yes. In families that included both a husband and wife, male counselors had better success in getting husbands to come in than did female counselors. Male counselors also had slightly better success in getting wives to come in. In both instances, the differences were statistically significant. They also more frequently saw both husband and wife in the same family.[5]

Women counselors more often saw only one partner, usually the wife, while husbands seldom came in unless the wife was also seen, regardless of the sex of the counselor. Husbands apparently prefer a joint approach to family problems, one that also involves their wives, although not necessarily in the same interview. Perhaps men also feel more comfortable in discussing their marital and family problems with a man and less fearful that he may side with their wives in conflict issues.

Still another explanation suggests itself. Could it be that the greater success of male counselors in reaching husbands stems from their more frequent use of newer modalities, such as joint interviewing of husband and wife and group treatment?[6] Since men are more heavily represented among the newer entrants to the field and are generally younger,[7] they may find the shift to these newer modalities easier. Did their heavier use of joint interviews with both spouses make it easier for male counselors to get the husbands to come in? Or were they able to make heavier use of such interviews because they were more successful in getting husbands to come in? The present study does not provide the answer. ∎

Who are the counselors and how satisfactory is the relationship?

COUNSELORS' AND CLIENTS' EVALUATIONS OF THEIR RELATIONSHIP AND EXTENT TO WHICH THEY AGREE

Chart 48

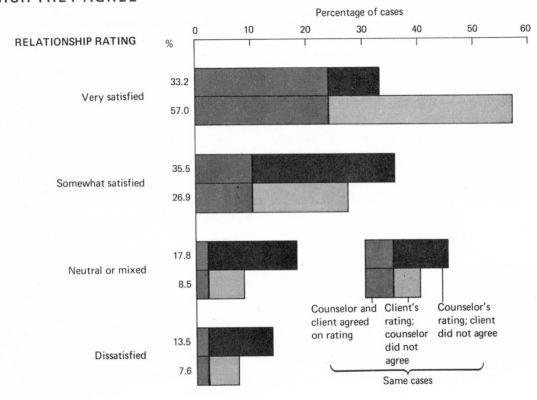

Percentage of cases

RELATIONSHIP RATING %

0 10 20 30 40 50 60

Very satisfied
33.2
57.0

Somewhat satisfied
35.5
26.9

Neutral or mixed
17.8
8.5

Dissatisfied
13.5
7.6

Counselor and client agreed on rating | Client's rating; counselor did not agree | Counselor's rating; client did not agree

Same cases

Because the counselor-client relationship is fundamental to effective treatment, both counselors and clients were asked how satisfied they were with the relationship. More than eight in ten of the clients, but less than seven in ten of the counselors, reported that they were satisfied with this relationship. Nearly six clients in ten reported that they were "very satisfied" with the relationship, whereas

their counselors gave a similarly high rating for their relationship with only one client in three. At the opposite end of the range, only about half as many clients as counselors reported that they were "dissatisfied" with the relationship. The explanation for the consistently lower ratings by counselors is not clear. Perhaps their less favorable view is the result of higher expectations about the characteris-

tics of a good therapeutic relationship.

Agreement between counselor and client about how satisfactory their relationship had been not only was lower than expected but also varied by level of satisfaction. Agreement was highest for "very satisfied" where more than half of the ratings agreed. For "somewhat satisfied," it dropped to one-third. For "neutral" and "dissatisfied," agreement was minimal. Overall, only 38 percent of those submitting ratings agreed with the other party in the interaction on how satisfactory the relationship was.

Occasionally clients complained in no uncertain terms about their relationship with their counselor. The following are direct quotations from the mail questionnaire replies: "She tended to regard each 'case' as a stereotyped situation"; "He wasn't as sympathetic as I'd have liked. At times I even felt hostility"; "The counselor was too busy and too pressured for time even to give more than a brief telephone report"; "I felt like the 50,000th person they had to see that day—just someone else with a problem"; "It was like talking into a tape recorder."

Fortunately, such responses were rare and were counterbalanced by numerous ratings of "very satisfactory." Appreciative comments referred to the friendliness of the counselor, her "genuine interest," how she had "opened the door" between the parents and the daughter, the fact that the counselor "helped put things in proper perspective," provided a "safety valve," or "gave courage." How important these good relationships are both to completion of the service needed and to favorable outcomes will become evident in later findings. ∎

Factors associated with a satisfactory counselor-client relationship

Because of the central importance of the counselor-client relationship to effective treatment, a search was made for clues as to what enhances this relationship. To facilitate the search, the two available views of whether the relationship was satisfactory—that of the counselor and that of the client—were merged into a single scale.[8] These merged ratings, when correlated with other factors, revealed the following patterns:

Client characteristics associated with relationship

The largest and most significant negative correlation ($r = -.42$) was that between these relationship scores and the disagreement score.[9] Major perceptual differences between the two parties clearly pose problems for the relationship. (For further discussion, see chart 51.) Much smaller but still statistically significant negative correlations also were found with two other client characteristics: severity of the total problem complex and total number of problems seen at intake.

The reverse side of the same picture was also evident from two small but statistically significant positive correlations with client characteristics: the relative ease of the type of problem which was the focus of treatment[10] and the amount of improvement predicted by the counselor at intake. In short, the easier the task, the better the relationship.

In combination, these findings reaffirm the well-known but tragic predicament of many clients: The more difficult and the more numerous their problems and the more they are psychologically in need of a warm positive relationship, the more difficult it often is for them to develop the relationship that they need. The challenge to the practitioner is to break through these barriers and achieve an in-depth relationship of warmth, trust, genuineness, empathy, and mutual positive regard in spite of the overwhelming problems and needs of these clients.

In contrast to these highly individualized diagnostic indicators, the objective characteristics of clients apparently have little effect on the achievement of a good relationship. There was, for example, no statistically significant association with socioeconomic status, race, family size, number of environmental problems, external factors affecting outcomes, or age of the family head. To the extent to which there was any perceptible variation at all, the more positive relationship ratings tended to be reported by both white and nonwhite clients from the lower half of the socioeconomic scale. These findings suggest that, in the main, counselors are able to relate successfully across socioeconomic and racial barriers that often impede communication in other settings.

Service characteristics associated with relationship

The highest positive correlations between relationship and service patterns were found associated with an increased number of interviews and an increased number of services. These findings serve only to support the obvious: The more the client and his family are satisfied with the relationship, the longer they will continue to use the service. Lower but still statistically significant positive correlations were found with the matching of the sex of the counselor with that of the client seen most. Apparently sex-matching slightly eases certain strains in the relationship. Matching of the counselor and client on race showed no statistically significant correlation with the ratings of level of satisfaction in the relationship.

A few small negative correlations were also found with service factors. For example, use of interviews involving more than one family member as a primary modality showed a low negative but significant correlation with a good counselor-client relationship. Perhaps the need to share the counselor with other family members places certain strains on the relationship that are less likely to present problems in the one-to-one interview. Perhaps it is simply a matter of case selection, intervention in the more complex problems being more likely to require interviewing jointly two or more family members. A second low negative association was found with length of time on the waiting list. This would suggest that being required to wait may stir up hostilities that later erode the relationship. There was also a minor negative association with transfer to a different counselor.[11] Here a negative reaction to transfer may be involved. No other service characteristics examined showed any significant association, either positive or negative, with the degree of satisfaction in the counselor-client relationship. Probably this relationship stems primarily from the extent to which the personalities of the counselor and the family participants achieve a meshing rather than from the more formal aspects of treatment modality as such. ∎

COUNSELOR-CLIENT DISAGREEMENTS ABOUT TREATMENT ISSUES

Chart 49

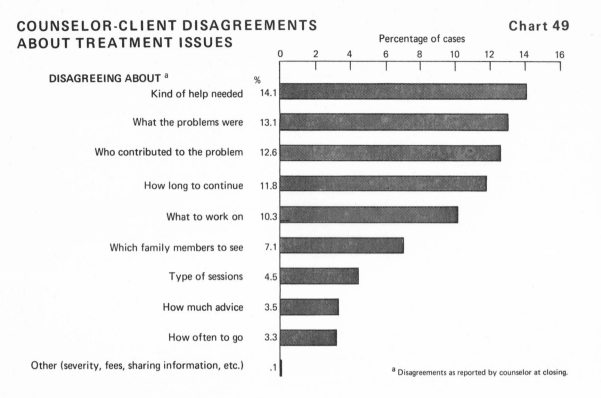

Percentage of cases

DISAGREEING ABOUT [a]   %

Kind of help needed	14.1
What the problems were	13.1
Who contributed to the problem	12.6
How long to continue	11.8
What to work on	10.3
Which family members to see	7.1
Type of sessions	4.5
How much advice	3.5
How often to go	3.3
Other (severity, fees, sharing information, etc.)	.1

[a] Disagreements as reported by counselor at closing.

Another significant dimension of the counselor-client interaction is the extent to which the two parties disagree about the core issues under discussion. Chart 49 provides detail about disagreements on certain treatment issues. Counselors reported some disagreement in this area in more than one case in three and an average of over two disagreements for each such case. Since clients were not directly asked about these treatment issues at follow-up, the information shown reflects only the counselors' impressions.

Disagreements about treatment issues most commonly focused on the kind of help needed or such related issues as what the client's problems were and who contributed to them (whether self, spouse, other family members, or situations outside the family). A second major group of disagreements related to the approach to be used—who was to be seen, whether they should be seen separately or together, how frequently, for how long, how much advice should be given, and the like.

A few direct quotations from the clients themselves will illustrate common areas of disagreement. Complaints often related to lack of advice and direction: "expected counselor to tell me what to do"; wanted "more con-crete suggestions"; "expected to be led by the hand"; "wanted a little advice even though it was against policy rules"; or received "no clearcut answers as to what we should or shouldn't do." Other expectations included: "expected help with present depression rather than past life"; expected counselor to show "husband where he was wrong"; or "expected worker to tell me what my wife said." Frequently clients expected that a child would be seen and worked with individually rather than through the parent, that a psychiatrist or psychologist would see them, that they would be seen as a couple instead of in a group, or that they would be seen individually instead of in an intake group. One client protested over having to "listen to a bunch of women who have the same problem and can't help me." Another wanted more home visits. A third commented that he felt it a "waste of time" since he and the counselor "did not agree on the nature of the problem."

Counselors on the whole reported more disagreements with white than with nonwhite clients and with upper and middle-status clients than with lower, perhaps because the former were more familiar with treatment issues and alternatives and more inclined to communicate their differences of opinion.

Disagreements about the kind of help needed was the one exception to this pattern. They were slightly more frequent when clients were from the lower end of the socioeconomic range, both white and nonwhite. Even this difference was minimal and not statistically significant. Probably what is reflected here is the greater need of the lower socioeconomic groups for types of practical services that family agencies can not provide. ■

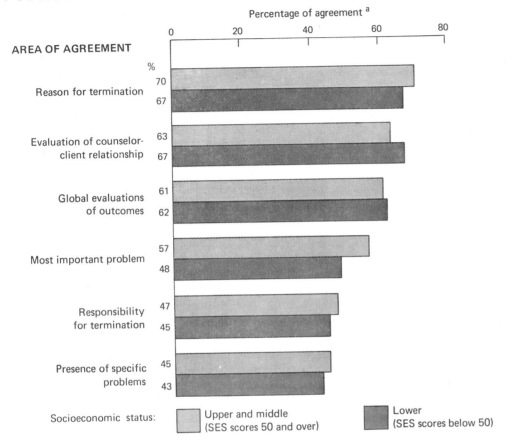

Percentage of agreement [a]

AREA OF AGREEMENT

	%	
Reason for termination	70	
	67	
Evaluation of counselor-client relationship	63	
	67	
Global evaluations of outcomes	61	
	62	
Most important problem	57	
	48	
Responsibility for termination	47	
	45	
Presence of specific problems	45	
	43	

Socioeconomic status: Upper and middle (SES scores 50 and over)   Lower (SES scores below 50)

[a] Based on comparison of reports from counselors and clients.

plored, there is no way to tell whether these figures are above, below, or at the expected level.

The comparisons by socioeconomic status show surprisingly little variation. Differences were not only small but inconsistent in direction. The only statistically significant difference among the six was that for most important problem.[13] This exception points to the need for special care in communication across sociocultural and ethnic barriers in matters relating to problem identification.

It is also important not to overestimate the significance of the differences between counselors and clients reflected in these figures. For example, the lack of agreement on the problem often reflects merely a difference in naming or classification or in the attribution of responsibility. A counselor might report a parent-child relationship problem while the client might report the same concrete situation as a problem in child behavior, a school problem, a recreational problem, or the like. Another example is reason for termination. Here clients tended to see the decision as their own while counselors reported it as mutual. While disagreements in any particular area may not be significant, taken as a whole they are related to outcomes, as will be shown in chart 88. For this reason, study of these differences in depth in small samples may well yield new clues that will contribute to improved practice. ■

Chart 50 provides a convenient summary of the extent of counselor-client agreement in a wide range of areas. All items are based on direct comparisons between counselors' and clients' responses to the same items for the same cases. Agreement was highest on reason for termination and lowest for the presence of specific problems.[12] Two closely related issues—the most important problem and who made the decision to terminate—took more intermediate positions. Since the extent of counselor-client agreement has seldom been ex-

Who are the counselors and how satisfactory is the relationship?

To supplement the information in chart 50 on counselor-client disagreements in specific areas, some overall indication of the extent of counselor-client disagreement was needed. A composite disagreement index was therefore constructed using eleven indicators of disagreement available from the counselors' and clients' reports.[14] The disagreements included in this index were concerned with what the problems were, what kind of help was needed, what kinds of changes took place in the course of agency service, how satisfactory the counselor-client relationship was, and what the reason was for termination.

The resulting scores showed that clients and counselors disagreed on the average on about four of these eleven items. This relatively high count should not be construed as reflecting overt or conscious disagreement since in many cases neither party to the interaction was aware that the other had submitted reports that differed from his own.[15]

In chart 51, averages for this index are used to answer two questions: (1) To what extent does disagreement in the perception of relevant issues vary with the level of satisfaction in the counselor-client relationship? (2) Does the average level of difference vary by socioeconomic status? The answer to the first is that the association with the counselor-client relationship is substantial (r= −.42). The better this relationship, the less extensive the discrepancies between the two reports. Obviously a certain circularity is involved here. Similarities in perception of key issues contribute to ease in the relationship. Likewise, a good relationship fosters open communication,

DISAGREEMENT BETWEEN COUNSELOR AND CLIENT BY RELATIONSHIP RATING

Chart 51

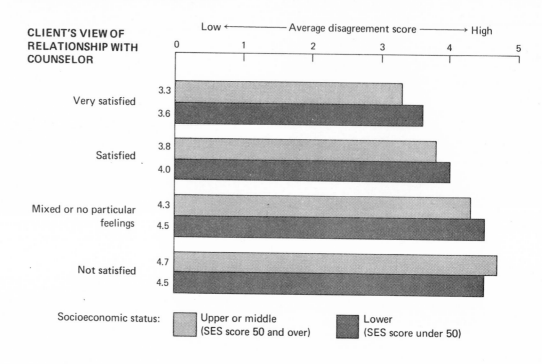

which in turn helps in the working through of differences.

The answer to the second question is that the extent of disagreement is minimally but inversely related to socioeconomic status.[16] Except for the few clients who were definitely dissatisfied with the counselor-client relationship, disagreement scores were slightly higher for those in the lower half of the socioeconomic range. Overall disagreement scores

were very close: 3.7 for the upper and middle group and 3.8 for the lower. There was also no significant difference in disagreement scores either by race of the client or by whether client and counselor were of the same race. Differences between counselor and client in the perception of critical treatment issues are apparently a universal problem and one that has important consequences, as will be shown later.

6
WHEN AND WHY
IS SERVICE
TERMINATED?

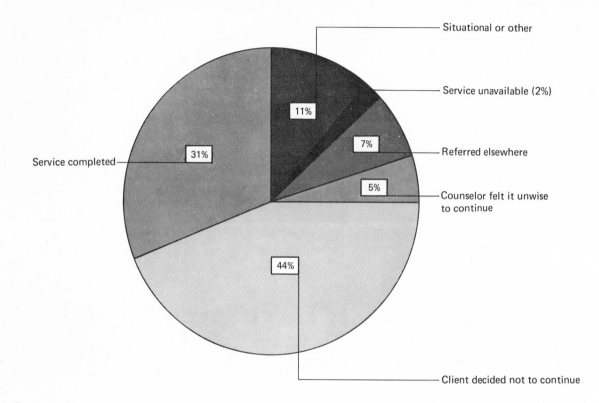

Situational or other

Service unavailable (2%)

11%

7%

31%

Referred elsewhere

5%

Service completed

Counselor felt it unwise
to continue

44%

Client decided not to continue

referral were especially frequent for environmental problems and for cases involving crime, delinquency, alcoholism, mental illness, and mental retardation. An additional 2 percent, although also seeking a service not available at the agency, were not referred. Perhaps the needed service did not exist in the community. Possibly the client simply preferred to try to manage on his own.

In 5 percent of the closings, the counselor felt it was unwise to continue with agency service. In some instances, the client was receiving treatment elsewhere—for example, at a mental health center or with a private psychiatrist—and overlapping responsibility seemed inadvisable. In other instance, the counselor felt that improvement was unlikely, that the service was not proving helpful, or that the client was not sufficiently motivated to make progress.

In about one case in nine, situational or other factors were primary. The client had moved, become ill, gone on vacation, or found agency hours inconvenient. In a few cases treatment was interrupted because the counselor left the agency or because the project involved was terminated. Eligibility was a factor in only about one case in 100.

In the 1960-70 decade, trends in reason for closing are obscured by classification changes. The largest change was a substantial drop in referrals elsewhere because the service needed was not available at the agency.[2] For the same agencies, the decline for this category was from 19.6 to 7.2 percent. This is probably largely the result of greater community knowledge of agency services and, secondarily, of the expansion in the range of services available elsewhere. Both reasons reflect gains for the community at large. ■

Two reasons[1] for termination were cited by counselors as primary more frequently than all others: (1) The service the agency could provide had been completed, and (2) the client himself decided not to continue. Corresponding reports from clients sometimes gave positive reasons for this latter decision—they were satisfied with the gains made or were finding their problems less stressful. Others complained that the service was not helping. The

high proportion terminating on client initiative without completion of service presents a problem which is discussed further in connection with charts 57, 58, and 59.

The "referred elsewhere" category includes applicants seeking services not available at the agency but provided elsewhere in the community. Here the counselor's role was one of orientation, removal of roadblocks, and facilitation of the referral. Terminations because of

At follow-up clients were asked: "Why did you stop going to the agency?" In response, about two-thirds of the clients gave positive or at least neutral reasons. The most frequent explanation was simply that the problem was solved or less stressful. Such reports frequently included appreciative comments about the service.[3] One in eight had decided to handle their problems on their own or go elsewhere. One in thirteen gave as their primary reason a decision reached either by the counselor or by them both mutually. A few cited crises unrelated to service as their reason—a death in the family, moving, vacation, or some other situation. Others simply explained that they had gone as far as they could.[4]

The other third of the clients cited less positive reasons for terminating. The most common complaint, expressed by 12 percent, was that the service either had not helped or could not help. Another 2 percent felt their situation had actually worsened or had ended unsatisfactorily. Objections from other family members were cited by 9 percent. For 8 percent, the problem was with office hours, fees, having to wait, or the counselor having gone on vacation. Complaints about counselors were infrequent (3 percent); those that were offered came from a group that tended to report more complaints in general.[5] At times the counselor was blamed because some practical service the client had requested—money, testing, or the like—had not been provided. In-depth probing of such complaints can provide important clues for the improvement of service. When clients' open-ended responses were compared with counselors' checklist responses on reasons for closing, they were found to agree in about three-quarters of the cases (71 percent). ■

When and why is service terminated?

Percentage of cases with follow-up report

POSITIVE OR NEUTRAL REASONS   %

Reason	%
Problem solved or less stressful	30.6
Decided to handle on own or go elsewhere	13.1
Situational reason	7.3
Worker initiative or mutual agreement	6.8
Has not stopped or plans to resume	4.2
Went as far as could with agency	3.2

NEGATIVE REASONS

Reason	%
Service not helpful or no help expected	11.6
Other family members unwilling	8.9
Problems with arrangements (fees, hours, distance, waiting)	8.3
Dissatisfaction with counselor or treatment plan	3.4
Situation worse or ended unsatisfactorily	2.0

CLIENT'S REASON FOR TERMINATION BY RELATIONSHIP

Chart 54

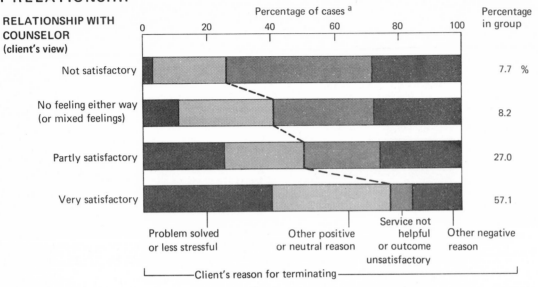

RELATIONSHIP WITH COUNSELOR
(client's view)

Percentage of cases [a]

Percentage in group

Not satisfactory — 7.7 %

No feeling either way (or mixed feelings) — 8.2

Partly satisfactory — 27.0

Very satisfactory — 57.1

Problem solved or less stressful | Other positive or neutral reason | Service not helpful or outcome unsatisfactory | Other negative reason

——Client's reason for terminating——

[a] Based on follow-up cases with answers to both questions.

Clients' reasons for terminating showed a strong association with their views of the counselor-client relationship. When clients rated this relationship as "very satisfactory," 40 percent reported terminating because their problem was solved or less stressful; only 7 percent complained that the service had not been helpful or that outcomes were unsatisfactory. On the other hand, when clients rated the relationship as "not satisfactory," only 3 percent reported their problem solved or less stressful while 46 percent described the service as not helpful or the outcomes as unsatisfactory.

Was this marked association the result of the client's rating the relationship retrospectively according to whether he felt he had been helped? Or was a good relationship itself a major contributor to the positive or negative results that he reported? To untangle insofar as possible which came first, counselors' ratings of relationship (instead of the clients') were examined in relation to clients' reports on reason for termination.[6] The findings indicated that when counselors rated the relationship as "very satisfactory," 45 percent of the clients reported terminating because the problem was solved or less stressful; only 7 percent terminated because the service was not helpful or the outcomes unsatisfactory. On the other hand, when the counselors rated the relationship as "not satisfactory," only 16 percent of the clients reported terminat-ing because the problem was solved or less stressful, while 22 percent reported that the service was not helpful or the situation worse. Thus a strong association remained in spite of the use of a relatively independent rating for the relationship.[7] In combination, these data suggest that a report of a good relationship is not merely an indicator of a good outcome but actively contributes to such an outcome[8] —which is what counselors have believed all along.

In comparison with relationship, other factors were clearly secondary influences on reason for termination. For example, for white clients socioeconomic status was not related to the proportion of negatives in reason for closing. For nonwhite clients there was a difference—the negatives being higher for the upper and middle-status group than for the lower.[9] A search for reasons again revealed problems with arrangements as the major source of the discrepancy. Probably, once again, it was the problem of evening and Saturday hours for working parents that was causing difficulty.[10] ■

Who decides when it is time for counseling to end? Chart 55 gives the answer from the counselors' viewpoint. They saw the majority of terminations (51 percent) as based on a mutual decision and most of the rest as initiated by the client or his family (41 percent). As socioeconomic status declined, there was a gradual increase in terminations that counselors attributed to their own initiative. A similar pattern was noted in 1960.[11] Apparently, as in many aspects of life, those who are more comfortably situated tend to be and can be more independent in their decisions than those for whom the range of choice is more limited.

The contrast by race was particularly marked. Nonwhite clients were about double white clients on terminations on counselor initiative (14 percent versus 7 percent), a difference that probably reflects the nature of the service provided.[12] A client receiving temporary financial assistance or some other tangible service, such as caretaking, may have to be terminated or referred because of limited agency resources rather than because these services are no longer needed. Whether other factors than these are involved in this statistically significant difference is not known.

Clients were not asked directly about who made the termination decision. Clues were derived indirectly from their narrative answers to the question: "Why did you stop going to the agency?" When tabulated against counselors' views for the same cases, the differences were striking: 76 percent of the clients but only 39 percent of the counselors indicated that it

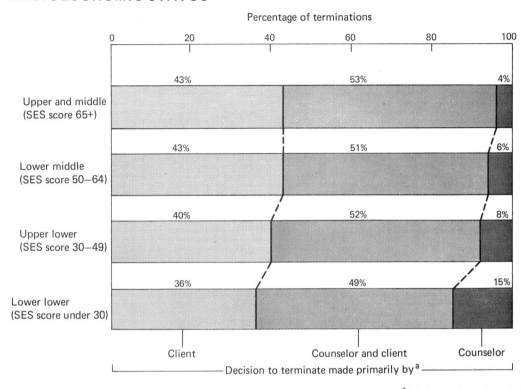

Percentage of terminations

Upper and middle (SES score 65+): Client 43%, Counselor and client 53%, Counselor 4%

Lower middle (SES score 50–64): Client 43%, Counselor and client 51%, Counselor 6%

Upper lower (SES score 30–49): Client 40%, Counselor and client 52%, Counselor 8%

Lower lower (SES score under 30): Client 36%, Counselor and client 49%, Counselor 15%

Client — Counselor and client — Counselor

Decision to terminate made primarily by[a]

[a] In judgment of counselor at closing.

was the client's decision; only 12 percent of the clients but 56 percent of the counselors saw the decision as mutual; and 12 percent of the clients but only 5 percent of the counselors saw it as the counselor's decision only.[13] While these contrasts probably exaggerate the difference,[14] it is still clear that clients view as their own many termination decisions that counselors report as mutual. Clients apparently see themselves as acting autonomously in making this important decision.

In spite of these indications of client initiative, nearly three-fifths of all closings were planned in advance. In this respect there was no significant difference between white and nonwhite clients. Both showed more unplanned closings among clients of middle socioeconomic status than among those at either the lower or upper extremes. This is consistent with the relatively high disengagement rate for this same group of clients shown in chart 58 on page 86. ∎

When and why is service terminated?

conditions. What a family agency can do in these latter areas through counseling on individual cases is necessarily limited.

A look at the reasons counselors gave for terminating by plan in the first interview showed this group to be relatively high on terminations because some simple service had been completed or needed service was not available at the agency. Many of the latter clients were referred. Terminations resulting from the applicant's decision not to continue were infrequent for those terminating within the first interview but were more characteristic of clients dropping out between the first and second interview (18 versus 61 percent). Such clients probably were ambivalent or negative from the beginning about the use of agency service but did not want to admit this in their first face-to-face contact.

An examination of racial differences in the frequency of terminations in the first interview showed that nonwhite clients significantly exceeded white clients in this respect (17 versus 9 percent). Counselors' reports on these cases showed the figures for nonwhite clients to be significantly above those for white clients on terminations because service was completed (55 versus 41 percent). Services they had received included financial assistance, legal aid, and other direct services. On the other hand, terminations by nonwhite clients were lower than those by white clients for reasons of referral (16 versus 21 percent) or because the client was unwilling to continue (14 versus 20 percent). Neither of these latter differences is statistically significant. There was no difference between white and nonwhite clients on terminations because the counselor felt it was unwise to continue (6 percent for both). ■

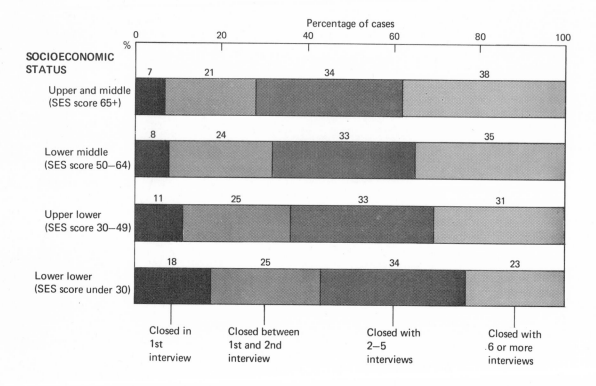

The various socioeconomic subgroups demonstrated somewhat different patterns in the timing of their terminations. In general, the lower the socioeconomic status of the applicant, the higher the proportion terminating early and the fewer continuing to the sixth interview or beyond. Only the proportion terminating between two and five interviews remained relatively constant. The pattern was roughly similar though more extreme in 1960.[15]

The explanation for this consistent pattern probably lies in the changing problems and service needs of applicants as socioeconomic status decreases (see charts 19 and 36). In general, concern over family relationship and personality adjustment problems at the upper levels tends to shift at the lower levels to relatively heavy engagement with problems related to basic family supports and survival in the face of difficult and often hostile external

CLIENT DISENGAGEMENT BY COUNSELOR-CLIENT RELATIONSHIP [a]

Chart 57

Percentage of clients deciding not to continue [b]

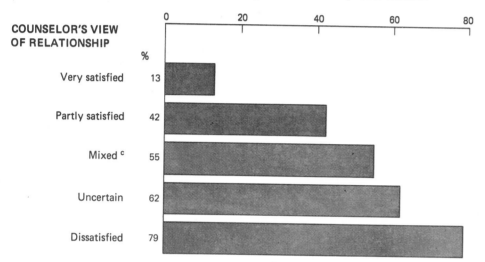

COUNSELOR'S VIEW OF RELATIONSHIP

	%
Very satisfied	13
Partly satisfied	42
Mixed [c]	55
Uncertain	62
Dissatisfied	79

[a] Disengagement refers to cases in which the primary reason for termination was the client's decision not to continue.
[b] Based on total cases in each relationship category.
[c] Satisfied with relationship with some family members but not with others.

Reason client decided not to continue (counselor's opinion)	Percentage of clients deciding not to continue [a]
Satisfied with gains made or found problem less stressful	40
Uncomfortable about treatment process or about going to agency for help	32
Unwilling to continue because some other family member was unwilling to participate	29
Discouraged or doubted that agency could help	27
Disagreed with counselor on some issue	9
Denied having problem or claimed that he no longer had problem	7
Objected to fees charged	5

[a] Since more than one reason was sometimes cited, percentages total more than 100.

Reason client decided not to continue [a] (client's opinion)	Percentage of clients deciding not to continue [b]
Problem solved or less stressful	24
Service not helpful or situation worse	18
Other family members unwilling to participate	15
Problems with arrangements	11
Decided to handle problem on own	10
Situational factors	6
Dissatisfied with counselor or with treatment	5
Counselor suggested termination (or decision was mutual)	5
Felt had gone as far as could go with problem	3
Other reason	2

[a] The clients responded to an open-ended question: "Why did you stop going to the agency?" rather than to the checklist the counselors used. Therefore, the reasons do not match up.
[b] Since there was usually only one answer per follow-up, the percentages do not exceed 100.

Chart 57 begins a series on client-initiated disengagement.[16] It shows that the proportion of clients who decided to terminate varied markedly according to how satisfied the counselor was with the relationship. But what is cause and what effect? Did the clients terminate because they, also, were dissatisfied with the relationship? Or did the counselor rate the relationship as unsatisfactory because the client decided to withdraw prematurely?

Actually, the situation was much more complex. Some reasons cited by the counselors for their clients' deciding not to continue are shown in the first table. Other explanations included client objections to distance, appointment time, having to wait, and transfer to an-other counselor, plus reports that the client had moved or encountered situations that interfered.

The clients themselves reported a somewhat different set of reasons for their decision to terminate. See second table.

Both lists suggest that clients' decision to terminate may reflect gains made and thus have positive rather than negative implications. The reasons for termination may also be totally unrelated to agency service. In spite of the apparently close association with the counselor-client relationship shown in the chart, clients identified problems in this area in only 5 percent of all disengagements.

When and why is service terminated?

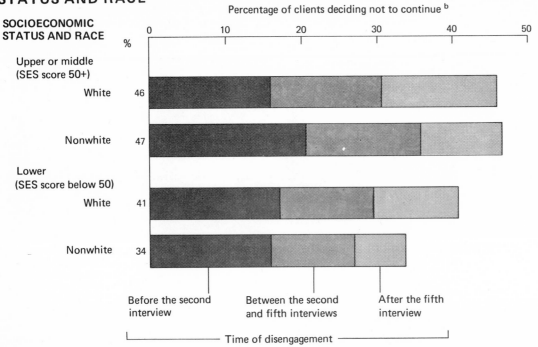

SOCIOECONOMIC
STATUS AND RACE

Percentage of clients deciding not to continue [b]

0   10   20   30   40   50

%

Upper or middle
(SES score 50+)

White   46

Nonwhite   47

Lower
(SES score below 50)

White   41

Nonwhite   34

Before the second interview

Between the second and fifth interviews

After the fifth interview

Time of disengagement

[a] Disengagement refers to cases in which the primary reason for termination was the client's decision not to continue.

[b] Based on total cases within each socioeconomic and racial group.

Terminations because of the client's decision not to continue accounted for more than four in ten of all family agency closings. At what point in service did these closings occur? Were they more frequent with some types of clients than with others? Both questions are answered by chart 58.

Clients from upper and middle socioeconomic groups were more prone than those from the more improverished groups to decide on their own not to continue. Within the lower-status group, disengagement was more frequent among white than nonwhite clients. These findings suggest more hesitation and resistance about using agency service among upper and middle-status clients than among lower, a pattern that runs counter to the assertion that family agency service is primarily a middle-class service.

The most usual time for client-initiated termination was between the first and second appointments. Apparently, after the initial interview experience, clients tend to retreat to assess within themselves and with other family members whether the approach to their problems through agency service is actually right for them. Almost one client in six withdrew at this point. Once this critical first decision to continue was made, the attrition rate declined. Total drop-out between the second and the fifth interviews hardly equaled that after the first (13 versus 17 percent), while total client disengagement for all interviews beyond the fifth was slightly less.[17] The low disengagement rate for lower-status nonwhite clients beyond five interviews was particularly conspicuous and serves to equalize the high rate of nonwhite closings in the first interview (see page 84).

When planned closings in the first interview were added to the disengagement figures shown in this chart, the proportion of white applicants who stayed with agency service without drop-out became 42 percent for the upper and middle and 39 percent for the lower-status white group. For the nonwhite group, the pattern was reversed. More lower-status nonwhite clients continued (37 percent) than did upper and middle-status nonwhite clients (34 percent). This discrepancy helps to explain the low average interview count of this latter group (see chart 37). It is one of several clues in the data[19] to some unidentified problem in the provision of family agency service to the upper and middle-status nonwhite client. ■

Chart 59 is directed to the question: Does matching of the counselor and principal client on sex and race have any effect on whether the client decides on his own initiative not to continue? It also looks at whether this disengagement occurs before or after the second interview.

When the client seen most was a woman, she was less likely to terminate on her own initiative if she was assigned to a counselor of her own sex. The difference was statistically significant and supported by significantly better relationship ratings when women clients were assigned to women counselors.

Male clients also had a slightly lower overall disengagement rate with women than with men counselors, though their disengagement before the second interview was higher with women than with men counselors. Men also terminated before the second interview significantly more frequently with female than with male counselors for reasons other than disengagement (25 versus 11 percent). The combined effect of early disengagement and other one-interview closings was that men continued on the average for only five interviews when assigned to a female counselor as compared with eight interviews with a male counselor,[19] statistically a highly significant difference. All in all, the results seem to favor sex matching for both men and women clients.

Contrasts for race matching were more startling. Black clients assigned to white counselors showed a significantly higher disengagement rate (both before the second interview and overall) than those assigned to black counselors. White clients also disengaged somewhat less frequently when seeing a black counselor, though this difference was not statistically significant. There was practically no difference in disengagement before the se-

SEX MATCHING [b]

Percentage of clients deciding not to continue [c]

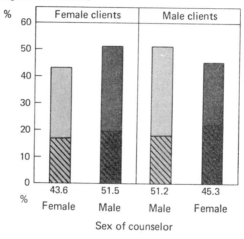

Sex of counselor

Time of disengagement:

After 2 or more interviews

Before second interview

Matched   Not matched

RACIAL MATCHING [b]

Percentage of clients deciding not to continue [c]

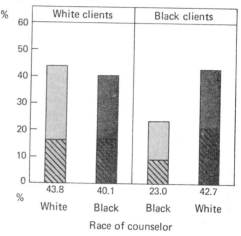

Race of counselor

[a] Disengagement refers to cases in which the primary reason for termination was the client's decision not to continue.

[b] Classification based on family member seen most. Deliberate assignments to achieve matching are not implied.

[c] Based on all cases in each of the four subcategories plotted for each topic.

cond interview between white clients seeing white counselors and those seeing black counselors.

While the findings with regard to sex and race matching are more definitive for the female counselor with the female client and the black counselor with the black client, all of the combinations appear, on balance, to favor consideration of both race and sex matching in case assignments when this is feasible.[20] For male clients with male counselors, the initial holding power and the increased average number of interviews are persuasive. Regarding white clients with black counselors, the position in favor of race matching is based on

the relatively low number of black counselors available (see page 72) and the striking reduction in the disengagement of black clients assigned to black counselors.

The data tell little about the source of these differences. Probably in the stressful situations that bring clients to agencies, many applicants feel more at ease with persons that they define from easy visual clues as more like themselves and therefore better able to empathize with their difficulties. Why this does not appear to apply to white clients with a black counselor is not clear. This aspect of the findings will be discussed further in connection with chart 94. ■

When and why is service terminated?

Other facts on termination

Planning for termination:

57 percent of closings were planned in advance.

At the point of closing 60 percent of clients were offered further service.

Relation to type of problem given most attention:

Reports of "problem solved or less stressful" were most frequent for family and home-management cases.

Negative reasons for terminating were highest for marital problem cases.

Relation to severity of total problem situation:

Service was reported completed for 49 percent of mild cases, 36 percent of moderately severe cases, and 23 percent of severe cases.

Relation to unmet needs:

When clients reported no unmet needs, their most frequent reason for terminating was "problem solved or less stressful."

When clients reported one or more unmet needs, their most frequent reason for terminating was "service not helpful."

Relation to primary treatment modality:

Family group treatment cases more often than others gave as their reason for closing, "problem solved or less stressful" (40 versus 34 percent).

Joint interview cases more often than others gave as their reason for closing "other family members unwilling" (13 versus 10 percent).

Group treatment cases more often than others gave as their reason for closing some external situation or arrangement problem (40 versus 17 percent).

Group treatment cases less often than others gave as their reason for termination, "service not helpful or situation worse" (9 versus 15 percent).

Satisfaction with service:

Positive comments about agency service were volunteered more than two-and-one-half times as often as negative comments —and this in spite of the fact that there were many probes for negative comments but no question about whether clients were satisfied with agency service.

Willingness to return:

In response to a question on willingness to return if need arose, clients answered:

Yes, unqualified	88%
Yes, qualified	4
No	8

Yes responses were slightly higher for lower than upper and middle-status clients and, within each group, for nonwhite than white clients.

Explanations for *no* responses were as follows:

Service did not help	28%
Complaint about counselor	21
Needed service unavailable	14
Complaint about agency (fees, hours, waiting, etc.)	10
Other resource	10
Will not be necessary	9
Situational reasons	4
Other family members unwilling	3

■

7
WHAT ARE THE OUTCOMES?

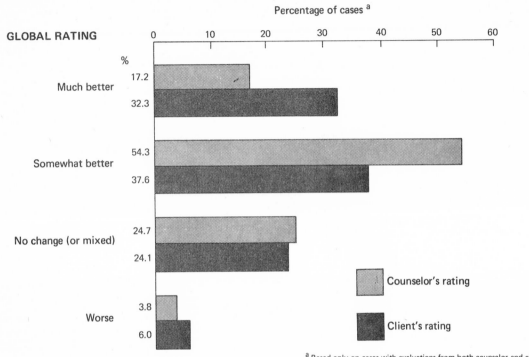

Percentage of cases [a]

GLOBAL RATING

a Based only on cases with evaluations from both counselor and client.

and client. Additional ratings from counselors only were available for cases with no follow-up report. When these were added in, the picture from counselors was somewhat less positive: 14 percent, "much better"; 52 percent, "somewhat better"; 29 percent, "no change"; and 5 percent, "worse."

Chart 61 changes the focus from the overall frequency of global improvement to the extent of agreement on which cases improved. Each bar is divided into two parts: one for ratings on which the two informants agreed and the other for those where they did not. Agreement was highest for "somewhat better," next highest for "much better," slightly less for "no change," and almost nonexistent for "worse." Here informants agreed in only eight cases. The sources of these disagreements will be discussed on pages 104-105.

The overall level of agreement for these global evaluations was 40 percent. If the two levels of improvement ("somewhat better" and "much better") are merged, the level of agreement increases to 62 percent. Viewed statistically, both levels of agreement exceed chance expectations by a highly significant margin.[2]

After clients had made their global rating, they were also asked whether other family members would agree with their rating.[3] A high proportion (73 percent) said they would; 6 percent that they would not; 8 percent that some would and some would not; and 13 percent that they were unable to say. Of those few who acknowledged disagreement, only one-third indicated that the disagreement related to outcomes. For the rest, the disagreement was in some other area—what the prob-

Charts 60 and 61 begin a series of charts on outcomes. They provide two views of the extent to which the client's total problem situation improved during the period of treatment: The first focuses only on overall frequencies; the second details the extent of agreement between counselor and client on individual cases.

Almost twice as many clients as counselors reported their total problem situation as "much better," while about one-third more counselors than clients checked "somewhat better." If the

two categories are merged, both counselors and clients are found to have reported about seven out of ten cases as improved. The tendency of counselors to select more moderate evaluations than clients was also evident in reports on deterioration. Counselors reported the total problem situation as "worse" in 4 percent; clients, in 6 percent. Both reported "no change" in about one case in four.[1]

For purposes of comparison, these ratings were limited to those cases for which a global evaluation was available from both counselor lem was, how severe it was, who contributed to it, what action should be taken, whether divorce or separation was the answer, or whether the agency should have been asked to help. Disagreement between family members was particularly frequent in marital cases.

When either party reported that things were worse, they were also asked for details. In descending order of frequency, counselors mentioned deterioration in family functioning or relationship, a worsening of the behavior or mental health of some family member (return of symptoms, depression, and so on), break-up of the marriage, some adverse development in external conditions, declining physical health, or some major crisis. Clients more often than counselors cited adverse changes in external conditions to explain what was worse. Otherwise they confirmed the same general range of problems.

Counselors and clients together reported twenty-four major crises. Some were unrelated to agency service, such as a death in the family from natural causes. Others involved tragic situations where the call for help came too late. Serious developments that the agency had failed to prevent included criminal or delinquent behavior, attempted or actual suicide, drug overdose, and children's running away from home. The client frequently blamed the counselor, not for causing the episode, but for failing to forestall it.[4] Usually, agency contact had been brief and both informants had reported an unsatisfactory relationship with the counselor. Some closed with a bitter tone. For example, a man whose daughter had attempted suicide re-

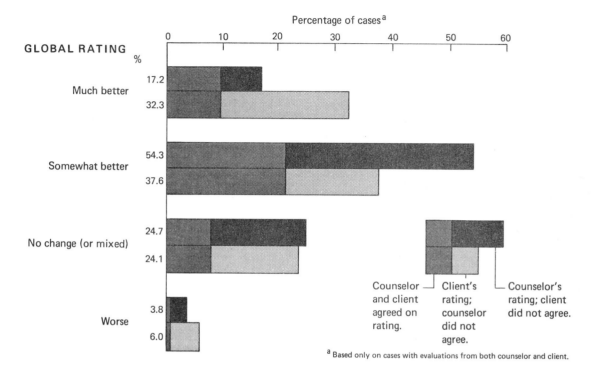

Percentage of cases[a]

GLOBAL RATING

Much better — 17.2 / 32.3

Somewhat better — 54.3 / 37.6

No change (or mixed) — 24.7 / 24.1

Worse — 3.8 / 6.0

Counselor and client agreed on rating.

Client's rating; counselor did not agree.

Counselor's rating; client did not agree.

[a] Based only on cases with evaluations from both counselor and client.

turned his questionnaire unanswered, commenting: "I am not interested in anything because no one was interested in me when I had a problem."

Fortunately, relatively few of the desperately serious situations brought to agencies end negatively. For example, a nineteen-year-old drug user, who reported that she "was in despair and suicide seemed inevitable" when she first came to the agency, as a result of agency service was helped to tackle her problems, to get much-needed medical care,

and to return home to her family.

On a more general level, twelve times as many clients reported improvement as deterioration. Those who had benefited spoke often of agency service with real appreciation: "a great blessing," "am grateful," or "helped a lot." Some were more specific: "I got more incentive to look for work"; "We got a better look at ourselves and our behavior"; "Truly the homemaker was a lifesaver for me"; "We got out of it the answers we needed to save our marriage."

What are the outcomes?

MAIN REASON FOR CHANGES REPORTED
(Client's view)

Chart 62

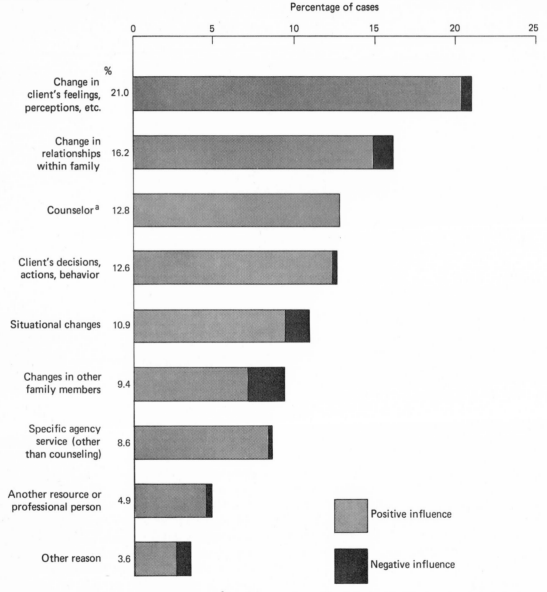

Percentage of cases

Change in client's feelings, perceptions, etc.	21.0
Change in relationships within family	16.2
Counselor[a]	12.8
Client's decisions, actions, behavior	12.6
Situational changes	10.9
Changes in other family members	9.4
Specific agency service (other than counseling)	8.6
Another resource or professional person	4.9
Other reason	3.6

Positive influence

Negative influence

[a] In no instance was the counselor cited as a negative influence under main reason for change.

At follow-up, clients were also asked what they throught was the main reason for the changes they had reported. Most frequently, answers gave credit to changes in the client's own feelings or perceptions—his reduced worries about his problems, his more realistic ideas about ways out, his more comfortable, positive feelings about himself, and his improved image of himself generally.

Changes in relationships within the family, including better communication, came next. In the main, clients attributed these changes to what they themselves had done or what the family had done together. The counselor as the main reason for change was mentioned third. Especially stressed here was the chance to talk things over with an impartial outsider. The fourth item—changes the client made in his own behavior, actions, or decisions —was mentioned with almost equal frequency. Again, clients were seeing the changes as their own achievements. This is consistent with a view of counseling as primarily a healing and enabling process that frees the client to take responsiblity for finding and choosing his own solutions to his problems.

Situational factors related to health, income, housing, and the like were mentioned by one in nine; help from such a resource as a minister or Alcoholics Anonymous, by one in twenty. Other factors credited included reading, meditation, religion, and the passage of time.

Practically all the influences mentioned were considered to have had positive rather than negative effects. Negative reports mainly mentioned changes in other family members and situational changes. ■

Section seven

INFLUENCE OF AGENCY SERVICE AND EXTERNAL FACTORS ON OUTCOMES

Chart 63

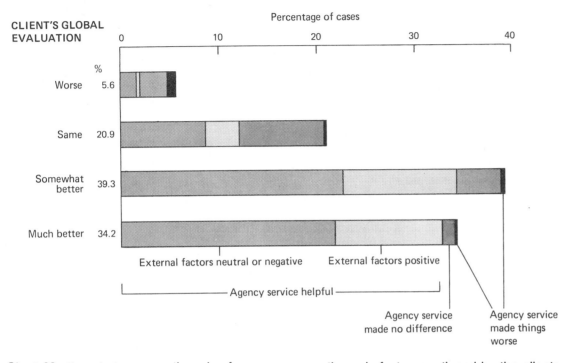

CLIENT'S GLOBAL EVALUATION

Percentage of cases

	%
Worse	5.6
Same	20.9
Somewhat better	39.3
Much better	34.2

External factors neutral or negative — External factors positive — Agency service helpful — Agency service made no difference — Agency service made things worse

Chart 63 attempts to assess the role of agency service in the changes reported. Since it was thought unlikely that clients would be able to rate directly the role of agency service in the reported changes, the issue was approached obliquely through questions on the helpfulness of agency service, the direction and extent of change, and the influence of external factors.[5] Chart 63 examines the combined role of external factors and agency service in the changes reported.

In the "better" categories, one finds large segments indicating that agency service was helpful and external influences were neutral or negative. For this group, agency service

was the only factor mentioned by the clients as contributing to improvement. Smaller components represent situations where agency service was helpful but external conditions were also positive, leaving open the issue of the degree to which agency service contributed to the reported improvement. Finally, a small proportion (3 percent) achieved improvement apparently independently of either agency service or positive external factors. These cases provide testimony to the capacity for comeback and healing after crises and for growth against odds that are part of the human potential.

In the "same" category, the proportion in

which "agency service made no difference" increased substantially, while the proportion of positive external influences declined. Reports of "agency service made things worse" were few in any category but were largest proportionately in the "worse" category.

When the global ratings were consolidated into two groups, "improved" and "not improved," the total figures became:

	Percentage of cases[a]
Improved:	
Agency service helpful—	
External factors neutral or negative	44.3
External factors positive	22.7
Agency service made no difference	6.0
Agency service made things worse	0.5
Total improved	73.5
Not improved:	
Agency service helpful	14.1
Agency service made no difference	11.5
Agency service made things worse	0.9
Total not improved	26.5

[a]Includes only follow-up cases answering these component questions.

The foregoing data support the tentative conclusion that for nearly half the group the influence of agency service was the major factor in improvement. In another fifth it was one of several contributing factors. For another one in seven, service was reported helpful even though it did not result in improvement. In such cases it may have prevented deterioration or slowed its pace. Both are important functions of agency service in situations where improvement can not be expected. ■

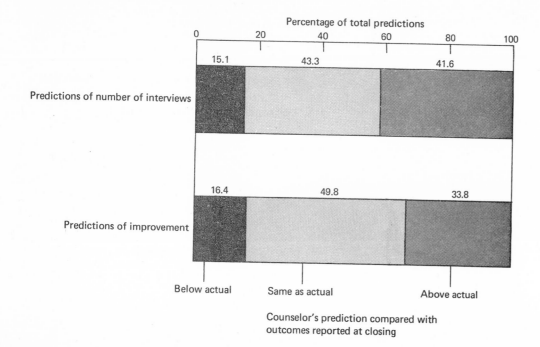

Percentage of total predictions

Predictions of number of interviews: 15.1 | 43.3 | 41.6

Predictions of improvement: 16.4 | 49.8 | 33.8

Below actual   Same as actual   Above actual

Counselor's prediction compared with
outcomes reported at closing

Their predictions on outcomes were "above actual" twice as often as they were "below actual," and their "predictions of number of interviews," three times as often. To the extent that this atmosphere of "therapeutic optimism" helps set in motion the predicted changes, it is in the best interests of clients. It made little difference to the accuracy of the prediction whether the counselor who made the initial prediction also carried the case to termination, indicating that the urge to report confirmation of one's original prediction was not a significant factor in the rating of outcomes at closing.

Exploration of factors associated with the accuracy of predictions produced the obvious finding: The higher the predicted outcome, the more likely it was to be too high and the lower the prediction, the more likely it was to be too low.

Other factors somewhat related to the accuracy of predictions were problem severity, socioeconomic status, and race. The more severe the problem situation at intake, the more likely the prediction was to be too high. Predictions were most often correct for mild cases. Irrespective of status level, predications for white clients were more often correct than were those for nonwhite clients. For white clients, socioeconomic status showed no relation to accuracy of prediction. For nonwhite clients, initial predictions tended to be too high, especially for clients at the upper and middle socioeconomic levels. The whole issue of prediction is obviously complicated by culturally patterned expectations and by the minimum information available at intake. ∎

To what extent is it possible for a counselor to predict accurately at intake whether an applicant can be helped? If accurate predictions should prove possible, selective intake could improve the allocation of scarce agency resources.

A look at chart 64 suggests that such a policy is neither feasible nor safe. When tested against closing ratings, counselors' intake predictions proved to agree with actual outcomes only about half the time. While this record of agreement is highly significant statistically,[6] it is not sufficient to use for screening purposes. In fact, a higher record of accuracy could have been attained simply by predicting that everyone would show some improvement. Not enough is yet known about who will and will not benefit from counseling for clients to be denied service on the basis of intake predictions except in special circumstances.

Counselors' predictions of number of interviews agreed with actual interview counts less than half the time. Again, this record was highly significant statistically. It was also better than could have been achieved by a standard prediction for all cases. Nevertheless, it was again too low to have practical utility.

A second conclusion from chart 64 is that counselors are strong optimists.

In addition to the global ratings, both counselors and clients were asked to report their own perceptions of the direction of change (not the amount of change) for a large number of specific items selected from four major areas: changes in problems that received attention, changes in component steps in problem-coping, changes in aspects of family relationships presenting problems, and changes in individual family members. Chart 65 reports the proportion of improvement ratings for each of these major areas.

The results provide impressive confirmation of the reality of progress on family problems achieved with the help of family agencies. Clients' improvement ratings reached a high of 66 percent of all ratings in the problem-coping area. Even in the lowest category —changes in family members—they nearly reached the halfway mark. Counselors' ratings also reached impressive levels. Their range was from a high of 63 percent for problem-coping changes to a low of 32 percent for changes in family members. Almost all other ratings were no-change reports. Only 2 percent of counselors' ratings were ratings of worse, and only 5 percent of clients' ratings.

In addition to providing evidence of progress, these ratings yield important clues as to why counselors' ratings did not agree with those of clients. Note, for example, that agreement on the proportion of improved ratings was within three percentile points for specific problems and for aspects of problem-coping. However, for family relationships, clients reported about one-fifth more improvement ratings than did counselors, as well as a third more for changes in individual family members.

IMPROVEMENT IN FOUR COMPONENT AREAS INCLUDED IN CHANGE SCORE

Chart 65

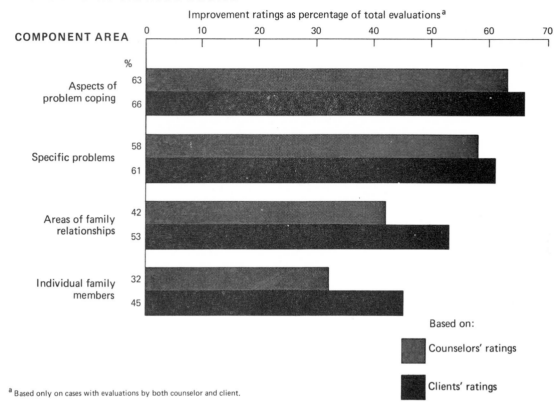

Improvement ratings as percentage of total evaluations[a]

Based on:
Counselors' ratings
Clients' ratings

[a] Based only on cases with evaluations by both counselor and client.

These contrasts serve to remind one that in evaluating outcomes, counselors face a major information handicap. They must depend for their information mainly on what is reported or observed in weekly interviews largely focused on specific problems and their solution. Clients, in contrast, have access to a wider spectrum. They live throughout the week with themselves, their family, and their external world. They have numerous contacts with family members and others whom counselors never see. Because their problems are so real, intense, and critical to their well-being, they are also more alert to small changes, secondary effects, and unanticipated consequences. No wonder, then, that they report more changes in family relationships and individual family members than do counselors. These are realities to be pondered in relation to a central evaluation issue: Who is the best reporter of change? ∎

Percentage reporting improvement [a]

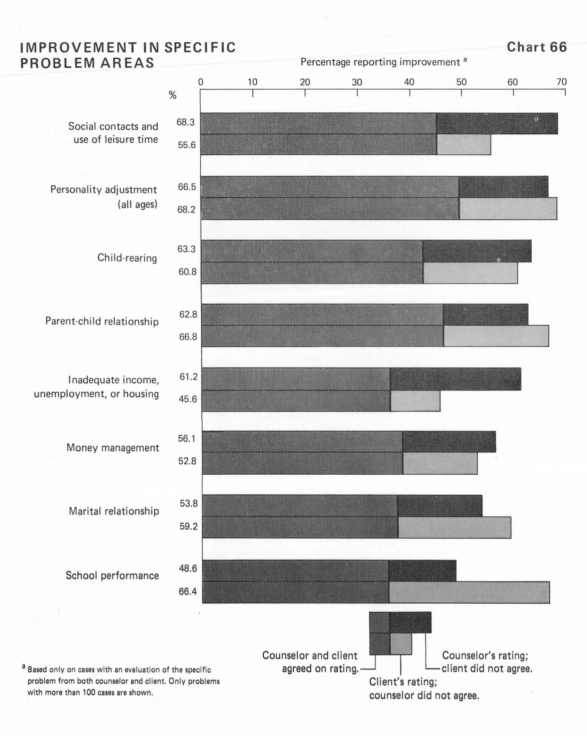

	%
Social contacts and use of leisure time	68.3
	55.6
Personality adjustment (all ages)	66.5
	68.2
Child-rearing	63.3
	60.8
Parent-child relationship	62.8
	66.8
Inadequate income, unemployment, or housing	61.2
	45.6
Money management	56.1
	52.8
Marital relationship	53.8
	59.2
School performance	48.6
	66.4

Counselor and client agreed on rating.

Counselor's rating; client did not agree.

Client's rating; counselor did not agree.

[a] Based only on cases with an evaluation of the specific problem from both counselor and client. Only problems with more than 100 cases are shown.

Chart 66 reports on improvement for all specific problems for which 100 or more dual evaluations were available. A search for patterns in the seeming sameness reveals a tendency for clients to report more improvement ratings for family relations, personality adjustment, and school behavior than counselors but less improvement than counselors in the areas of money, work, housing, and leisure. Perhaps differences in expectations were a factor in both. Clients may expect less from counseling in the area of family and personal problems and hence be more likely to report small gains, whereas their expectations of tangible relief in such areas as income, housing, and employment and their disappointment when these goals are not attained may militate against their reporting as progress certain small instrumental gains, such as improved use of community resources, that might be noted as progress by counselors. Perhaps more important, the major methods of intervention available to family agencies are better suited to giving significant help with internal family problems than with problems with external institutions.

Reports of deterioration were infrequent and came primarily from clients. They were highest for marital problems, where they reached 13 percent.[7] Even here, however, reports of improvement were more than four times as frequent as reports that the situation was worse (59 versus 13 percent). For all problems combined, informants agreed that deterioration had occurred in less than one percent of the problems evaluated. ∎

ASPECT OF PROBLEM-COPING

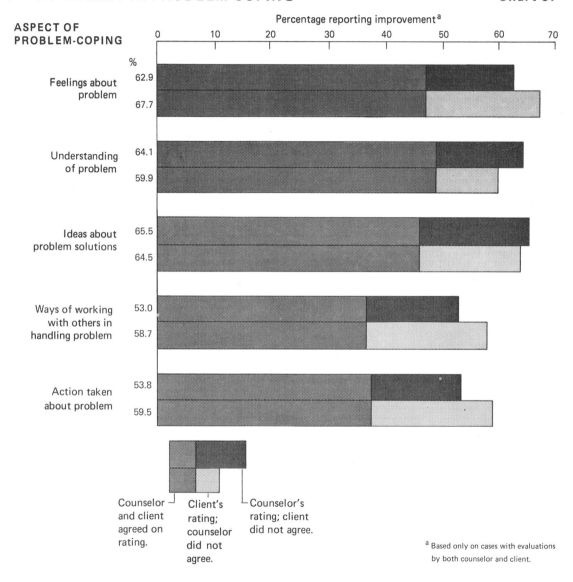

Percentage reporting improvement[a]

Aspect	%
Feelings about problem	62.9 / 67.7
Understanding of problem	64.1 / 59.9
Ideas about problem solutions	65.5 / 64.5
Ways of working with others in handling problem	53.0 / 58.7
Action taken about problem	53.8 / 59.5

Counselor and client agreed on rating.

Client's rating; counselor did not agree.

Counselor's rating; client did not agree.

[a] Based only on cases with evaluations by both counselor and client.

In addition to rating specific problems, both counselors and clients were asked to evaluate their progress in terms of more universal steps in problem-coping. These steps were conceptualized on the basis of an earlier exploratory study in New London.[8] This approach was adopted because it seemed essential to reflect changes that fell short of complete problem solution and also to include some universal items not tied to specific problems.

The results amply affirmed the suitability of the approach. Not only did the problem-coping area show higher proportions of improvement generally than did the pooled ratings in the other three areas; they also showed the highest level of counselor-client agreement on improvement ratings of any area.

The returns for specific categories also revealed interesting and consistent patterns. Changes in the two perceptual areas—"understanding of problem" and "ideas about problem solutions"—were rated slightly higher by counselors than by clients. Perhaps here clients were less aware than counselors of the subtleties of the gradual and mostly unconscious perceptual changes in their mapping of the problem and its potential solutions. Clients reported more improvement than did counselors in the way they felt about their problems, in actions taken, and in ways of working with others in handling problems. Both reported behavioral and action changes less frequently than feeling and perceptual changes, perhaps because the latter more nearly represent the final steps in problem-coping. Negative changes (not shown) were low for all these items—never over 6 percent.[9] In short, the total pattern of responses about problem-coping changes mirrors the central tasks of counseling and suggests the importance of this area to evaluation generally. ■

What are the outcomes?

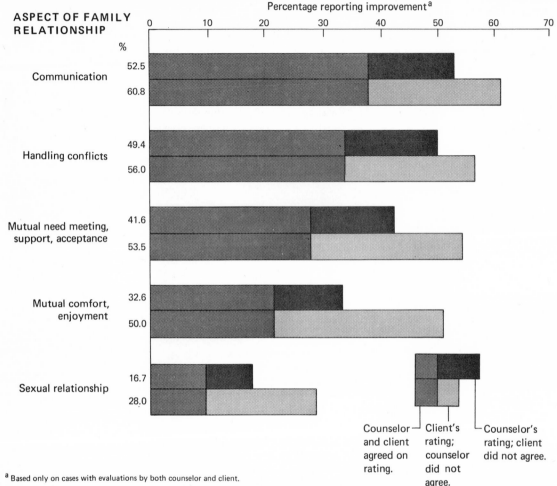

ASPECT OF FAMILY
RELATIONSHIP

Percentage reporting improvement[a]

Communication
52.5
60.8

Handling conflicts
49.4
56.0

Mutual need meeting,
support, acceptance
41.6
53.5

Mutual comfort,
enjoyment
32.6
50.0

Sexual relationship
16.7
28.0

Counselor
and client
agreed on
rating.

Client's
rating;
counselor
did not
agree.

Counselor's
rating; client
did not agree.

[a] Based only on cases with evaluations by both counselor and client.

To provide a total family perspective on change, clients were also queried about changes in family interaction.[10] Those living in families were asked to rate five dimensions of this interaction. Those not living in families rated similar aspects of their relationships with significant others. When their ratings were compared with those of their counselors on the same items, the results were striking in four respects:

1. In every area except the sexual, more than half of clients' ratings were reports of improvement—and this in spite of the typically brief service they had received and the fact that family interaction was often not the primary focus of service.

2. In every area clients reported significantly higher percentages of improvement than did counselors. The more the topic differed from typical counseling themes, such as inadequate communication and interpersonal conflict, the greater this excess. For all five areas combined, 42 percent of counselors' ratings and 53 percent of clients' ratings were reports of improvement.

3. Case-by-case agreement on improvement declined in direct proportion to the remoteness of the behavior rated from the possibility of direct observation in multiple-client interviews. Agreement was closest on changes in communication and conflict and least for changes in sexual relationships. For family interaction, the overall percentage of agreement on improvement for the same cases was 28 percent, a lower level than that for either specific problems or problem-coping.

4. Reports of deterioration (not shown) were very infrequent. They were exceeded by improvement reports in the ratio of fourteen to one for counselors' reports and seven to one for clients' reports. Actual reports of deterioration by clients were most frequent in the sexual area (13 percent).

In combination, these data reflect substantial gains in improved family interaction patterns among those receiving help from family service agencies.[11] They also provide convincing evidence of the importance of going directly to the consumer for ratings in these areas.   ■

Chart 69 introduces still another dimension of improvements through casework counseling—improvement in individual family members. It is based on responses from both counselors and clients when they were asked which family members had improved and which had become worse during the treatment period. The improvements reported for husbands and wives when they were classified by whether or not they were seen support four conclusions:

1. Who is seen makes a significant difference in who improves. For both husbands and wives, the percentage improving was significantly higher when they were seen than when they were not. Best results were reported when both were seen. This conclusion holds regardless of who does the rating.

2. Differences in improvement according to who was seen were more conspicuous in counselors' than in clients' reports. There was also a greater difference between the two ratings for husbands than for wives. Probably both differences stem from the counselor's lack of information about changes in those not seen or seen less often.

3. Progress was not limited to spouses seen, especially in terms of clients' ratings. Apparently, marital partners sometimes do improve even without being seen. Perhaps the stimulus here is some change in how they are treated by the partner who has been seen. This finding offers some hope for improvement even when a spouse refuses to participate in treatment.

4. Improvements in wives seen were significantly more frequent than improvements in husbands seen. The reasons for this sex difference are not apparent in the data. Perhaps wives have more at stake than husbands in

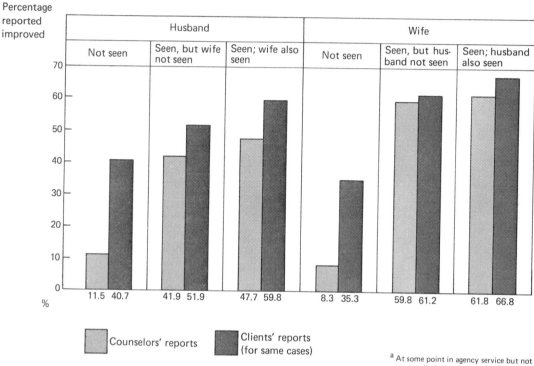

IMPROVEMENT IN HUSBANDS AND WIVES BY WHO WAS SEEN[a]
(Husband-wife families)

Chart 69

Percentage reported improved

Counselors' reports
Clients' reports (for same cases)

[a] At some point in agency service but not necessarily in the same interview.

the solution of marital and family problems and hence are more highly motivated to made maximum use of counseling.

In all these respects, the responses seem to follow logical patterns. This suggests that the data reflect not haphazard ratings, but a clear positive response by both husbands and wives to the counseling service provided by the agency. Judged from this perspective, husbands have been a neglected group in agency service. In the counseling provided to intact families in the present study, 90 percent of the wives were seen but only 66 percent of the husbands. This is an area in which expanded office hours could perhaps make a significant difference. ■

What are the outcomes?

IMPROVEMENT IN CHILDREN BY WHETHER THEY WERE SEEN

Chart 70

Percentage of children reported improved [a]

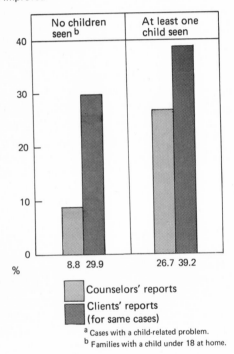

No children seen [b] : 8.8 29.9
At least one child seen : 26.7 39.2

%

☐ Counselors' reports

■ Clients' reports (for same cases)

[a] Cases with a child-related problem.
[b] Families with a child under 18 at home.

Chart 70 is the final one in the series focused on changes in specific areas. It relates to two questions regarding children's improving when there is a child-related problem: What proportion of children improve in cases with child-related problems? Does it make any difference whether or not the children themselves are seen? The findings suggest the following answers.

1. Counting both the children seen and those not seen, counselors reported that 19 percent of the children improved; clients reported that 35 percent improved.

2. It does make a difference whether the children are seen. A much higher proportion of children improved in families with children's problems when one or more of the children were seen than in families in which no children were seen. The difference was highly significant statistically.

3. Clients reported many more children improving than did counselors. When no children were seen, clients reported more than three times the proportion of children improving as did counselors. When at least one child was seen, differences were less, but clients' reports were still more than one-third higher than those from counselors.

These findings underscore the major information gap counselors face when they attempt to rate all family members on the outcomes of treatment.

4. Counseling of adult family members when children's problems are present has important effects on the children themselves even if they are not seen. In the present sample, even when no child was seen, clients reported 30 percent of the children improved. Here the effects on the children are obviously an indirect result of changes in the parents, in their relationships with their children, and in the patterns of family interaction generally. Since family agency clients have an above-average number of children (see page 16), these indirect changes have much significance for prevention.

These unexpectedly high reports of changes in children underscore the importance of basing outcome ratings on the total family. They also give graphic testimony to the wealth of information and increased perspective that clients can provide in this area if they are asked. In addition, they suggest that a greater investment in seeing the children may pay dividends in improved outcomes. ■

Explanation of the change score

All the charts in the rest of this section and the next two use what is referred to as a change score. This score represents a composite of all available evaluations in four areas: changes in specific problems, changes in problem-coping, changes in family relationships, and changes in individual family members. It was designed to provide the following.

1. A sensitive and flexible index that would reflect the types of gains typical of casework counseling—multiple, small, interrelated gains specific to the problem at hand but which often spread throughout the family.

2. An index of family rather than individual change.

3. A score that would reflect the core of family service—facilitation of improved coping with family problems.

4. A score that would utilize all evidence available to the rater, both tangible and intangible.

5. A procedure that would require no assessment of amount of change and would utilize instead multiple judgments of the direction of change.[12]

6. A procedure that would not require advance value judgments of what constitutes improvement or deterioration but instead would leave this decision to those who know best each actual situation.

7. A score that would not be diluted by the inclusion of items not germane to the service for a particular case.

8. A score that would utilize components that could be obtained in parallel form from both counselors and clients.

9. A procedure that would not require outside raters, research interviewers, or review of case records.

10. A score that would be simple enough to be computed eventually by a local agency without undue expense.

The scoring procedure devised utilized data on scope of change as a substitute for ratings of amount of change. The inferences as to amount of change were derived from the extent of spread to other areas and persons, plus indicators of changes in problem-coping in general. The change score therefore reflects scope and direction of change rather than amount, depth, or duration of change. The score is incapable of reflecting prevention of deterioration. In fact, reported changes can not necessarily be assumed to result from agency service. The contribution of service is separately assessed.

Scores were computed by totaling the number of checks for "better," "same," and "worse" in the specified areas, subtracting the worse ratings from the better, giving double weight to certain key items, and dividing the net number of improvement ratings by the number of items rated.[13] The result was multiplied by ten, yielding a scale with a theoretical range +10 to −10. The answer represents the net ratio of positive ratings to total items evaluated. Scores were computed for all cases that met certain minimum requirements.[14]

Readers should note that a high plus score means that some positive change was perceived in many areas and a low plus score that positive change was seen in only a few areas or that gains were mainly offset by losses. A zero means either no change on all items or an exact balance between gains and losses. A minus score means that losses out-weighed gains, if any. Scores seldom reach either extreme. Even when they do, they do not necessarily indicate major changes in life-style or level of functioning, but merely that some improvement (or deterioration) was reported on almost all items rated.

The change scores derived from counselors' reports were based on an average of sixteen evaluations, of which 43 percent were "better"; 55 percent, "the same"; and 2 percent, "worse." Change scores derived from clients' reports were based on an average of seventeen evaluations, of which 54 percent were ratings of "better"; 41 percent, "the same"; and 5 percent, "worse." The need to subtract negatives from positives occurred infrequently.

No estimate of reliability was feasible.[15] The best validation available for the change scores was a check of their internal consistency with the global ratings (which were not utilized in computing the change score itself). Change scores based on counselors' item evaluations correlated with counselors' global ratings of outcomes at the +.74 level. Change scores based on clients' item evaluations correlated with clients' global ratings of outcomes at the +.70 level. All these correlations were statistically significant at the .001 level. In spite of these close relationships, the change scores proved to be considerably more sensitive to the influence of client and treatment characteristics than were the global evaluations. On the other hand, the relationship between counselors' and clients' change scores was relatively low ($r = +.34$), although still highly significant statistically. The reasons for this low relationship are discussed fully in connection with chart 72. ∎

Chart 71

DISTRIBUTION OF CHANGE SCORES

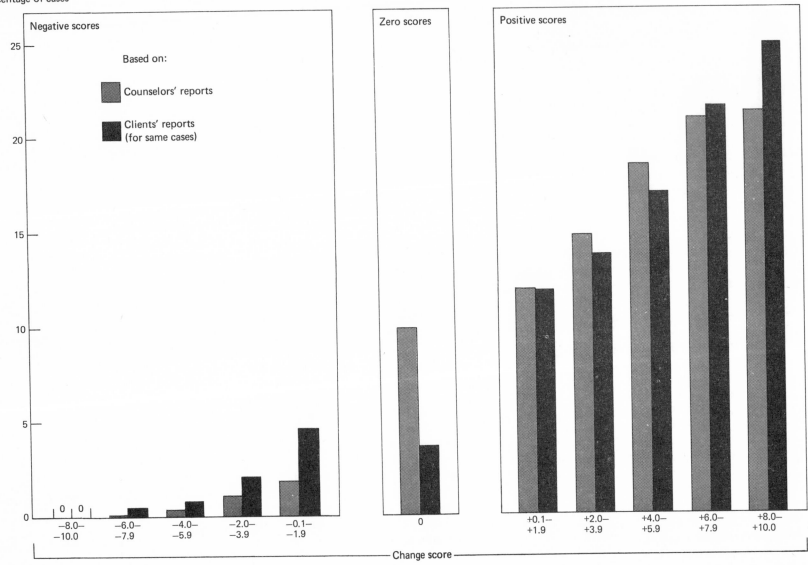

Percentage of cases

Negative scores

Based on:

Counselors' reports

Clients' reports
(for same cases)

Zero scores

Positive scores

25

20

15

10

5

0

−8.0—
−10.0

−6.0—
−7.9

−4.0—
−5.9

−2.0—
−3.9

−0.1—
−1.9

0

+0.1—
+1.9

+2.0—
+3.9

+4.0—
+5.9

+6.0—
+7.9

+8.0—
+10.0

——— Change score ———

Section seven

Chart 71 shows how actual change scores, computed as described on the previous page, were distributed. The most obvious finding is that of the strong preponderance of positive over negative scores. Improvement scores outnumbered negative ones in the ratio of twenty-nine to one for counselors' reports and eleven to one for clients' reports. More than one case in five reached the top change score category according to counselors' ratings, and nearly one in four according to those of clients.

Although individual scores varied widely,[16] they produced a composite profile strongly skewed to the right as compared with the normal curve. For this reason, averages fell near the middle of the positive range—at +4.8 for scores based on counselors' reports and at +5.0 for scores based on clients' reports.

To facilitate comparisons, scores for cases with no follow-up were omitted from the chart. When these were added in, the overall average for change scores based on counselors' reports was +4.3. The effect of the non-response group on the average change score for clients is discussed in connection with chart 73.

Comparisons of counselors' and clients' reports indicate that clients' change scores were concentrated more at the extremes, both positive and negative, than were those of counselors. Counselors' change scores, in contast, were conspicuously high in frequency for the zero score, no-change category and slightly higher than clients' at the lower end of the positive scores—up to +6.0. This tendency for counselors' ratings to cluster more narrowly than those of clients was also noted in the global ratings (see chart 60). The sources of these and other differences are discussed in connection with chart 72.

For most readers, these are new and strange scores that have little inherent meaning. How should they be interpreted? Some clues are provided by the average change scores for each global rating shown below:

Average change scores[a]
(same cases)

Global ratings	Counselors' reports[b]	Clients' reports
Much deterioration	−1.5	−1.5
Some deterioration	+0.1	−0.3
No change	+0.8	+1.0
Mixed change	+2.7	+3.0
Some improvement	+5.5	+5.6
Much improvement	+8.0	+7.7

[a]Averages cited for clients apply to clients' global ratings; those for counselors, to counselors' global ratings.
[b]When all cases including those with no follow-up report are used, counselors' averages become −0.2 and −1.8 for the deterioration categories. Other figures change little.

Another way to visualize these scores is to remember that for the average client report with seventeen component ratings, an increment of 0.6 in the change score is equivalent to a net addition of one more improvement rating. Viewed in these terms, the findings as a whole were remarkably positive.

To what extent does this indicate that more progress was achieved with the help of family agency service than would have been achieved without it? Unfortunately, in the absence of a control group, it is not possible to be sure. One simply can not tell what would have happened if equally motivated and involved applicants seeking help at the point of crisis had been denied such help. Family agencies have not been willing to put such clients to the test of denial of service. In most other stud-ies the control groups utilized, and the treated groups also, have been captive groups not motivated for or actively seeking service. Often they were likewise not at the point of crisis.[17] Hence, one can not tell from these studies what kinds of gains occur simply from the normal process of self-healing after crises. What one does know from these other studies is that the changes associated simply with the passage of time are typically more balanced between positive and negative changes. For example, Ludwig L. Geismar et al., following a general population control group of 175 young urban families over a three-year period, reported positive overall movement in family functioning during this period in 39 percent, negative movement in 47 percent, and no change in 14 percent.[18] Consequently, if it were not for the differences in the rating procedures used and the unsolved issue of the extent of self-recovery after crisis, one could presume that the preponderance of positive changes shown here reflect, in the main, changes set in motion by counseling. Some supporting evidence of the minimal role of other factors has already been presented (see chart 63). Further evidence linking these positive changes more clearly to the counseling service provided by agencies will be presented in section 9. ∎

COUNSELOR-CLIENT DIFFERENCE IN CHANGE SCORE
BY COUNSELOR'S GLOBAL EVALUATION

Chart 72

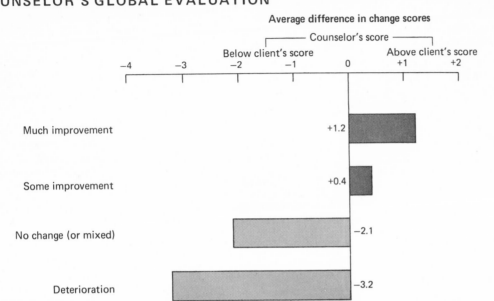

Average difference in change scores

⌐—— Counselor's score ——⌐

Below client's score   Above client's score

| -4 | -3 | -2 | -1 | 0 | +1 | +2 |

Much improvement   +1.2

Some improvement   +0.4

No change (or mixed)   -2.1

Deterioration   -3.2

On an average basis, counselors' and clients' change scores agreed closely. For all cases with both scores, the average for clients' ratings exceeded that for counselors' reports by two-tenths of a point, a difference too small to be statistically significant. Unfortunately, this similarity in overall averages was the result of a close balance between positive and negative differences and not of agreement on specific cases. When the absolute differences between scores for the same cases were added without regard to which of the two scores was higher, the average difference rose to 3.0, a highly significant difference. Do the data throw any light on the sources of these marked differences?

Chart 72 illustrates one such source. When either party gave an extreme rating, particularly a rating of "worse," the other tended to rate the changes more conservatively. For example, when counselors reported "much improvement," counselors' scores averaged 1.2 points higher than those from clients. When counselors reported "deterioration," counselors' scores averaged 3.2 points lower than those of clients. This pattern was statistically highly significant.[19]

Somewhat similar and equally significant patterns were evident when the data were analyzed by clients' rather than counselors' global scores. When clients reported the situation as "worse," their scores averaged 4.5 points below those of

counselors. When clients reported "much improvement," their scores averaged 1.7 points higher than those of counselors. This tendency of both parties to moderate the extreme views of the other would suggest that some merging of the two scores would give a reasonably conservative picture of actual change.

A second major source of counselor-client differences was some difficulty or friction in their relationship. Regardless of who was doing the rating, the highest differences were found when either rated the relationship as unsatisfactory. High disagreement scores were also associated with large differences in change scores. Both patterns were statistically highly significant.[20]

A third factor that clearly contributed was the counselors' lack of information about what was happening to the clients. This was confirmed by counselors' reports about how much evidence was available to them. Thirty-nine percent reported very little; 42 percent, a moderate amount; and only 19 percent, a substantial amount. Change score differences decreased as available evidence increased. When there was little evidence, counselors' scores averaged 1.5 points below those of clients; when the amount was moderate, counselors' ratings averaged 0.5 point above those of clients; when it was substantial, they averaged 0.6 point above. However, even when there had been ten or more interviews, counselors still rated the evidence available to them as substantial in only half of the cases.

That counselors' lack of information contributed to the difference was also confirmed by a highly significant inverse relationship between number of interviews and change score differences. When there had been only one interview, clients' scores exceeded those of counselors by a considerable margin. As number of interviews increased and counselors gained access to more outcome information, counselors' scores rapidly caught up with and then exceeded those of clients (see chart 84). The same pattern was evident as the number of family members seen increased (see chart 89).[21]

The tendency of counselors to report higher scores than clients as the amount and intensity of the contact increased suggests that differences in their views about what gains are important may be another factor contributing to counselor-client differences. For example, counselors may be more aware than clients of certain intermediate steps in problem-solution and more likely to see them as improvements.[22] The same may be true for certain subtle attitudinal and emotional changes that counselors have learned to note and value. The extent to which counselors' ratings were also influenced by their professional expectations of progress with certain types of clients and service input can not be ascertained from the data.

Counselor-client differences were also less when an in-person interview rather than a mail questionnaire was used. To what extent this difference resulted from interviewers' efforts through probing to increase the accuracy and completeness of the responses and to what

extent from clients' hesitation to report negatives in a face-to-face contact can not be definitely established.

Another influential factor related to the follow-up process was the amount of delay in contacting the client. As this lag increased, so did the differences (both positive and negative) between counselors' ratings at closing and those reported by clients. Absolute differences increased from 1.9 points when delay in follow-up was under two weeks to 3.6 points when the delay in follow-up was substantial. This pattern was statistically significant[23] and understandable in the absence of any post-treatment contact.

Only two client characteristics were found significantly associated with counselor-client change score differences: severity of the total problem situation and influence of external factors on outcomes (see chart 80). Both suggest that an additional factor in these differences is the inherent difficulty and complexity of the rating task itself. In the case of external developments affecting outcomes, the counselor's lack of knowledge about such changes probably again contributed.

Background characteristics of the client were not found significantly associated with these counselor-client differences. Indicators that were tested in this area included education, race, and socioeconomic status. Treatment approaches tested and not found significant included whether the counselor and client were matched on race and sex, whether the focus was on relationship problems, and whether multiple-client interviewing was the primary modality. A final factor of obvious inherent relevance was the high variability of the change scores themselves.

In summary, the evidence appears to support the following factors as contributing to the relatively large case-by-case differences between counselors and clients in their change ratings.

1. The tendency of an extreme view by one party to be linked to a much less extreme view by the other.

2. Dissatisfaction with the relationship.

3. The inadequate information on outcomes available to the counselor.

4. Differences in the types of changes noticed and valued.

5. Differences in the type of feedback encouraged by different follow-up methods.

6. A major discrepancy in the time when the two ratings were made.

7. The complexity of the situation being evaluated.

8. The high variance of the change scores themselves.

How much of the total variation do these factors account for when considered in combination? If both the direction and the amount of difference are taken into account, the best answer available is about half.[24] How much of the remaining variance is owing to reliability problems with the instrument itself and how much to other types of real but still unidentified differences in the views of counselors and clients on outcomes is not yet known. Research involving direct discussions between counselors and clients of their separate ratings is needed to throw light on these issues, as well as further testing of the instrument itself. Such explorations are essential if the field is to move toward use of clients' outcome reports as a primary source of information on the results of agency service. ∎

Throughout this report, great care has been taken to base all counselor-client outcome comparisons on the same cases. This has meant that slightly less than half of the cases (45 percent) could be included because no follow-up report was obtained on 47 percent of the sample and one or both scores could not be computed for another 8 percent.[25] A crucial issue therefore requires attention: In what way and to what extent did this omission influence the findings reported? The answer must be approached through attention in sequence to two intermediate questions: How did cases with a follow-up report differ from those without one? How much effect did these differences have on the overall findings?

The follow-up sample compared with the nonresponse group

Cases that counselors saw as having favorable outcomes were more likely to be in the follow-up sample than those given lower ratings. This is evident from the discrepancy in chart 73 between counselors' average change scores of +4.8 for the follow-up group and +3.7 for those with no follow-up. This difference is statistically highly significant.

The follow-up group differed significantly from the nonfollow-up group in certain key dimensions related to outcomes: Those followed up had completed more years of school (twelve as compared with eleven years), had higher socioeconomic scores (53 versus 45), scored higher on the index of client involvement in seeking help, had a more positive counselor-client relationship, and received more interviews (7.8 versus 5.9). Families where marital, child-related, or adult personality problems were primary responded more often than those with environmental or major

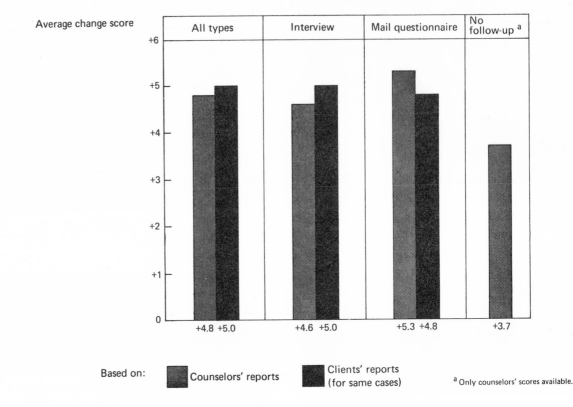

Based on: ▨ Counselors' reports   ■ Clients' reports (for same cases)   [a] Only counselors' scores available.

social or behavioral problems, and mild cases more often than severe. Terminations for the follow-up group were more often planned, based on a mutual decision by the counselor and client, and the result of the completion of service. Thus, the follow-up sample tended to show a consistently higher proportion of those qualities normally associated with more favorable outcomes than did the nonresponse group. The incompleteness of the follow-up sample clearly introduced a favorable bias.

What accounts for these differences between the follow-up and nonfollow-up groups? Agencies' reports on failed follow-up attempts suggest a partial answer. In 44 percent the client could not be located. Many of these were brief service, drop-in cases in which the counselors knew little about the client and received little or no feedback about the effect of agency services; hence they had little evidence on which to base change ratings. If reached, these clients might well have reported more favorably than did their counselors. An additional 33 percent of the nonresponse group were unwilling to participate in the follow-up. If they had participated, some of their reports undoubtedly would have been negative. The agency itself felt that follow-up was contraindicated for an additional 5 percent because of confidentiality problems, the hostility or unreliability of the client, or the type or brevity of the service. These selective omissions leave major information gaps that present problems in interpretation.

To local agencies conducting their own follow-up studies, where closer control can be exercised, the challenge of this nationwide experience is to develop staff commitment to and ingenuity in following up the full range of their clientele regardless of transiency, attitude, or nature of service.

Estimates for the total sample

When the counselor change scores were averaged for all cases for which they were available rather than just for those with a corresponding client change score, the overall counselor score dropped from +4.8 to +4.3. To what extent would the overall client change score average of +5.0 also have been different if a follow-up report had been obtained for all cases where there was a counselor change score? The answer required some form of estimate for the cases with no follow-up. The procedure chosen substituted for each missing client score an estimated score that differed from the counselor's score for that same case by the same amount as did actual client's scores when paired with counselors' scores at the same change score level. This process yielded the following estimates for the nonresponse group and the sample.

	Average change scores	
Type of case	Counselors' scores	Clients' scores
Cases with both counselor's and clients' change scores (N = 1,606)	+4.8	+5.0
Cases with only counselors' change scores (N = 1,440)	+3.7	+4.6 (estimated[a])
All cases with counselors' change scores (N = 3,046)	+4.3	+4.8 (estimated[b])

[a]Estimates based on the differences between counselors' and clients' change scores for the 1,606 cases where both were available.

[b]Estimated by combining the actual scores for 1,606 cases with the estimated scores for 1,440 additional cases having a counselor's score.

The results of this estimating process brought the two groups closer together than was anticipated. The reason is evident from chart 72. When the counselors reported "no change" or "deterioration," as they did for many of the nonresponse group, clients usually tended to see the results in a more favorable light. The estimating process therefore more often added to than subtracted from the counselors' scores. Thus, the estimated client average for the total group was only 0.2 below the average for the follow-up group.

These findings suggest that client figures limited to the same cases probably approximate fairly closely how the total client group would have responded if they had been reached. For counselors, the difference is more pronounced but is easier to take into account since counselors' scores are available for nearly the total sample. These scores have been watched throughout the study. When consideration

of the total sample would make a significant difference in the conclusions (which is unusual), the reader is alerted.

Effect of type of follow-up

A third question germane to chart 73 is also of concern to agencies: Does the type of follow-up affect the outcome findings? Three-quarters of all follow-ups were by personal interview, one-quarter by mail questionnaire. There was more selection in a favorable direction in the mail questionnaire than with the interview form of follow-up. This is apparent from the lower response rate to the mail questionnaire (56 versus 72 percent, where an attempt was made), the counselors' significantly higher scores for the mail questionnaire group, and the fact that those who returned mail questionnaires tended to have characteristics associated with more favorable outcomes.[26] The favorable bias in the mail questionnaire group is, however, offset in the client scores by the tendency of the mail responses to be less favorable than those from interviews[27] when viewed in the light of corresponding counselor scores.

These findings pose a dilemma for agencies: The mail approach will yield richer and less restrained comments with less expense but will introduce more selection owing to nonresponse. The personal interview will provide more adequate coverage, more complete reporting, and more opportunity to probe complaints. It also will assist in locating those who have moved. At the same time it will be more expensive and may inhibit client feedback. Probably a combination of these approaches will be needed if local agencies are to secure full follow-up returns without undue expense

CHANGE SCORES BY AREA EVALUATED

Chart 74

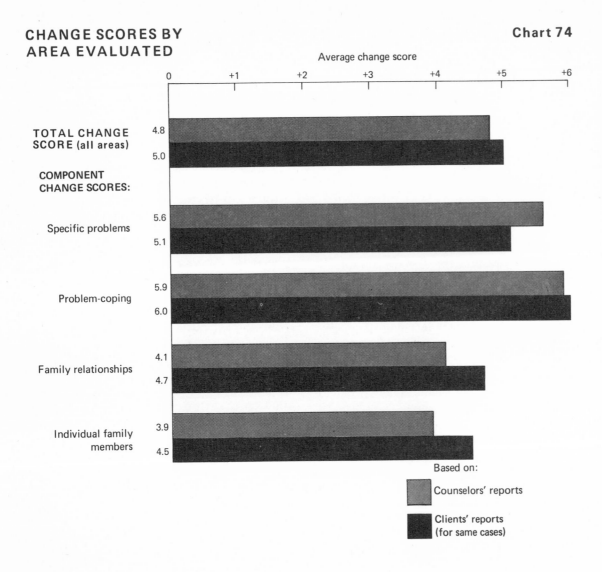

Average change score

0	+1	+2	+3	+4	+5	+6	

TOTAL CHANGE SCORE (all areas) — 4.8 / 5.0

COMPONENT CHANGE SCORES:

Specific problems — 5.6 / 5.1

Problem-coping — 5.9 / 6.0

Family relationships — 4.1 / 4.7

Individual family members — 3.9 / 4.5

Based on:

Counselors' reports

Clients' reports (for same cases)

Chart 74 should help the reader visualize the four subareas included in the overall score. Since each was computed by the same procedure used in computing the total score, comparisons can be meaningful.

All these area scores present a reasonably consistent picture of change.[28] Greatest gains were reflected in the problem-coping area. Next highest gains were those for specific problems. Changes in individual family members and in family relationships both showed lower average scores than either of the other two areas. These differences suggest that, of the areas studied, the problem-coping area probably reflects most closely the content and focus of casework counseling.

Comparison of the two averages for each area, one for counselors' scores and one for clients' scores, reveals the same pattern for both as far as relative rank is concerned. The figures for problem-coping were almost identical. Changes in family relationships and individual family members were the most divergent. Probably this difference reflects the typical content of counseling interviews. Issues related to problem-coping no doubt receive almost universal attention, whereas changes occurring in family relationships and individual family members might or might not be discussed depending on their relevance to the core problem.

The only area in which counselors' ratings exceeded those from clients was that for specific problems. Possibly this reversal reflects a definition of problem improvement by counselors that includes gains in instrumental steps toward problem resolution, whereas clients may define problem improvement primarily in terms of effective relief of stress. ■

8

HOW DO CLIENT
CHARACTERISTICS
AFFECT
OUTCOMES?

Chart 75

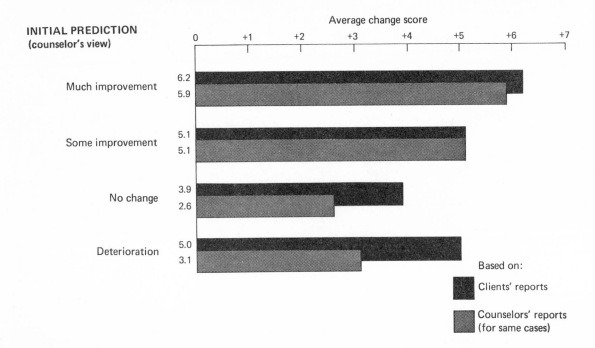

INITIAL PREDICTION
(counselor's view)

Average change score

Much improvement	6.2 / 5.9
Some improvement	5.1 / 5.1
No change	3.9 / 2.6
Deterioration	5.0 / 3.1

Based on:

■ Clients' reports

▨ Counselors' reports (for same cases)

Chart 75 begins a series on the relation of client characteristics to average change scores (see page 101 for explanation of change scores). Among the more marked associations was that with the counselor's own prediction at intake about how much improvement would occur before closing. These predictions, which can be thought of as very rough prognostic assessments, were asked for on the intake report whenever further service was planned. Much improvement was predicted for 14 percent of such cases; some improvement for 74 percent; no change for 8 percent; and deterioration for 4 percent. How did these predictions relate to actual outcomes?

As chart 75 indicates, the two improvement predictions showed the expected relationship to the change scores. For the "no change" and "deterioration" predictions, counselors' and clients' change scores showed the same general pattern, but clients' scores greatly exceeded those of counselors.[1] (This pattern also appears in chart 72.) Obviously, counselors tend to underestimate the chances of achieving gains when initial prognostic indicators appear unpromising. Because this group is a relatively small one, counselors' and clients' scores on an overall basis showed a highly significant correlation with initial predictions.

Another anomaly of the present chart is the fact that, regardless of source, the lowest final scores were found for the "no change" predictions, not for those where "deterioration" was anticipated. The reason for this unexpected finding is not clear.[2] Perhaps clients are more easily mobilized to maximum effort if the alternative they visualize is a worse situation than their present one than if it is continuance of the status quo.

These mixed findings lead one to ask: Under what circumstances did counselors predict "improvement" and when did they predict "no change" or "deterioration"? Some clues can be obtained from the correlation of these initial predictions with available information on client characteristics. Two factors showed a significant but low positive association with favorable predictions: extent of client involvement in seeking help and whether the problem that was to be the major focus of service was one where improvement was relatively frequent. Four characteristics showed a significant but low association with unfavorable predictions: severity of total problem situation, number of problems identified at intake, number of environmental problems, and age of family head. There was no significant association between the counselor's prediction of outcomes and the size of family, the client's socioeconomic status or race, or whether the family was receiving public assistance.

These patterns suggest that counselors assess prognosis not from formal facesheet data but from individualized case-by-case considerations. Later findings support this approach (see chart 83), but it is apparent that counselors are still underestimating some of the hidden strengths of applicants who on first contact appear unlikely to achieve positive change. ■

Average change scores also showed a close and consistent relationship to the severity of the total problem situation as estimated by the counselor at intake. Change score averages were highest for applicants with mild problems and lowest for those whose problems were most severe. This pattern held regardless of whether scores were based on counselors' or clients' reports. In fact, the averages for the two informants agreed closely. The same pattern also prevailed but at a lower level when cases without a follow-up were included in the averages[3]. In each instance the relation of the change scores to severity was highly significant statistically.

Since nearly half of all cases served by family agencies are concentrated in the severe category, it is most fortunate that agencies actually are able to help such families cope with their desperately difficult problem situations. This fact is confirmed by the levels of improvement reported both by counselors and by clients for these severe cases. As shown in chart 76, the averages for severe cases represent a net balance of about seven more "better" ratings than "worse" ratings. These gains were not achieved, however, without a relatively large time investment. Mild cases achieved their higher scores with an average of only 4.5 interviews. The intermediate scores for the moderately severe cases required 8.1 interviews to achieve; the lower scores for the severe cases represent an investment of 6.6 interviews. The lower figure for the severe cases results, in part, from premature termination on client initiative.

Like the ratings of predicted improvement, these severity ratings represent counselors' evaluations at the time of intake. What kinds of cases did counselors tend to rate as severe?

How do client characteristics affect outcomes?

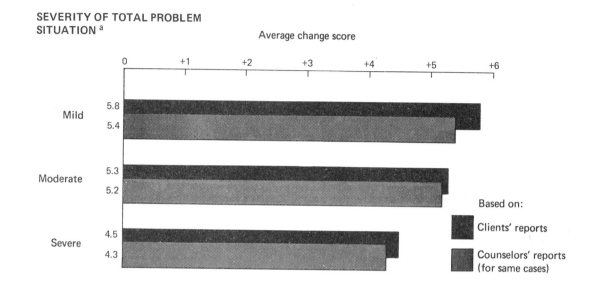

SEVERITY OF TOTAL PROBLEM SITUATION [a]

Average change score

Mild — 5.8 / 5.4
Moderate — 5.3 / 5.2
Severe — 4.5 / 4.3

Based on:

■ Clients' reports

▨ Counselors' reports (for same cases)

[a] As judged by the intake counselor.

Judging by the correlation findings, they were the cases with more problems and with types of problems resistant to improvement, such as delinquency, alcoholism, and mental illness. Age showed a slight but statistically significant negative association with severity, suggesting that young applicants bring somewhat more severe problems than older applicants. Client characteristics, such as socioeconomic status, race, and size of family, were not significantly related to these severity ratings.   ■

CHANGE SCORES BY DEGREE OF CLIENT INVOLVEMENT IN SEEKING AGENCY SERVICE

Chart 77

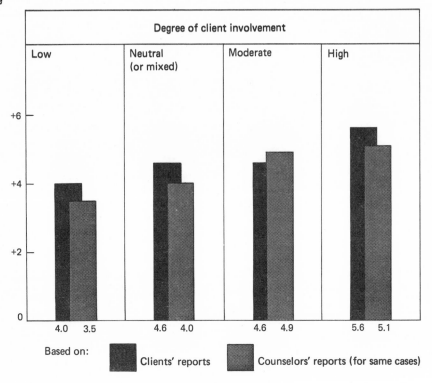

Average change score

Degree of client involvement

| Low | Neutral (or mixed) | Moderate | High |

| 4.0 | 3.5 | 4.6 | 4.0 | 4.6 | 4.9 | 5.6 | 5.1 |

Based on: ■ Clients' reports ▨ Counselors' reports (for same cases)

Chart 77 focuses on the effect on outcomes of client involvement in seeking service. Since counselors were not asked in this study to rate motivation directly, a special index had to be constructed using all available indicators.[4] The results, classified into four levels of involvement in seeking service, indicated that 10 percent of the cases with a follow-up report were in the low involvement group, 12 percent in the neutral or mixed group, 36 percent in the moderately involved group, and 42 percent in the highly involved group.

As chart 77 indicates, this index of client involvement also showed a consistent and highly significant relationship both to counselors' and to clients' change scores. This pattern continued to prevail for the counselors' scores when those without a client follow-up were added in.[5] It was likewise evident when the involvement scores were related to clients' global outcome ratings.

These findings throw into question the conclusions about the outcomes of casework that have been based on control and treated groups selected without regard for the interest or active investment of those in the sample in the help-seeking process.[6] Because of the ethical considerations involved in denying service to those actively seeking it, investigators have usually chosen to conduct their experiments with some easily identified population, such as welfare recipients, housing project residents, or school children, because in such situations the control group could be randomly selected and watched for change without interference with the lifestyle of members of the control group, without denial of service, and often without their knowledge. While this procedure has usually met the scientific requirements for equality between the experimental and control groups, it has placed the evaluation of casework at a gross disadvantage in two respects: (1) It has tested casework service on types of families that seldom are agency clients, and (2) it has tested this service largely with relatively unmotivated families where success is least likely. In spite of these handicaps, the results have sometimes been interpreted as an evaluation of casework service as a whole.[7] ■

Chart 78 examines for three separate problem groups how change scores vary according to where a client believes his problem lies.[8] The same basic patterns were found for the three principal problems shown—marital problems, children's problems, and problems related to the personality adjustment of an adult. Averages were highest when the client defined his problem as located within himself, next highest when he defined it as involving a relationship in which he participated, and distinctly lower when he attributed the problem to another family member, such as a spouse, child, or parent. Except for marital problems, scores were lowest when the problem was defined as situational. The exception for marital problems perhaps reflects the profound effect on marital balance of major situational and life-cycle changes.

These patterns were much less clear when other problem areas were the primary focus of service, perhaps because external situations were more likely to be a primary influence when the problem was a practical one. The worst record was found when the client maintained that he had no problems but came at the insistence of someone else, such as a spouse or a legal authority. This "no problem" group showed change score averages of only +3.0 for counselors' reports and +2.9 for clients' reports.

Together, these findings suggest that the client's definition of where his problem lies may itself provide an important prognostic clue to how much counseling can help. If the client is right in seeing the situation as outside of himself, he may be limited in what he can do to change it. If he is not right, his denial of involvement makes progress more difficult. ■

How do client characteristics affect outcomes?

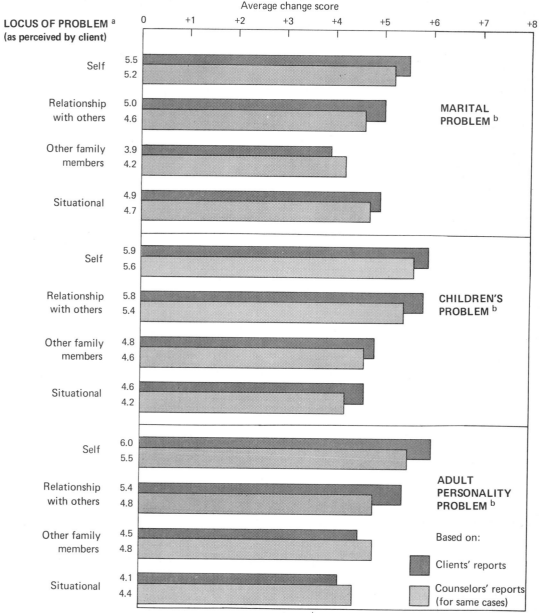

CHANGE SCORES BY TYPE AND LOCUS OF PROBLEM   Chart 78

Average change score

LOCUS OF PROBLEM [a]
(as perceived by client)

[a] Based on clients' problem descriptions at follow-up.

[b] Most important problem at either intake, closing, or follow-up.

Based on:

Clients' reports

Counselors' reports
(for same cases)

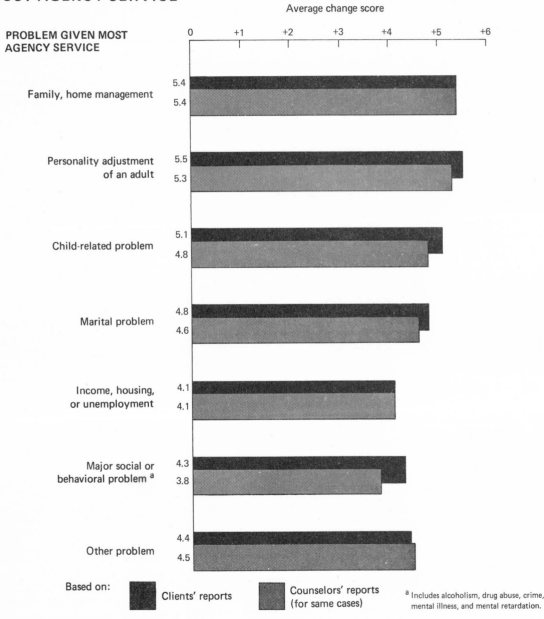

Average change score

PROBLEM GIVEN MOST AGENCY SERVICE

Family, home management
5.4
5.4

Personality adjustment of an adult
5.5
5.3

Child-related problem
5.1
4.8

Marital problem
4.8
4.6

Income, housing, or unemployment
4.1
4.1

Major social or behavioral problem [a]
4.3
3.8

Other problem
4.4
4.5

Based on:
Clients' reports
Counselors' reports (for same cases)

[a] Includes alcoholism, drug abuse, crime, mental illness, and mental retardation.

The gains achieved through agency service vary substantially according to the problem focus. For both counselors and clients, scores were highest for family and home management problems and adult personality adjustment problems; they were intermediate for marital and child-related problems, with marital problems the lower of the two; they were lowest for major social and behavioral problems and problems related to income, housing, and unemployment.

Viewed in the context of related studies, the high averages for family and home management bring to mind the findings of Ludwig L. Geismar and others on the relatively high gains in instrumental (as contrasted with expressive) areas such as family relationships.[9] The two lowest categories present special difficulties for the achievement of gains: Major social and behavioral problems are often complicated by both major pathology and an adverse subculture; environmental problems often involve the impossible task of rallying enough external supports to make a significant difference to an individual family.

The low averages for major social and behavioral problems also suggest the difficult context in which most controlled studies of the effectiveness of casework have been conducted. In many instances the samples used have involved delinquents, predelinquents, or multiproblem families[10]—types of cases that tend to concentrate in this lowest group in chart 79. When cases of these specific types were separately examined, the pattern of low gains remained.[11] All too often, casework has been tested not with a typical clientele but rather with types of cases and problems that are the most resistive to positive change. ■

INFLUENCE OF EXTERNAL FACTORS
(client's view)

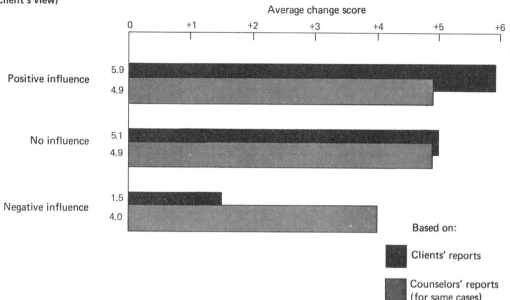

Average change score

	Clients' reports
Based on:	
	Counselors' reports (for same cases)

were situational in nature. Relatives and friends were cited in about equal proportions among the positive and negative influences.

The effect of agency service can best be assessed when external influences are not seen as a factor.[14] This pattern is given in the second column of the table below:

Client's global rating	Percentage of cases		
	External factors positive (N=502)	External factors neutral[a] (N=943)	External factors negative (N=51)
Much better	36	35	4
Somewhat better	45	39	8
No change (or mixed)	17	21	47
Worse	2	5	41
Total	100	100	100

[a]Or no external factors reported.

When external factors were neutral, about three-quarters of the clients reported improvement in their global ratings while their change scores averaged +5.1. Both of these indicators provide a remarkably favorable record for the outcomes associated with agency service. ∎

The impact of external factors[12] on the outcomes of counseling was surprisingly marked —at least when judged by clients' ratings. This is evident both in chart 80 and in the table beneath. When external influences were positive, clients' scores reached +5.9 on the average; when they were negative, the scores fell to +1.5. The same marked patterns were repeated for clients' global ratings. When external factors were positive, 81 percent reported improvement; when they were negative, only 12 percent reported improvement.

Judged by their reports, counselors often know little about the external developments in clients' lives.[13] Counselors' and clients' scores agreed closely when neither reported any external influences. When external factors were positive, clients' ratings were a full point higher than those of counselors; when they were negative, clients' scores fell a full 2.5 points below counselors' ratings.

Fortunately, cases in which external influences were negative were infrequent. Only 51 cases, or 3 percent of the follow-up sample, mentioned negative influences. About a third mentioned some positive influence; the rest (64 percent) reported either no external influences or only neutral ones. Nearly half of the positive influences involved other professional persons. Nearly half of the negative influences

Average change score

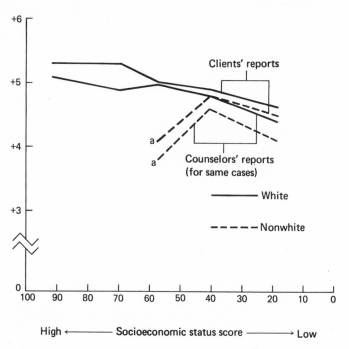

High ←——— Socioeconomic status score ———→ Low

a Nonwhite cases not plotted beyond this point
because of small samples.

greater than those by socioeconomic status. Despite the fact that the scores for nonwhite clients paralleled closely those for white clients at the lower status levels, the difference, considering all levels, was sufficient to be highly significant statistically for counselors' scores both for the same cases and for the total sample. The difference in clients' scores by race was not statistically significant.[17] In the main this difference is traceable to one small subcategory—the lower-middle-status group. The relatively low outcome record for the forty-seven nonwhite clients at this level is not only marked but also consistent with their record on number of interviews (see chart 37). While special problems of some type are obviously interfering with reaching and helping this group, they can not be adequately identified in the present study. The sources of these problems deserve early and close study by both practitioners and researchers.

In the larger context of previous research and theory, this chart is an encouraging one. As phrased by Geismar and documented from research both in casework and psychiatry, it has been a common contention that "the traditional approaches of casework are relatively ineffective in helping individuals and families who belong to lower socioeconomic status groups."[18] This contention is not supported by the findings of the present study. Perhaps the explanation lies in the improved awareness of and accommodation to the needs and problems of the disadvantaged that are inherent in the current multiservice approach of many agencies and in their increasing use of planned, short-term, crisis-focused service. ∎

Contrary to expectations, the socioeconomic status of clients proved to be a relatively minor factor in outcomes. Only a slight downward trend was evident for both counselors' and clients' scores as socioeconomic status declined. Although this association was sufficient to be statistically significant, the actual correlations were extremely low (r = +.05 and +.07 for counselors' and clients' scores respectively). The association was more marked for the total sample.[15] These minimum differentials in outcomes were achieved in spite of the greater handicaps faced by lower status clients—more problems, more difficult problems, less adequate environmental supports, and less knowledge of when and where to go for help.[16]

Racial differences in outcomes were slightly

Chart 82 focuses on an issue seldom explored in casework research[19]: Does the age of the client make any difference in the outcomes of counseling? The results were striking. Clients' scores showed a progressive decline, first slow and then faster, as age progressed up to a final category where there was a marked increase. Counselors' scores fell below those of clients up to about age fifty-five, at which point they rose to levels well above them. They also showed a sharp final rise. Clients' scores were associated with age at a highly significant level; counselors' scores were not. On the global ratings, both gave ratings that varied significantly with age. The chances of improvement through family agency service do appear to decline with age.

But why were clients' ratings at the higher age levels less positive than those of their counselors? The answer does not appear to lie in any variation in the treatment provided since there was no evidence of any significant decline in number of interviews as age progressed. It is more likely to be related to a growing sense of depression in older clients about the widening gap between what they would like and what agencies can actually provide. In comparison with their younger counterparts, families with older family heads tended to have lower socioeconomic scores, to report more problems but less difficult types of problems, and to be less able to pay fees. They were also less likely to have been personally involved in seeking help. Their counselors tended to anticipate less progress, possibly because they sensed both a lessened flexibility and the closing-in of opportunities.

These patterns suggest a pile-up with age of the problems of daily living, combined with a

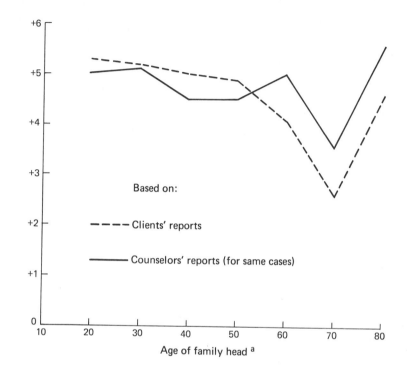

Average change score

Based on:

- - - - Clients' reports

———— Counselors' reports (for same cases)

Age of family head [a]

[a] Or of primary individual if not a family.

certain loss of initiative and opportunity for doing something about them. Perhaps it is no wonder that clients' reports of outcomes at the higher age levels were less positive than those of their counselors.[20]

The one bright note is the final upswing in both scores at the end of the life-cycle. Undoubtedly these higher ratings reflect the results of very practical agency services, such as help in obtaining needed health care, housing, caretaking, escort service, or basic support. The final section will consider in further detail the needs and the services provided to those sixty-five and over. ■

How do client characteristics affect outcomes?

RELATIVE POWER OF VARIOUS CLIENT CHARACTERISTICS TO PREDICT CHANGE SCORES

Relative power to predict change scores [a]

Chart 83

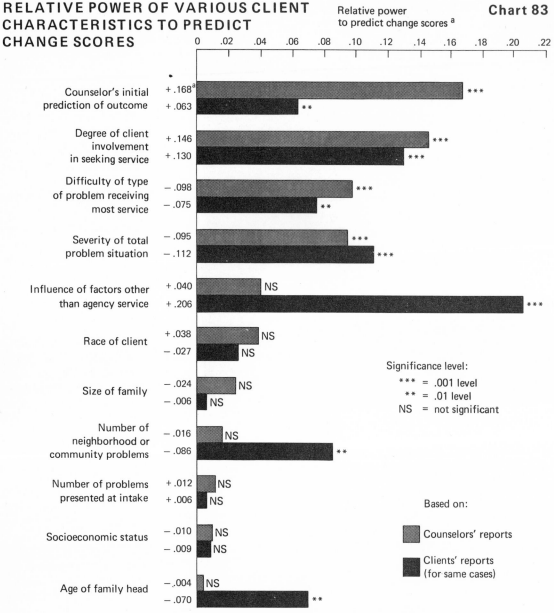

Counselor's initial prediction of outcome	+ .168[a] *** / + .063 **
Degree of client involvement in seeking service	+ .146 *** / + .130 ***
Difficulty of type of problem receiving most service	− .098 *** / − .075 **
Severity of total problem situation	− .095 *** / − .112 ***
Influence of factors other than agency service	+ .040 NS / + .206 ***
Race of client	+ .038 NS / − .027 NS
Size of family	− .024 NS / − .006 NS
Number of neighborhood or community problems	− .016 NS / − .086 **
Number of problems presented at intake	+ .012 NS / + .006 NS
Socioeconomic status	− .010 NS / − .009 NS
Age of family head	− .004 NS / − .070 **

Significance level:
*** = .001 level
** = .01 level
NS = not significant

Based on:

Counselors' reports

Clients' reports (for same cases)

[a] Figures shown are standardized regression coefficients in which the influence of all other client characteristics listed is held constant.

When all available client characteristics are considered jointly, which ones have the greater influence on outcomes? Chart 83 attempts an answer, using bars of various lengths to represent the relative power of each available client characteristic to predict counselors' and clients' change scores.[21]

Striking differences are immediately apparent between the predictors for the two types of change scores. For counselors' scores, the best predictors were the highly individualized characteristics of the client and his situation that counselors commonly assess in the initial exploratory interviews. Ranked from highest to lowest in order of relative predictive power, these were: the counselors' own prognostic estimate, the extent to which the client was personally involved in seeking service, the difficulty of the type of problem receiving the most service, and the severity of the clients' total problem situation. No client characteristic beyond these four was a significant predictor of counselors' change scores when all other client characteristics were held constant.

The same list also proved predictive for clients' scores, though mostly at lower levels and in a somewhat different order. The most conspicuous addition was the influence of factors other than agency service, a predictor which outranked all others for clients' scores. Number of environmental problems and age of the family head also were predictive at a highly significant level statistically. All three suggest that clients' perspectives on change differ substantially from those of counselors. Two of the factors added represent areas that clients know a great deal more about than counselors.[22] The third factor, age of the family head, further confirms the pessimistic view older clients commonly hold about the outcomes of agency service (see charts 82 and 106).

Equally meaningful are the factors which were not significantly related to outcomes when other client factors were controlled. One of these—total number of different problems identified at intake—suggests that it is the nature and seriousness of the problems and their interrelationships rather than any count of the total number present that are indicative of the kind of progress that can be expected.

Three simple demographic characteristics identifiable from facesheet data were also tested: socioeconomic status, race, and size of family. Size of family was not found predictive, either with or without other factors controlled.[23] Socioeconomic status was predictive for both counselors' and clients' scores before other factors were controlled; race was predictive for counselors' scores only. However, neither was significant when other factors closely related to them were controlled, for example, number of environmental problems and influence of external factors. These findings are consistent with the conviction of many caseworkers that it is the total problem configuration and the unique strengths and vulnerabilities of the particular applicant that combine with the type and quality of the service to determine what can and can not be accomplished, rather than any formal characteristics of the client—be they education, occupation, income, or race.

Two other client characteristics—locus of problem and years married—were not included in this summary analysis since they were germane only for subgroups within the total sample. Findings in these areas are shown in charts 78 and 103. Two other important client characteristics, motivation and ego strength, also could not be included because no questions were asked in these areas. These factors warrant attention in smaller studies where definitions can be carefully monitored.

Still another client characteristic—whether the client was or was not receiving public assistance—was examined at an earlier point. Interest in this variable stemmed from the use of public assistance caseloads as the sample for certain key studies of casework outcomes.[24] When the data were confined to cases having both change scores, there was no statistically significant difference in relation to receiving public assistance. Receipt of public assistance was therefore dropped as a category from the final summary analysis. Public assistance status did, however, show a significant relationship to counselors' scores when tests were made on all cases rather than only on those having both a counselor's and a client's change score. For this larger group, counselors' change scores averaged +3.9 for clients receiving public assistance and +4.3 for those who were not—a statistically significant difference.

The fact that public assistance was dropped as a factor in predicting the change scores does not mean that public assistance samples of the type utilized in various control group studies can be considered similar in outcome potential to the caseloads of family agencies generally. They differ in a most fundamental respect not characteristic of the present study: The public assistance recipients included in these controlled studies were not families that had sought out counseling on family and personal problems on their own initiative. This critical difference was shown in chart 77.

One final question: How much of the outcome associated with use of family service is predictable from all these eleven client characteristics taken together? When all were combined into a single multiple correlation coefficient, the amount of variation accounted for was surprisingly low. Only 9 percent of the variance in counselors' scores and only 10 percent of that in clients' scores could be accounted for by all these eleven characteristics combined.[25]

Perhaps this is actually good news for future clients. The limits of what a family agency can do to help are apparently not predetermined either by the client's formal characteristics or by the number, type, and severity of his problems, at least insofar as present evidence can demonstrate. The service provided by the agency and the quality of the counselor-client relationship appear to be much more powerful than any of the characteristics listed in chart 83. This conclusion will be documented in section 9. In addition, as previously mentioned, other characteristics that the client brings to the problem-solving task could not be assessed in the present study. Among those that undoubtedly contribute to favorable outcomes, perhaps the most important are motivation and ego strength.   ■

Explanation of the "predicted scores"

In the next section, findings of the type reported in chart 83 have been converted into a new type of score termed the "predicted score." Its purpose is to help the reader answer the question: Does a particular amount or type of treatment show results that significantly exceed or fall below the results to be expected solely on the basis of the characteristics of the clients who received the service?

Since clients in the sample were not assigned on a random basis to the various service alternatives, it was necessary for the study of service factors to develop a statistical procedure for offsetting, as far as possible, the influence of client characteristics on the change scores reported. The method adopted involved the use of a multiple regression analysis. With the help of the computer, the eleven client characteristics listed in chart 83 were used to establish a mathematical equation that could predict the most probable change score for each case, taking into account the particular combination of these eleven factors represented by this case. As would be expected, this process yielded higher predicted scores for cases with more favorable characteristics (for example, younger, fewer problems, less difficult problems, more involvement in seeking treatment, less environmental stress, and so on) than for those with the opposite, less favorable characteristics. Two sets of predictions were developed, one for counselors' scores and one for clients' scores. This step was necessary because the factors on which the predictions were based related differently to the two scores, as is evident in chart 83. (For further technical details, see "Technical Explanation of Methods of Analysis" in the Appendix.)

As the probing of service factors proceeded, the predictions were further refined by the addition of certain service factors to the prediction equations. The predictions used in chart 84 are based only on the eleven client characteristics. Those cited in charts 86, 87, and 88 add number of interviews as a twelfth predictor. All the remaining charts in the section also take account of three additional predictors —number of different services, the rating of the counselor-client relationship, and the disagreement index. This is a total of fifteen predictors.

The intent throughout is to provide for each subgroup a kind of statistical norm against which the influence of specific treatment inputs can be more clearly assessed. The level of these average predicted scores (the norms) is indicated for each category in each chart in section 9 by means of a broken line zigzagging horizontally across the entire chart area. The level changes from category to category because the types of cases involved change from one group to another and because the predictions for the same case differ according to whether they were based on counselors' or clients' reports.

The differences between the actual scores (shown by bars) and the predicted scores (shown by the broken line) may or may not be statistically significant. If they are not significant, no stars appear at the bottom of the bars. If they are statistically significant, the number of stars, as interpreted in the key on the chart, indicates the level of significance of the difference. If they are significant, this indicates either (1) that the specific factor under consideration is contributing to this result, or (2) that it is associated with some hidden uncontrolled factor that is influencing the findings. On the other hand, if the actual and predicted scores are closely similar, this indicates either (1) that the factor under study yields about average results for the types of cases involved or (2) that its influence is masked by unidentified factors that are offsetting its effect.

Seen in another perspective, this approach provides a somewhat imperfect statistical substitute for an experimental comparison group, which would normally be secured by the random assignment of cases to different treatment approaches and to different counselors. The latter would be the design of choice in rigorous experimental studies but was not a feasible procedure on a nationwide basis. ∎

9

HOW DO SERVICE CHARACTERISTICS AFFECT OUTCOMES?

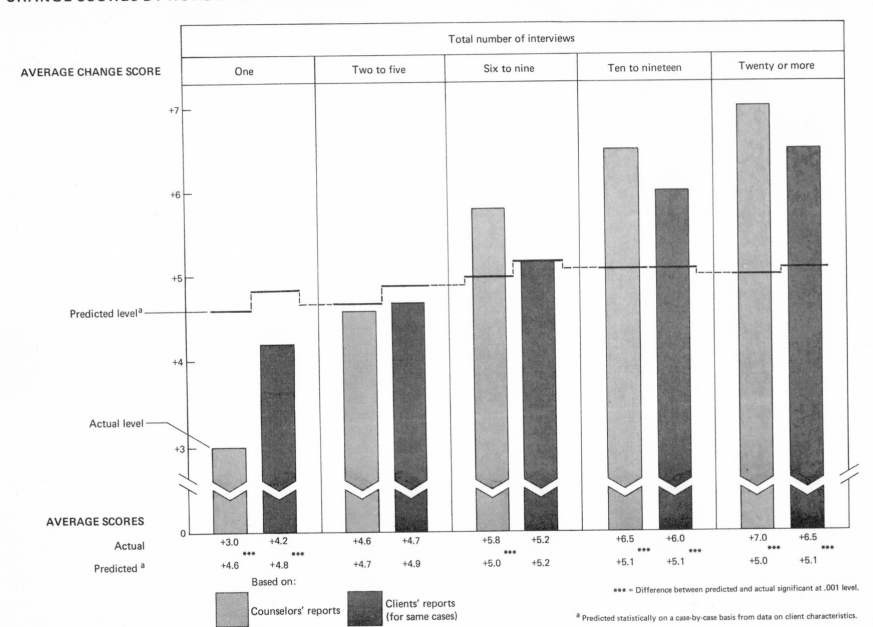

AVERAGE CHANGE SCORE

Total number of interviews

| One | Two to five | Six to nine | Ten to nineteen | Twenty or more |

Predicted level[a]

Actual level

AVERAGE SCORES

Actual   +3.0   +4.2   +4.6   +4.7   +5.8   +5.2   +6.5   +6.0   +7.0   +6.5
             ***   ***   ***   ***   ***   ***   ***

Predicted[a]   +4.6   +4.8   +4.7   +4.9   +5.0   +5.2   +5.1   +5.1   +5.0   +5.1

Based on:

Counselors' reports   Clients' reports (for same cases)

*** = Difference between predicted and actual significant at .001 level.

[a] Predicted statistically on a case-by-case basis from data on client characteristics.

Chart 84, on number of interviews with the family, is the first of a series on service input in relation to outcomes. Immediately apparent is a marked and consistent increase in average change scores as one moves from the one-interview, minimum investment category on the far left to the twenty-or-more interview category on the far right. These increases proved to be highly significant statistically (at the .001 level), both for counselors' and clients' scores.[1]

Could this association perhaps result not from the treatment input but from the early drop-out of unpromising cases? The predicted line is designed to answer this question. It tells what the average change scores for each category would have been if each case in that group had received the average amount and type of service received by all clients having the same characteristics as that case. (See explanation on page 120.) Using the predicted line as a base, one notes first that the one-interview cases fell considerably below the expected scores for that group. This difference was statistically significant at the .001 level. As the number of interviews increased, actual scores approached predicted levels. In the six-to-nine interview category, counselors' scores exceeded expectations. For clients' reports, the excess began in the ten-to-nineteen category. In statistical terms, all these differences were highly significant.[2]

Note also that the predicted line itself showed an early but less marked upward trend. This is the result of the early drop-out of some unpromising cases. Fortunately, the predicted lines make it easy to discount for this selection factor.

These findings are directly relevant to the issue: Does casework work? If the predicted line is accepted as a norm, these findings support two conclusions: (1) Minimum service as reflected by the one-interview cases results in significantly less gain, as measured by the change score, than does average service for cases of the same type; and (2) service at the level of ten or more interviews produces significantly more improvement than average service for corresponding cases. If the counseling received had had no effect on the changes reported, one would expect to see not this sharp and highly significant upward trend by amount of service, but bars at a fairly even level (except for random fluctuations) regardless of service input. These positive findings add a new perspective to the controversy over the effectiveness of casework.

Some details still require explanation: Why do averages based on clients' reports exceed those from counselors up to five interviews?[3] The reasons seem obvious. Counselors simply do not receive enough feedback, especially from one-interview cases, to assess adequately the gains made. The client, being in touch with what follows the interview contact, usually knows what has happened and what these changes have meant to his family. He also may value more highly the emotional relief of talking over his problems with an understanding and impartial outsider.

But why is there a reversal in the six-to-nine category? Perhaps counselors, as they came to know clients better, gave more weight than clients to intermediate problem-coping efforts or to subtle changes in perceptions and attitudes.

These explanations are consistent with the changes by number of interviews in the component scores reported in Appendix table 2. There it is evident that counselors' higher ratings in the later interviews stem almost entirely from higher reports on changes in specific problems and in problem-coping. For family relationships and persons changing, counselors' scores begin very much lower than those of clients and rise only to approximate equality as the number of interviews increases.

These shifts also clarify a related issue: Why were the average ratings of clients for the sample as a whole higher than those of their counselors? Clearly, this was the result of clients' higher change scores for the one and two-to-five interview groups, coupled with the termination of two-thirds of all clients by the sixth interview.

Still another question of significance for practice is not directly answered by this chart: Is there a level beyond which additional interviews are, on the average, unproductive? Detailed trends beyond twenty interviews indicate that scores based on counselors' reports peaked in the forty to forty-nine interview range; clients' scores, in the thirty to thirty-nine interview range.[4] For both measures there was a slowing down of the rate of gain after ten to fifteen interviews. Whether this pattern of declining gains is real, or whether it results from some insensitivity in the change score to the types of gains that come from extended treatment, can not be determined from the data.[5] ∎

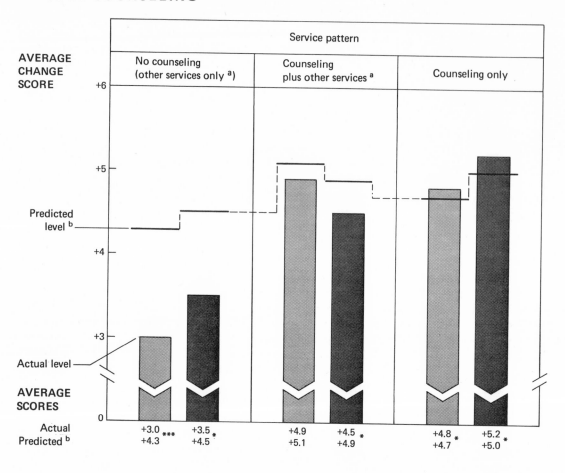

CHANGE SCORES BY WHETHER SERVICE INCLUDED COUNSELING

Chart 85

	Service pattern		
AVERAGE CHANGE SCORE	No counseling (other services only [a])	Counseling plus other services [a]	Counseling only

Predicted level [b]

+6

+5

+4

Actual level

AVERAGE SCORES

	Actual	Predicted [b]
No counseling	+3.0 ***	+3.5 *
	+4.3	+4.5
Counseling plus other	+4.9	+4.5 *
	+5.1	+4.9
Counseling only	+4.8 *	+5.2 *
	+4.7	+5.0

Based on:

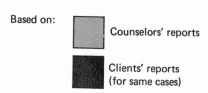

Counselors' reports

Clients' reports (for same cases)

*** = Difference between predicted and actual significant at .001 level (* = .05 level).

[a] Includes referral, caretaking services, financial assistance, and legal and advocacy services.

[b] Predicted statistically on a case-by-case basis from data on client characteristics, number of interviews, number of services, and counselor-client relationship.

Chart 85 provides a second type of comparison group that can serve as a yardstick, as did the one-interview group in chart 84. In this case, the minimum service group is the one that received various practical services but no counseling.[6] What evidence does it provide about the outcomes of counseling?

Again, one finds strong confirmation that casework counseling does make a difference. Change scores for those who received no counseling fell markedly and significantly below predicted scores, whereas those that received counseling more nearly approximated expected levels.[7] In addition, the overall association between both types of change scores and the receipt of counseling was statistically highly significant.

Similar patterns were evident in the component areas that comprise the change score. For both counselor and client, improvement of scores in all four areas was greater for those receiving than for those not receiving counseling. However, for the noncounseling group, the improvements that occurred were primarily in specific problems or in problem-coping. In the areas of family relationships and persons' changing, averages for the component scores for the noncounseling group were minimal—usually only two-thirds, or sometimes much less, of those for cases receiving counseling. (See Appendix table 2 for details.) In addition, except for counselors' ratings for specific problems, the component area scores were all significantly higher for cases receiving counseling than for those not receiving counseling.[8] While these findings support the utility of relevant practical services for the solution of many specific problems, they also suggest that substantial progress on family relationships and personal adjustment problems is dependent to a significant degree on the provision of counseling service.

But why, it may be asked, did those who did not receive any counseling show any change at all? The answer lies partially in the helpfulness of other services they received. For the group shown, these consisted of such services as home care, financial assistance, advocacy, day care, legal services, and referral. This group also received an average of 2.2 interviews, some of which no doubt provided opportunity for ventilation and emotional support in relation to their problems. What is not yet known is what the scores would have been in the total absence of any agency service.

A secondary query is also stimulated by chart 85: Why did the scores for cases receiving only counseling significantly exceed the predicted scores, although those for the group that received both counseling and direct services fell below predicted scores? In the abstract, one would expect the opposite—that counseling plus tangible services would be more effective than counseling alone, especially since those receiving both types of service also received more interviews than did those receiving counseling services only (10.1 versus 7.5).

The reasons for this unexpected finding are obscure until the two groups are compared on the types of counseling and other services provided. Services for the group that received only counseling concerned marital or children's problems or individual personality adjustment more often than did those for the multiservice group, and these are problems that are associated with high or intermediate change scores (see chart 79). In contrast, service for those who received counseling plus other services more often concerned problems related to income, housing, unemployment, unmarried parenthood, vocational problems, travel problems, or major social and behavioral problems—categories for which outcomes tended in the main to be comparatively low.[9] Possibly an additional factor was a lesser motivation for counseling among those receiving more than one type of service, although this can not be directly documented. What is known is that, as a natural consequence of the types of problems that brought them to the agency, a higher proportion of the initial service requests of the multiservice group were for services other than counseling. Moreover, a lower proportion of the counseling services they did receive had been requested by them at intake. Whether the absence of an intake request for counseling service in a particular area erodes the outcomes of counseling is not known, but it could well be a further explanation of the differential between these two groups.

While the findings for both the groups that received counseling appear reasonable, they in no way indicate that one approach is superior to the other. For some problems, the provision of multiple services is absolutely critical; for others, counseling is the only approach that makes sense. Regardless of the nature of the initial request or the services provided, both groups achieved significantly more positive change in problem-coping, family relationships, and individual adjustment than did the group that received no counseling. ∎

Chart 86

CHANGE SCORES BY NUMBER
OF AREAS OF COUNSELING

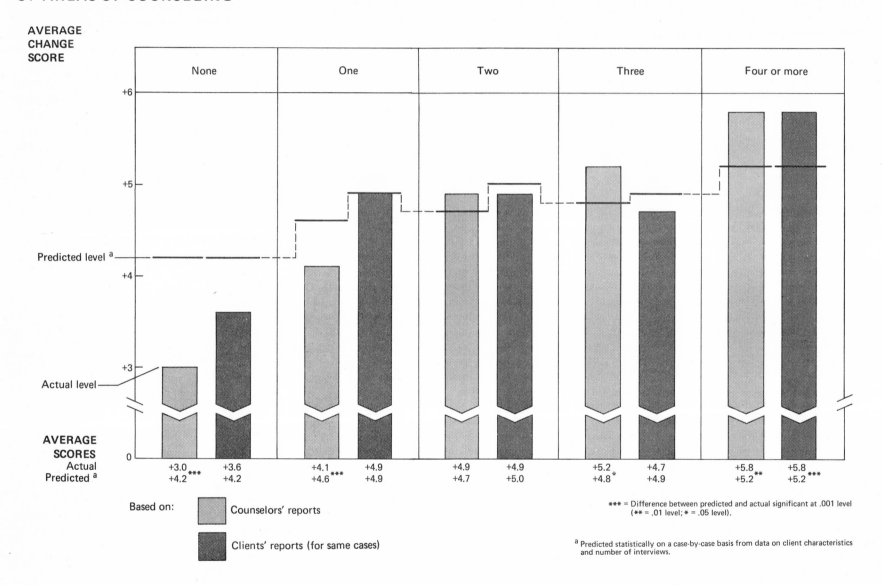

AVERAGE
CHANGE
SCORE

	None	One	Two	Three	Four or more

Predicted level [a]

Actual level

+6

+5

+4

+3

AVERAGE
SCORES
Actual
Predicted [a]

0

+3.0***	+3.6	+4.1***	+4.9	+4.9	+4.9	+5.2*	+4.7	+5.8**	+5.8***
+4.2	+4.2	+4.6	+4.9	+4.7	+5.0	+4.8	+4.9	+5.2	+5.2

Based on: ☐ Counselors' reports

■ Clients' reports (for same cases)

*** = Difference between predicted and actual significant at .001 level
(** = .01 level; * = .05 level).

[a] Predicted statistically on a case-by-case basis from data on client characteristics
and number of interviews.

Chart 86 is directed to the question: Does the number of areas in which counseling is provided make any difference in the outcomes as reflected in the change scores? In general, the answer again is yes. Counselors' scores increased steadily both in absolute terms and in relation to predicted levels as the number of areas involved in the counseling increased. Clients' scores showed substantial gains between none and one, but thereafter little gain until four or more of the client's life areas had been discussed. Nevertheless, for both types of scores, the overall relationship with number of areas in which counseling was provided was statistically significant and that for counselors' scores highly so. Findings showing this type of positive association would be highly unlikely to occur if counseling were, in fact, without effect, as some critics assert on the basis of the literature on control group studies.[10]

The same conclusions were confirmed when change score averages were assessed in relation to predicted levels and findings for other categories. For counselors' scores, averages for counseling in less than two areas were significantly below predicted scores and also significantly below the gains when counseling involved three or more areas. For clients' scores, only counseling that extended to four or more areas was significantly higher than predicted and also significantly above the no-counseling group. In other words, the relationship of counselors' scores to the number of areas in which counseling was provided was more marked and consistent than that for clients' scores.

For this analysis, counseling in each of the following areas was counted as one area: marital problems, parent-child problems, oth-er family relationships, individual personality adjustment, educational problems, unwed parenthood, vocational and employment problems, environmental problems, debt and credit problems, and problems of travelers and migrants.

In addition to counts on this basis, two other ways of counting services were tried. One approach was to add to the number of areas of counseling the number of other services provided. On this basis, the relationship to counselors' scores remained highly significant statistically; that for clients' scores was also statistically significant but not highly so.

The second approach was to consider all counseling simply as one service and to compute the total number of services, adding in one when any counseling was provided regardless of how many areas were involved. On this basis, the relationship of the count to the change score averages was not statistically significant. This fact suggests that the number of areas of counseling has a more powerful influence on outcomes as reflected in the change scores than does the total number of services counted in a way that minimizes counseling input.

In part, this minimal influence of services other than counseling probably stems from the nature of the change score itself. In fact, it would be expected since the change score was designed to reflect gains from counseling. However, the minimal difference also appeared to be related to the types of clients who were the heaviest users of services other than counseling. In the present study, these tended to be the clients with more problems and more severe problem situations generally. They also tended to be clients with slightly lower socioeconomic scores and lesser involvement in seeking service. It would appear that the difficulties such clients have in achieving progress with their problems approximately counterbalances the gains that would otherwise be expected from a multiple-service approach.

The fact that the total number of services computed in a way that minimizes counseling does not show increased gains associated with more service input is not in any case an argument for eliminating these supplementary services. Often they serve an essential family support function. What is noteworthy is the strength of the association between the number of areas discussed in counseling and the overall gains achieved. This finding further confirms the positive contribution of counseling to progress on family problems. ∎

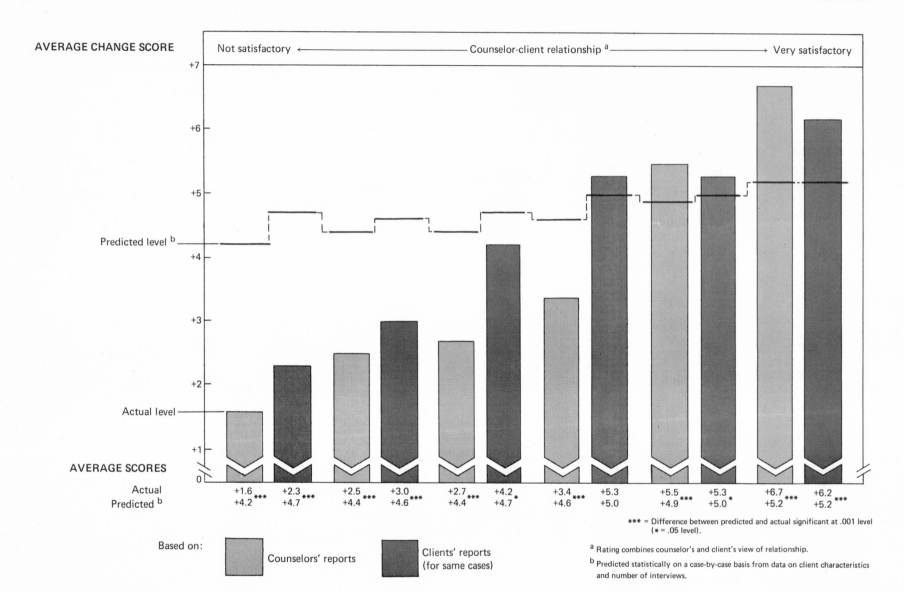

AVERAGE CHANGE SCORE

Not satisfactory ← —————————————— Counselor-client relationship [a] —————————————— → Very satisfactory

+7

+6

+5

Predicted level [b]

+4

+3

+2

Actual level

+1

AVERAGE SCORES

0

Actual	+1.6 ***	+2.3 ***	+2.5 ***	+3.0 ***	+2.7 ***	+4.2 *	+3.4 ***	+5.3	+5.5 ***	+5.3 *	+6.7 ***	+6.2 ***
Predicted [b]	+4.2	+4.7	+4.4	+4.6	+4.4	+4.7	+4.6	+5.0	+4.9	+5.0	+5.2	+5.2

*** = Difference between predicted and actual significant at .001 level
(* = .05 level).

Based on:
Counselors' reports   Clients' reports (for same cases)

[a] Rating combines counselor's and client's view of relationship.

[b] Predicted statistically on a case-by-case basis from data on client characteristics and number of interviews.

One of the most striking findings of the present study is the marked association of outcomes with the counselor-client relationship shown in chart 87. As ratings for this relationship move from "unsatisfactory" to "very satisfactory," change score averages show a substantial and consistent increase. This association was highly significant statistically. This was true not only for the patterns as a whole but also for all but one of the differences between predicted and actual figures for specific categories. When the relationship was "unsatisfactory," actual change scores fell far below predicted; when it was "very satisfactory," they exceeded scores predicted by a large and highly significant margin. Actual means also showed great contrasts. For counselors' ratings, they ranged from a low of $+1.6$ to a high of $+6.7$; for clients' ratings, from a low of $+2.3$ to a high of $+6.2$. Highly significant associations with relationship were also found for counselors' and clients' global outcome ratings. The same was also true for counselors' change scores for the total sample. This is the strongest association with outcomes found for any client or service characteristic analyzed in the present study.

The method used for rating this intangible relationship was elementary, direct, and admittedly only approximate. Clients and counselors were simply asked—each separately and confidentially—how satisfied they were with the relationship with the other. Their answers were then paired and averaged to provide an unbiased estimate of the actual relationship. Instances in which both counselor and client rated the relationship as "unsatisfactory" appear in the bottom category; those in which both rated the relationship as "very satisfactory" appear in the top category. In-termediate ratings and those reflecting some disagreement between the two raters appear in the intermediate categories. Fortunately for the clients, more than five out of eight counselor-client pairs gave ratings that placed the case in one of the top two categories; only one in twenty fell in the bottom category.

Also of interest in chart 87 is the slow but statistically significant rise in the predicted scores as relationship ratings improve. Apparently, the more promising cases, as estimated from the outcome predictors, tended to have slightly better relationship scores. This suggests that the initial characteristics of the client, as well as those of the counselor, contribute to a good relationship. This deduction is consistent with counselors' conviction that the client's initial capacity for relationship with a person from whom he is seeking help is an important prognostic clue.

From the point of view of cause and effect, which comes first? Does a good counselor-client relationship actually contribute to good outcomes? Or did the positive outcomes merely encourage a good relationship at termination? Unfortunately, no conclusive answer is possible in the present study since both ratings were made at the close of the treatment period.[11] What is clear is that the association is not simply a reflection of clients' gratitude since a substantial and highly significant association remained when clients' outcome reports were analyzed by counselors' ratings of the relationship and counselors' outcome reports were analyzed in relation to clients' ratings of the relationship.[12]

The larger task of confirming what counselors intuitively believe—namely, that a good therapeutic relationship is actually an important precondition for positive casework outcomes—must be left to future research. Important related issues also need to be pursued: What is it about the counselor-client interaction that enables a client to trust the counselor enough to expose his weaknesses, guilt, and fears and to risk trying out new approaches to his problems? What counselor characteristics contribute? What client characteristics? How can these characteristics be identified in applicants to schools of social work? To what extent can they be improved through in-service training?

These issues have been studied by Charles B. Truax and his associates in noncasework settings.[13] It has long been their contention, supported by their research, that patients in psychotherapy get either better or worse according to the quality of the therapist-patient relationship. They have further identified three characteristics of the therapist that according to their findings appear central to good outcomes: accurate empathy, nonpossessive warmth, and genuineness.

While it was not feasible in the present study to collect data on these components, the overall findings strongly support the applicability of their conclusions to casework counseling. This is an area that deserves much more attention than it has yet received from researchers, administrators, and practitioners in the family service field. ∎

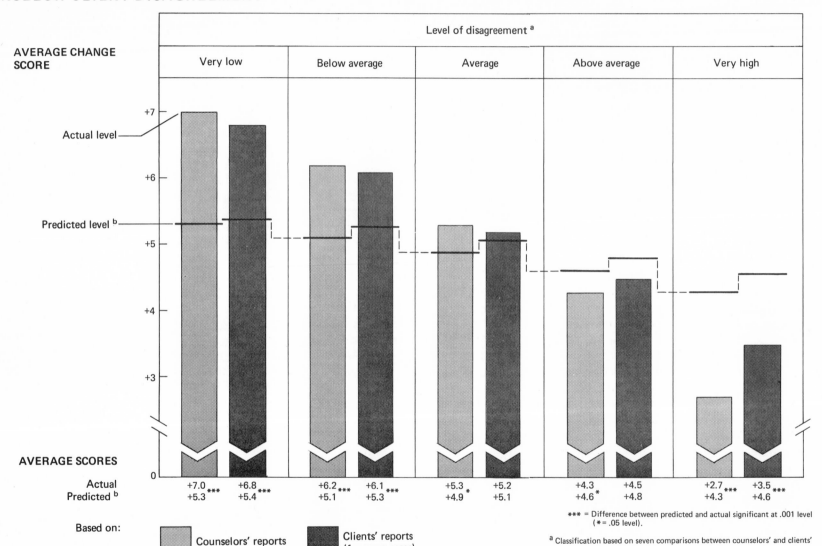

AVERAGE CHANGE SCORE

Level of disagreement [a]

| Very low | Below average | Average | Above average | Very high |

Actual level ⎯

Predicted level [b] ⎯

+7
+6
+5
+4
+3
0

AVERAGE SCORES

	Very low		Below average		Average		Above average		Very high	
Actual	+7.0 ***	+6.8 ***	+6.2 ***	+6.1 ***	+5.3 *	+5.2	+4.3	+4.5	+2.7 ***	+3.5 ***
Predicted [b]	+5.3	+5.4	+5.1	+5.3	+4.9	+5.1	+4.6 *	+4.8	+4.3	+4.6

*** = Difference between predicted and actual significant at .001 level (* = .05 level).

Based on:

☐ Counselors' reports   ■ Clients' reports (for same cases)

[a] Classification based on seven comparisons between counselors' and clients' reports and four additional items from counselors.

[b] Predicted statistically on a case-by-case basis from data on client characteristics and number of interviews.

Chart 88 focuses on a different question about the treatment interaction: Does it make any difference in outcomes whether the counselor and the client were in general agreement about the central issues related to their service experience? To find the answer, the same index of disagreement used in chart 51 was applied. As indicated earlier, this index utilized eleven available components, covering disagreements about what the clients' problems were, which problem was most important, what treatment approach should be used, who decided on termination, and how much improvement occurred.[14] Since most of the items were obtained by a direct comparison of counselors' and clients' responses rather than from overt questions about disagreement, a high score does not necessarily indicate that these disagreements were consciously perceived or discussed. The two may not even have been aware of their differences, or they may have passed them over as unimportant.

On the average, counselors and clients differed on nearly four out of eleven of the component items, a fact that suggests wide differences in perspective. Moreover, these differences were strongly associated with outcomes. In general, the less disagreement, the higher the change scores. This result was almost equally true of counselors' and clients' ratings. For both, the range from high to low was dramatic: for counselors' scores, from +7.0 to +2.7; for clients' scores, from +6.8 to +3.5. Considered on an overall basis, the association was highly significant statistically for both types of scores. The same was true for the relationship of disagreement to the counselors' and the clients' global ratings. In addition, most of the subgroup averages differed significantly from predicted levels and by level of disagreement. Viewed from every available angle, therefore, counselor-client disagreement showed a significant negative association with the change scores.

One key to the influence of disagreement on these change scores was the apparent tendency of disagreement to precipitate client-initiated disengagement before service was completed. When disagreement levels were in the top category, clients in the total sample averaged only 6.0 interviews as compared with 9.2 interviews, or more than half again as many as when disagreement was at a minimum.

Can anything be said about the kinds of cases in which there was a high level of disagreement between the counselor and the client? A look at the correlation patterns indicates that cases in which the disagreement level was high tended to have more problems, more severe problems, more environmental problems, less favorable outcome predictions, lower socioeconomic scores, and less personal involvement in seeking help. Thus, in general, the clients most in need of help were the same ones who were most likely to encounter disagreement barriers to the effective utilization of this help. Even these associations, however, are far from adequate to explain the patterns. This is evident from the relatively modest decline by disagreement level in the predicted scores that take all these factors and more into account.

A more major association was that with the counselor-client relationship itself. Here the correlation was r = −.42, a level more than twice as high as the correlations with most of the other factors listed above. In fact, the level is so high that one might ask: Is disagreement really an independent factor, or is it simply part of a larger relationship problem? Judging from chart 97, it has some independent influence on outcomes. When all other factors, including relationship, were held constant statistically, disagreement ranked second only to the counselor-client relationship as an independent predictor of counselors' change scores, exceeding all remaining factors in the multiple regression analysis.

The outstanding importance of these two factors and their close relationship suggests that the first place to look for a better understanding of counselor-client disagreement is in the therapeutic relationship itself. Sociocultural variations in how clients define their problems and what should be done about them provide a second source for clarification. This latter area has been extensively investigated by John E. Mayer and Noel Timms.[15] Together, these findings challenge the practitioner to become more aware of disagreements between himself and the client and to learn to cope more adequately with these differences, While they probably can not and sometimes should not be eliminated entirely, improved understanding of sociocultural variations and more accurate empathy for those involved can be expected to moderate the strong negative impact of counselor-client disagreements on outcomes. ∎

Chart 89

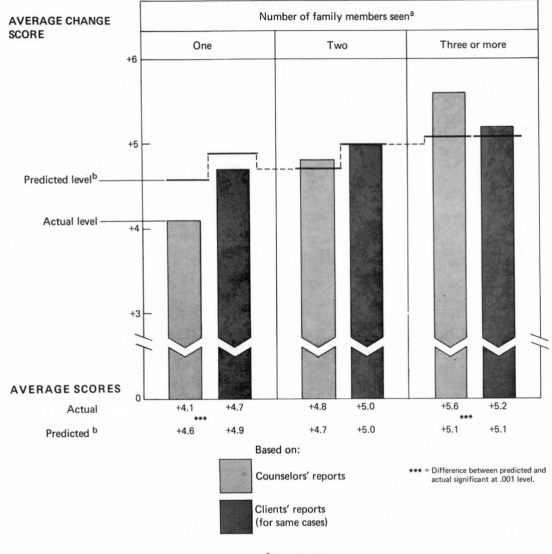

AVERAGE CHANGE
SCORE

Number of family members seen[a]

One	Two	Three or more

Predicted level[b]

Actual level

AVERAGE SCORES

	One		Two		Three or more	
Actual	+4.1	+4.7	+4.8	+5.0	+5.6	+5.2
	***				***	
Predicted [b]	+4.6	+4.9	+4.7	+5.0	+5.1	+5.1

Based on:

Counselors' reports

Clients' reports
(for same cases)

*** = Difference between predicted and
actual significant at .001 level.

[a] At any time during agency service.
[b] Predicted statistically on a case-by-case basis from data on client characteristics,
number of interviews, number of services, and counselor-client relationship.

Chart 89 examines a very elementary issue: Does seeing more family members during the course of agency service contribute to greater progress on family problems? Counselors' scores suggest that the answer is yes. On an overall basis, these scores showed highly significant differences in relation to the number of family members seen.[16] When only one family member was seen, actual scores fell below predicted levels by a highly significant amount. Gains were also significantly less when only one member was seen than when two or three were seen. Significant contrasts in a positive direction were evident when three or more family members were seen. Contrasts by number seen also persisted at highly significant levels when cases without a follow-up were included and when number seen was tested against counselors' global ratings for the total sample.[17]

For clients' scores, the answer was also in the expected direction but not at statistically significant levels.[18] Why this lesser effect? Probably counselors are more informed about changes when they have seen more family members. Undoubtedly, clients are more in touch with the effects of service on family members not seen.[19]

In spite of these uncertainties, chart 89 adds research support to the increasing conviction of practitioners about the importance of seeing more than one family member.[20] It also demonstrates that the increase since 1960 in the number of family members seen (see chart 42) represents progress. Nevertheless, the field still has a long way to go. Even in the present sample, only one family member was seen in one-third of the cases. ■

Chart 90 repeats for husband-wife families the same type of analysis reported in chart 89. This time the issue is: Does seeing both partners during the course of agency service result in more progress on family problems than seeing one partner only?

Once again the findings are very clear for counselors' scores but less definitive, though similar, for those from clients. When only the husband or the wife was seen, counselors' scores were significantly below predicted scores; when both were seen, they were significantly above. This was true even though predicted scores also rose.[21] When clients' scores were considered separately, the pattern was the same but less marked and not statistically significant. The small sample when only the husband was seen (forty-eight cases) is a factor. The scores for even a slightly larger sample yielding similar results for this category would have been significantly below predicted levels. Again clients' scores were higher than counselors' scores when only one partner was seen. When this person was the wife, gains approached predicted levels.[22]

Does it make any difference whether both partners are seen together in the first interview? The answer was similar. Seeing both husband and wife in this initial contact is significantly related to high scores from counselors but not from clients.

Considered as a whole, these findings confirm the conviction of practitioners about the importance of seeing both spouses.[23] They also provide reassurance that the increase in the 1960s in seeing both partners (see page 65) represents movement toward more productive service to clients. ■

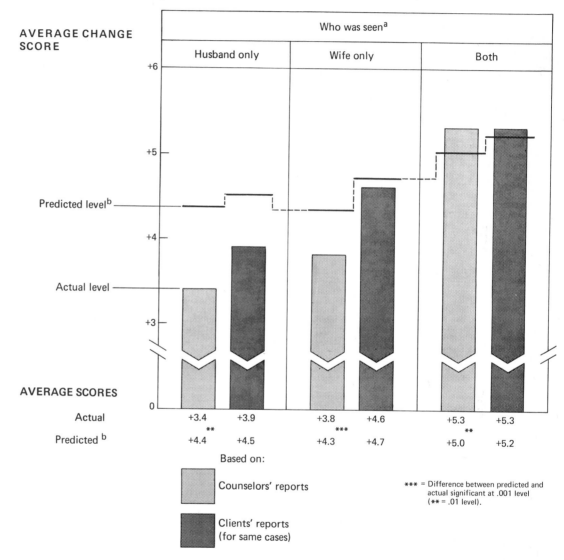

CHANGE SCORES BY WHO WAS SEEN **Chart 90**
(Husband-wife families)

AVERAGE CHANGE SCORE

Who was seen[a]

	Husband only	Wife only	Both

Predicted level[b]

Actual level

AVERAGE SCORES

	Husband only		Wife only		Both	
Actual	+3.4 **	+3.9	+3.8 ***	+4.6	+5.3 **	+5.3
Predicted[b]	+4.4	+4.5	+4.3	+4.7	+5.0	+5.2

Based on:

Counselors' reports

Clients' reports (for same cases)

*** = Difference between predicted and actual significant at .001 level (** = .01 level).

[a] At any time during agency service.
[b] Predicted statistically on a case-by-case basis from data on client characteristics, number of interviews, number of services, and counselor-client relationship.

How do service characteristics affect outcomes?

CHART 91

CHANGE SCORES BY PRIMARY TREATMENT MODALITY
(Families with three or more interviews)

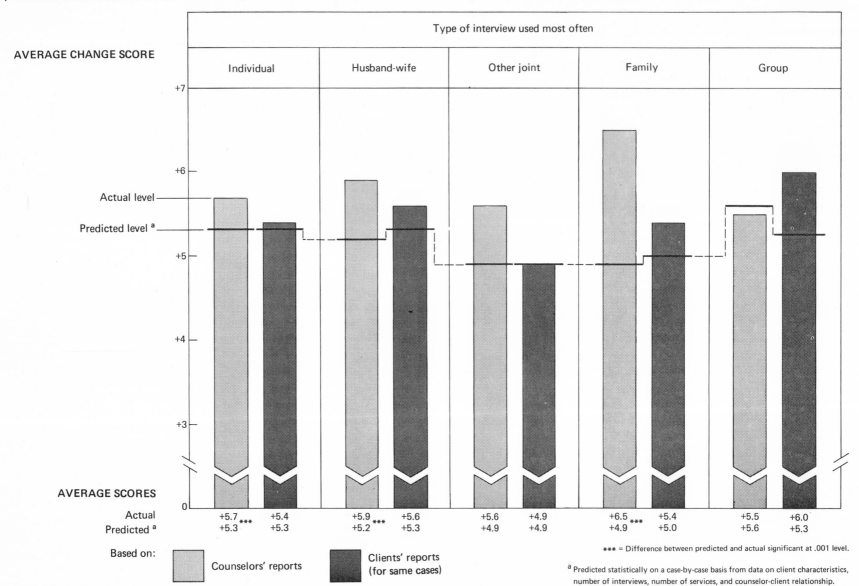

AVERAGE CHANGE SCORE

Type of interview used most often

| Individual | Husband-wife | Other joint | Family | Group |

Actual level

Predicted level [a]

AVERAGE SCORES

Based on: Counselors' reports   Clients' reports (for same cases)

	Individual		Husband-wife		Other joint		Family		Group	
Actual	+5.7 ***	+5.4	+5.9 ***	+5.6	+5.6	+4.9	+6.5 ***	+5.4	+5.5	+6.0
Predicted [a]	+5.3	+5.3	+5.2	+5.3	+4.9	+4.9	+4.9	+5.0	+5.6	+5.3

*** = Difference between predicted and actual significant at .001 level.

[a] Predicted statistically on a case-by-case basis from data on client characteristics, number of interviews, number of services, and counselor-client relationship.

The contrasts between the various treatment modalities were much less striking than those for the number of different family members seen. Apparently, outcomes depend less on who is seen with whom than on whether additional family members are seen at all. Nevertheless, the overall association between treatment modality and change scores was statistically significant for families receiving three or more interviews[24] when change scores based on counselors' reports but not on clients' reports were considered.[25]

When viewed in terms of the differences between specific modalities, counselors' reports showed gains with family interviews significantly above those for individual interviews (at the .01 level). This record was achieved with an average of 8.4 interviews as compared with 13.0 interviews for individual interviews for cases shown in the chart. Scores for family interviews were also significantly higher than predicted scores for the same cases. When viewed in terms of counselors' scores for component areas, family interviews were again the highest for any modality.[26] This approach also yielded the highest proportion improved when judged by counselors' global ratings.

This strong support for family group treatment held, however, only for counselors' ratings. Clients' change scores were highest for group treatment. Although this difference did not achieve statistical significance, this fact can be attributed to the very small sample for group treatment–forty-five cases. A similar differential in favor of group treatment was also consistently evident in the component area scores and in clients' global ratings.[27] Averages were particularly striking for the group treatment of married couples whose most important problem was a marital one.

For this group, change scores reached the striking average of +6.6, a figure higher than any average shown in this chart. Unfortunately, this sample included only sixteen cases. While none of these differences for clients' ratings was statistically significant, the pattern suggests that research on group treatment and on couples' groups in particular could be exceptionally productive.

Still another perspective on treatment modality can be obtained by a look at the following table showing for husband-wife families the proportion of husbands and wives improving with each modality.[28] Husband-wife interviews showed significantly more improvement in husbands than did individual interviews. Both husband-wife interviews and family interviews showed significantly more improvement

| Primary modality | Percentage reported improved[a] | | | |
| | Counselors' ratings | | Clients' ratings | |
	Husbands	Wives	Husbands	Wives
Individual interviews	40	70	55	69
Husband-wife interviews	63[b]	72	69[b]	71
Other joint interviews	28	57	54	58
Family interviews	51[b]	63	57	62
Group treatment	46	58	61	76

[a]Based on husband-wife families receiving three or more interviews. For number of cases on which each percentage is based, see footnote 28 for section 9 of text. This table is not controlled for the same cases. When percentages are computed for the same cases, the general pattern remains the same except for the counselors' reports on cases with group treatment. Here 63 percent of husbands were reported improved and 61 percent of the wives.
[b]Significantly above certain other modalities in same column. See text for details.

with husbands than did joint interviews in which both spouses were not seen together. Clients' reports also showed more frequent improvement in the husband with husband-wife interviews. For wives, group treatment showed somewhat better client ratings. Considered on an overall basis, counselors' and clients' ratings of improvement for husbands showed modality to be statistically significant. It was not significantly related to improvement in wives.

These several clues are consistent, but there was less clear confirmation of the special assets of husband-wife and family interviews than was anticipated from the current convictions of counselors about the value of these modalities. Probably a number of associated factors confound the picture. For example, there are sometimes subtle differences in the type and difficulty of the cases that are assigned to these various modalities. The modality itself also influences the amount of information on outcomes available to the counselor. This fact alone may explain some of the counselor-client differences noted. For example, if only one family member is involved, group treatment generates the least information on outcomes for the counselor, in contrast with family treatment, which yields the most information.

In addition, the modality groups themselves are not pure types. The labels reflect merely the predominant type of treatment. In most instances, several modalities were used. It is also probable that neither the method of computing the predicted scores nor the change score instrument itself is sufficiently sensitive to make possible the refined distinctions necessary for the comparative assessment of treatment modalities under the uncontrolled conditions that prevailed in the study. ∎

CHANGE SCORES BY ASSIGNMENT TO PLANNED SHORT-TERM TREATMENT
(Cases with three or more interviews)

Chart 92

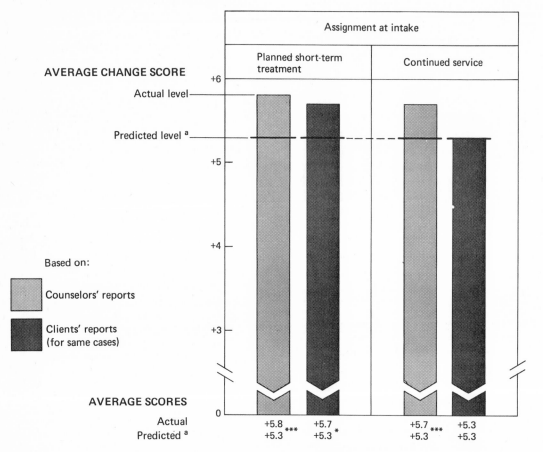

AVERAGE CHANGE SCORE

	Assignment at intake	
	Planned short-term treatment	Continued service

Actual level

Predicted level [a]

Based on:

Counselors' reports

Clients' reports (for same cases)

AVERAGE SCORES

	Planned short-term treatment		Continued service	
Actual	+5.8 ***	+5.7 *	+5.7 ***	+5.3
Predicted [a]	+5.3	+5.3	+5.3	+5.3

*** = Difference between predicted and actual significant at .001 level
(* = .05 level).

[a] Predicted statistically on a case-by-case basis from data on client characteristics, number of interviews, number of services, and counselor-client relationship.

The findings for planned short-term treatment showed less relationship to the change scores than was anticipated. When data were limited to cases receiving at least three interviews, as in chart 92, there was no significant difference between the two alternative approaches for scores based on counselors' ratings. In the case of clients' ratings, the difference was statistically significant at the .03 level.[29] Why these two informants did not agree on this issue is not clear.

In spite of the differences between counselors and clients in this area, the small margin in favor of planned short-term service re-

Item compared[a] (Clients' reports)	Planned short-term treatment	Continued service
Global outcomes rated improved	77.8%	71.5%[b]
Service evaluated as helpful	87.4	83.5
Improvement reported in husbands	62.1	58.5
Improvement reported in wives	68.3	70.3
Change scores for subareas:		
Changes in specific problems	6.2	5.3[c]
Changes in problem coping	6.5	6.4
Changes in family relationships	5.6	4.9
Changes in individual family members	5.0	4.9
Principal reason for termination (counselor's view):		
Service completed	39.7	31.3[c]
Client decided not to continue	34.2	40.0

[a] Limited to cases with three or more interviews.
[b] Difference came close to being statistically significant (chi square = 3.81).
[c] Difference statistically significant below .02 level.

ported by clients was further confirmed in the following related findings. (1) The multiple regression analysis of all service and client characteristics simultaneously showed a small but statistically significant difference in favor of planned short-term treatment for both counselors' and clients' change scores when all other factors were statistically controlled (see chart 97). (2) Significantly fewer clients decided after the first interview not to continue when the initial plan called for planned short-term service (48 versus 53 percent). In addition, the tabular comparisons based on clients' reports favor in balance the planned short-term approach.

Although the differences in these various items are individually small and in the main do not reach statistical significance, all but one favor planned short-term service. Moreover, these small advantages were obtained with an average of four fewer interviews (nine versus thirteen interviews).[30] These facts in combination suggest that planned short-term service on the average has a clear edge in cost-effectiveness.

It is interesting that the small difference in the one item that does not seem to favor planned short-term service, namely changes in wives, was also confirmed in counselors' reports.[31] It is also similar to the findings of Brenda J. S. Wattie, who found significantly greater positive changes in wives with continued service.[32] In combination, these findings suggest that planned short-term service under some circumstances may not be the treatment of choice. While it apparently represents a productive approach to helping families with specific problems and is particularly helpful in reaching husbands, it may contribute less under some circumstances to the improvement of wives than a longer period of treatment.

The reader should also take into account certain factors that contributed to blurring the contrasts between these two approaches in this study. There was, for example, no monitoring of the definition of planned short-term treatment. The classification used reflects whatever the intake counselor reported as the projected treatment plan for the case.[33] In addition, some counselors designated in their treatment plan more interviews than would normally be defined as planned short-term treatment. Finally, 11 percent of the cases originally assigned to short-term service were permitted to continue beyond fifteen interviews. In fact, this last group made the best record of all on outcomes, achieving an average change score of +7.1. This suggests that perhaps an initial time-limited contract combined with flexible time extensions based on later developments may be the most productive in many instances.

Viewed in the perspective of two other major studies, these findings take an intermediate position. The findings of William J. Reid and Ann W. Shyne at the Community Service Society of New York were strongly favorable to planned short-term service.[34] Those of Wattie at the Family Service Centre of Ottawa showed no overall statistically significant difference between the two approaches.[35] In terms of the average number of interviews reflected by the continued service category, the present study more closely approximates that of Wattie.[36] Perhaps the contrast between the two approaches increases with the number of interviews invested in continued service.

Another interesting similarity with the findings of Wattie also warrants comment. Through a complex factor analysis, she identified clients from the lower socioeconomic groups with multiple problems as particularly benefiting from longer service. This issue was not examined in the present study, but actual assignments of cases to continued service did show a slight tendency for counselors to assign to continued service clients from the lower socioeconomic groups and those presenting problems at intake that were above average in number, severity, and difficulty.

In combination, these findings suggest that planned short-term service, when utilized flexibly on the basis of professional judgment, can improve the cost-effectiveness of agency service. Its assets include both the reduction of premature drop-out and the achievement, with a lesser time investment, of improved outcomes, especially those for the husband, when judged from the perspective of the clients. ∎

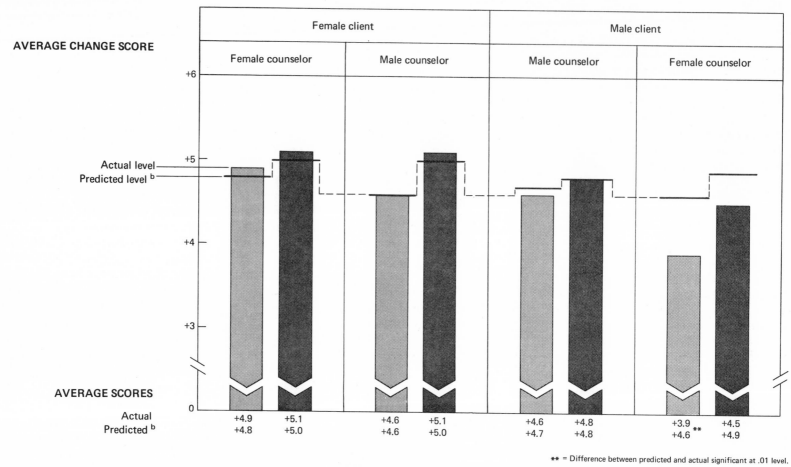

AVERAGE CHANGE SCORE

	Female client		Male client	
	Female counselor	Male counselor	Male counselor	Female counselor

AVERAGE SCORES

| | Actual | +4.9 | +5.1 | +4.6 | +5.1 | +4.6 | +4.8 | +3.9 ** | +4.5 |
| Predicted [b] | +4.8 | +5.0 | +4.6 | +5.0 | +4.7 | +4.8 | +4.6 | +4.9 |

** = Difference between predicted and actual significant at .01 level.

Based on: ▢ Counselors' reports   ■ Clients' reports (for same cases)

[a] Based on sex of counselor closing case (excluding students, social work assistants, and case aides) and sex of family member seen most.

[b] Predicted statistically on a case-by-case basis from data on client characteristics, number of interviews, number of services, and counselor-client relationship.

Chart 93 is directed to the issue: Does it make any difference in outcomes whether the counselor and the principal client are of the same sex? The answer seems to depend on whether the principal client is a man or a woman. Female clients were about equally successful in reaching the predicted score line regardless of whether their counselor was a man or a woman. For male clients, the sex of the counselor did appear to make a difference. When a man had a male counselor, actual scores approximated the predicted, but when he had a female counselor they fell substantially below. When a male client was assigned to a female counselor, the amount that the actual average fell below the predicted was statistically significant at the .01 level for counselors' scores. Clients' scores were also lower but not significantly so.[37]

A second observation is also suggested by the chart: Regardless of the sex of the counselor, outcome scores relative to predicted tended to be higher for female than for male clients. This difference was statistically significant at the .003 level. This fact complicates the analysis of sex matching as a factor in outcomes.[38]

Fortunately, there were other clues that help to clarify the issue. Evidence of the beneficial effects of use of male counselors with male clients included the following factors:

1. Male counselors were more successful than female counselors in getting to see the husbands in husband-wife cases (see chart 47). The difference was statistically significant.

2. Male clients treated by male counselors continued to more than a third again the average number of interviews of males assigned to female counselors (9.6 versus 6.9 interviews for the cases in the chart). The difference was statistically significant at the .001 level.

3. A higher proportion of male clients treated by male counselors reported improvement in their global ratings than did males assigned to female counselors (70 versus 64 percent). Because of the small sample size, this difference was not statistically significant.

One seemingly conflicting piece of evidence also appeared: Slightly more male clients treated by male counselors decided prematurely not to continue than was the case when male clients were treated by female counselors (see chart 59); however, the difference was not statistically significant.

There was also some support for sex matching when the principal client was a woman. Note the following results:

1. Female clients treated by female counselors were less likely to terminate prematurely than were those treated by male counselors (see chart 59). The difference was statistically significant.

2. Female clients treated by female counselors gave higher ratings to the counselor-client relationship than did those assigned to male counselors. The difference in average ratings was significant at the .006 level.

Again, one piece of contradictory evidence appeared: Female clients treated by male counselors continued on the average to slightly more interviews than those treated by female counselors (8.5 versus 7.0 interviews). However this difference was not statistically significant.

No other measures tested against sex matching, including client complaints, client compliments, and disagreement scores, showed any statistically significant differences or even any consistent pattern for or against sex matching regardless of whether the principal client was a man or a woman.

Even though sex considerations in counselor assignments in most instances do not present major difficulties, nevertheless, the balance of the findings in favor of sex matching does lead one to ponder meanings. Perhaps, each sex feels more confident of a sympathetic hearing, understanding of the issues involved, and needed support for decision-making and action when the counselor is of the same sex. Similarly, each may feel less hesitant about discussing sexual problems. To what extent such feelings are increased by the rising awareness of sex role issues or counterbalanced by cross-sex attraction can not be ascertained from the data. In any case, the consequences of the sex of the counselor deserve more attention in casework and research than they have as yet received. ∎

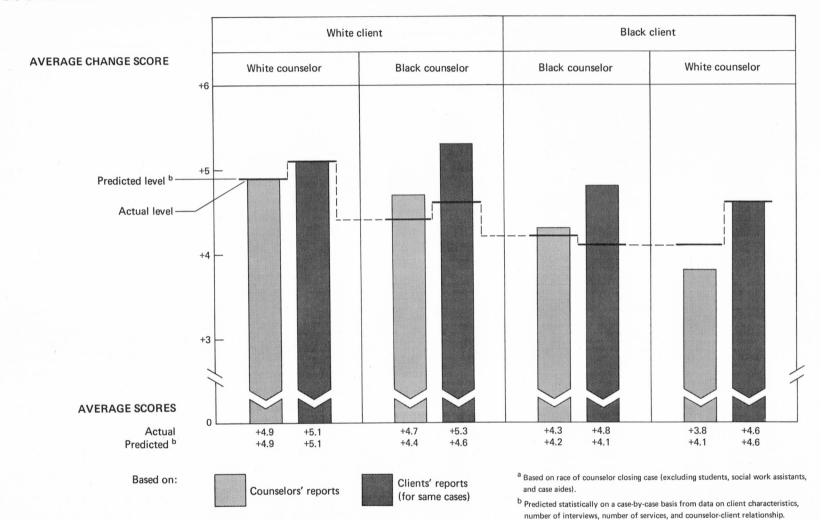

AVERAGE CHANGE SCORE

	White client		Black client	
	White counselor	Black counselor	Black counselor	White counselor

Predicted level [b]

Actual level

AVERAGE SCORES

	White counselor		Black counselor		Black counselor		White counselor	
Actual	+4.9	+5.1	+4.7	+5.3	+4.3	+4.8	+3.8	+4.6
Predicted [b]	+4.9	+5.1	+4.4	+4.6	+4.2	+4.1	+4.1	+4.6

Based on: Counselors' reports   Clients' reports (for same cases)

[a] Based on race of counselor closing case (excluding students, social work assistants, and case aides).

[b] Predicted statistically on a case-by-case basis from data on client characteristics, number of interviews, number of services, and counselor-client relationship.

Chart 94 examines differences in the average change scores according to whether white and black clients were matched with counselors of the same race.[39] Global evaluations for the same four combinations are given in the table below.

Both types of data suggest the same conclusion: Black clients do better with black than with white counselors. On the change scores, black clients matched with black counselors exceeded the predicted scores regardless of whether averages were based on counselors' or clients' reports. In contrast, black clients treated by white counselors fell below predicted levels in the case of counselors' reports and equaled predicted scores in the case of clients' reports. For both counselors' and clients' scores, clients treated by black counselors did better than those treated by white counselors. None of these differences reached statistical significance but, because of the consistency with other findings, one can presume that the lack of significance is mainly because of small sam-

| | Percentage of cases | | | |
| | White client | | Black client | |
Global rating	White counselor (N=1,326)	Black counselor (N=63)	Black counselor (N=52)	White counselor (N=190)
Counselor's rating				
Much better	18	25	25	9
Somewhat better	54	43	52	58
No change (or mixed)	24	24	23	29
Worse	4	8	—	4
Client's rating (same cases)				
Much better	33	29	25	27
Somewhat better	37	46	44	41
No change (or mixed)	24	16	23	26
Worse	6	9	8	6

How do service characteristics affect outcomes?

ple sizes.[40] The findings are also consistent with counselors' global ratings. In the case of the percentages for "much better," the difference (25 versus 9 percent) in favor of assigning black counselors to black clients was highly significant statistically. As was shown in chart 59, client disengagement figures also significantly favored racial matching for black clients. It is not clear why black clients' global ratings showed little difference by race of counselor.

For white clients treated by white counselors, the findings conform exactly with the predicted, which says nothing more than that the results were average. What was unexpected was the finding that white clients treated by black counselors showed better average results in relation to the predicted line than did those treated by white counselors, a reversal of the usual differential in favor of matching. Again, the differences between bars and the deviations from the predicted line were not statistically significant, perhaps because of sample size.[41] Nevertheless, the pattern was repeated for both types of change scores. Global ratings, however, in this instance did not confirm the pattern. Clients' global ratings favored racial matching for white clients, and counselors' global ratings showed more "much better" ratings and also more "worse" ratings when white clients were assigned to black counselors.

If one searches for further clarification in available data on the counselor-client relationship, disagreement scores, client complaints, and client compliments, one finds remarkably few clues and little variation of any type in relation to matching or nonmatching on race.[42] There was no evidence to support a conclusion that white clients had difficulty with black counselors. Neither was there

any support for the positive findings shown in the present chart. The picture was further confused by the finding that black clients having black counselors showed somewhat higher disagreement scores than those with white counselors.

If one disregards these cross-currents of evidence and accepts for purposes of discussion the apparent implication of chart 94 that white clients do better with black counselors than with white counselors, what might be various possible explanations? Has discrimination led to a tighter screening for black counselors so that they are, in fact, superior counselors? As recent entrants into the profession, are they perhaps younger and less given to psychological interpretations and more concerned about environmental problems and constraints? Are they perhaps less critical, warmer, more accepting? Are they for any reason less threatening to the insecure client? Since the change score differences shown in chart 94 in favor of black counselors for white clients are not statistically significant and are not supported by other variables, no firm interpretation is ventured.

What is clear, especially when considered in conjunction with other findings, is that black clients do somewhat better with black counselors while white clients achieve about equally good outcomes with or without racial matching. On the one hand, this finding underlines for agencies the importance of employing enough black counselors to permit black clients the advantages of matching. On the other hand, it can reassure and relieve any lingering fears and uncertainties on the part of black counselors and their supervisors as to the reception black counselors can expect to receive from white clients. ■

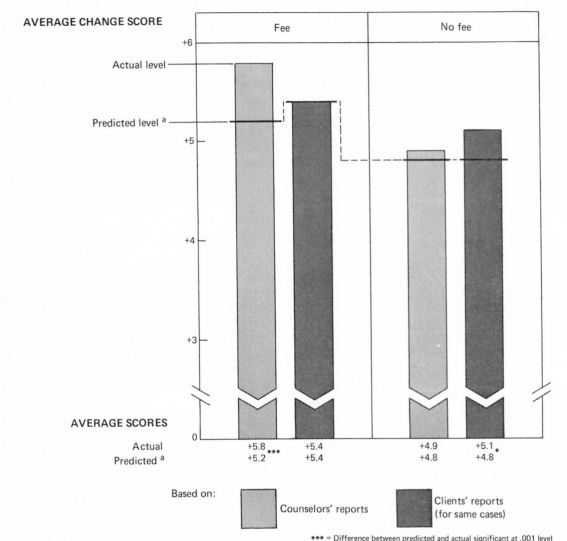

AVERAGE CHANGE SCORE

	Fee	No fee

Actual level

Predicted level [a]

AVERAGE SCORES

	Fee		No fee	
Actual	+5.8 ***	+5.4	+4.9	+5.1 *
Predicted [a]	+5.2	+5.4	+4.8	+4.8

Based on: Counselors' reports   Clients' reports (for same cases)

*** = Difference between predicted and actual significant at .001 level (* = .05 level).

[a] Predicted statistically on a case-by-case basis from data on client characteristics, number of interviews, number of services, and counselor-client relationship.

The findings on the association between payment of fees and change scores are puzzling. According to counselors' reports, when fees were paid, outcomes were not only significantly above those for clients not paying fees, but also significantly above the predicted level. This was true in spite of the fact that the predicted level itself was substantially higher for fee-paying clients. In contrast, clients' scores for nonfee-paying clients, although also below those for fee-paying clients, were significantly above predicted scores for that group.

Further exploration indicated that this pattern was not simply a result of the association of fee-paying with higher incomes and, hence, with higher socioeconomic status. The difference in counselors' scores between fee-paying and nonfee-paying clients held about equally within the lower and the upper socioeconomic groups and also within groups receiving incomes below and above $6,000. Moreover, it continued at a significant level when gains were classified by number of interviews. Counselors' global ratings also were significantly higher for fee-paying than nonfee-paying clients. A similar difference, also highly significant, persisted when the cases with no follow-up report were included and when global ratings were examined. Thus, regardless of how the data were analyzed, the difference associated with fee-paying remained consistently statistically significant, sometimes highly so, when ratings were derived from counselors' reports.

In sharp contrast, a similar analysis of change scores based on clients' reports consistently failed to show at any point a significant association between fee-paying and the progress reported. In a few instances the findings, although not statistically significant, were in the reverse direction. In fact, the analysis of variance revealed a highly significant interaction between who was doing the rating and whether payment of fees was found associated with favorable outcomes.

Client characteristics correlated with fee-paying perhaps provide a clue. The typical fee-paying case involved a well-motivated, upper- or middle-class, relatively young, white family with problems that were below average in number and severity. Counselors tend to expect this kind of client to do well. This image, plus a natural urge to see their service as worth the fees paid, may have slightly biased counselors' ratings in an upward direction. These same clients may have had higher than average expectations of what would be achieved by counseling, especially since they had paid fees. They may, therefore, have been less ready to report small changes as improvement.

While this explanation is at best only partial and unconvincing, the marked differences between counselors' and clients' reports on the outcomes associated with fee-paying suggest that agencies should not rush to conclude that paying fees in itself has a beneficial effect on outcomes. Were this true, one would expect that this finding would also have been confirmed by clients' reports. ■

Other service characteristics

A number of additional aspects of treatment were also examined for possible associations with outcomes. Of those not already illustrated by charts or discussed in connection with them, only two–whether the case was new or reopened and whether there was a transfer to a different counselor–were found significantly related to the change scores.[43] When other factors were controlled, new cases showed significantly higher gains than reopened cases on counselors' scores but no significant difference on clients' scores. Transfer, unexpectedly, was found to be positively and significantly associated (at the .03 level) with higher clients' scores, but not with counselors' scores (see chart 97). Since the reason for this latter finding is not apparent, other factors may be involved. For example, cases transferred were also more likely than others to be served through group treatment, to receive more interviews, and to have more family members seen. Possibly it is the association of involvement of a second counselor with these other treatment patterns known to be positively associated with favorable outcome reports from clients that acounts for this otherwise puzzling finding.

In addition, the following five service characteristics were tested for a possible relationship with the change scores and found to show no statistically significant association with outcomes under the conditions of the present study: (1) whether and how long the client was kept waiting, (2) whether the case was served through a specialized service department or project, (3) average number of interviews per month, (4) extent to which service was provided by social work assistants or case aides, and (5) whether the closing counselor was a student, social work assistant, or case aide. In most of these situations, interpretation is made difficult by the secondary nature of the factors tested, plus the complex interaction of treatment modality, patterns in case assignments, type of problem and type of service that they involve. The network of relationships is too complex to be untangled except in a study with an experimental design.

The problem is vividly illustrated by. the findings on social work assistants. These assistants tend to be selectively assigned to the simpler tasks and types of service and to the more motivated clients; in addition, they are usually closely supervised and more often than not assigned to work jointly with a trained counselor.[44] Under these circumstances, cases receiving some service from social work assistants yield outcomes similar to other cases. This fact, however, does not indicate what the outcomes would have been if social work assistants had been randomly assigned to full responsiblity for the same types of cases, problems, and functions as are normally assigned to fully trained counselors. ■

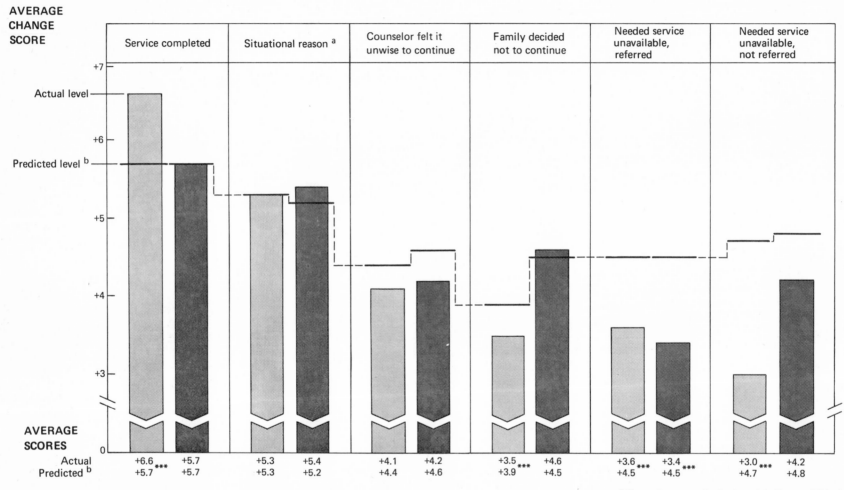

AVERAGE
CHANGE
SCORE

	Service completed	Situational reason [a]	Counselor felt it unwise to continue	Family decided not to continue	Needed service unavailable, referred	Needed service unavailable, not referred

Actual level

+7

+6

Predicted level [b]

+5

+4

+3

AVERAGE
SCORES

0

	Service completed		Situational reason		Counselor felt it unwise		Family decided		Needed service referred		Needed service not referred	
Actual	+6.6 ***	+5.7	+5.3	+5.4	+4.1	+4.2	+3.5 ***	+4.6	+3.6 ***	+3.4 ***	+3.0 ***	+4.2
Predicted [b]	+5.7	+5.7	+5.3	+5.2	+4.4	+4.6	+3.9	+4.5	+4.5	+4.5	+4.7	+4.8

*** = Difference between predicted and actual significant at .001 level.

☐ Counselors' reports   ■ Clients' reports (for same cases)

[a] Or other reason.
[b] Predicted statistically on a case-by-case basis from data on client characteristics, number of interviews, number of services, and counselor-client relationship.

Chart 96 indicates the differences in outcomes when service is and is not carried through to completion.[45] Clients who continued until their counselors considered the service completed achieved counselors' scores that exceeded predicted levels by a highly significant amount. These scores also exceeded by a significant margin the scores for each of the other categories. In fact, they were more than three points higher than those for the lowest group. Gauged by clients' scores, the record of this group was also the best of any,[46] although not in excess of predicted levels, which were also exceptionally high for this group.

Clients in the follow-up group who completed service also showed conspicuously high improvement when judged by the global ratings. Thirty-nine percent were rated "much improved" by their counselors and 43 percent, by the clients themselves. If those rated "somewhat improved" are added, the total reported improved becomes 91 percent using counselors' ratings and 79 percent using clients' ratings. This record, which was considerably better than that for the follow-up group (see chart 60), was achieved with an average of only 8.4 interviews.[47]

Clients terminating for situational reasons ranked next in outcomes, but achieved this level with three more interviews than were used by the completed service group. For this group, the two types of scores differed little from each other or from predicted levels. Again, this group had to be evaluated against relatively high predicted scores.

Scores for cases terminated because the counselor felt it unwise to continue were substantially less than those for either of the preceding groups. Nevertheless, they were not significantly below predicted levels, perhaps because the group included only sixty-nine cases. Such cases received an average of 7.0 interviews before they were terminated by their counselors.

Families who decided themselves not to continue broke contact somewhat sooner—after an average of 5.7 interviews. Their progress, as rated by their counselors, was significantly below predicted levels. Their predicted scores were also very low, suggesting a low potential for this group. Nevertheless, clients' scores for the same cases were unexpectedly high, even slightly above predicted levels. This finding is reminiscent of the many follow-up reports received from clients in this group indicating that they saw their problems as less stressful or were satisfied with the gains made.[48] These same clients were likewise higher than their counselors on their global ratings; 66 percent reported improvement as compared with only 57 percent of their counselors. Apparently, many saw changes of which their counselors were not aware.

Clients referred elsewhere for service not available at the agency represent in one sense a minimum service group. On the average, they received 4.0 interviews before referral, probably for limited consultation and help with the referral process. Their change score records were significantly below predicted levels on both counselors' and clients' scores. Their averages were also hardly more than half those for clients who completed their service with the agency.

A final group of only twenty-eight cases also needed service not available at the agency but were not referred. Instead they continued with the agency to an average of 8.8 interviews. Perhaps the service they needed was not available elsewhere. Perhaps they chose not to be referred or wished help in other areas. This group was also a minimum service group, not because of few interviews, but because the agency could not provide the primary service they needed. In comparison with the other groups, it was the lowest on counselors' scores. On clients' scores, however, it was remarkably high. Even though these clients did not receive the type of service they needed, they must have felt that they received meaningful help in other areas.

Each of these last two groups in their own way provide a minimum-service yardstick against which the contribution of completed service can be measured. What is evident is that a very substantial and highly significant increment is added to outcomes when clients receive what counselors refer to as completed service. It is also evident that outcome scores in general vary logically and significantly by reason for termination.[49]

Viewed in the context of other findings, this chart adds another type of evidence that change scores reflect more than random changes or the influence of factors unrelated to agency service. They appear to fit together with the other charts in section 9 to provide consistent, detailed, and logically coherent evidence that significant progress on family problems does occur in the context of agency service and is proportionate to the amount and type of service provided. ∎

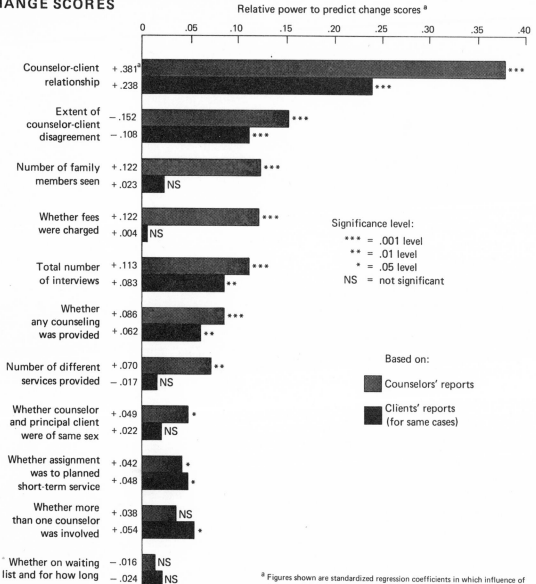

Relative power to predict change scores [a]

Counselor-client relationship	+.381[a]	***
	+.238	***
Extent of counselor-client disagreement	−.152	***
	−.108	***
Number of family members seen	+.122	***
	+.023	NS
Whether fees were charged	+.122	***
	+.004	NS
Total number of interviews	+.113	***
	+.083	**
Whether any counseling was provided	+.086	***
	+.062	**
Number of different services provided	+.070	**
	−.017	NS
Whether counselor and principal client were of same sex	+.049	*
	+.022	NS
Whether assignment was to planned short-term service	+.042	*
	+.048	*
Whether more than one counselor was involved	+.038	NS
	+.054	*
Whether on waiting list and for how long	−.016	NS
	−.024	NS

Significance level:
*** = .001 level
** = .01 level
* = .05 level
NS = not significant

Based on:
■ Counselors' reports
■ Clients' reports (for same cases)

[a] Figures shown are standardized regression coefficients in which influence of 11 client characteristics and 15 service characteristics is held constant.

Chart 97 is a summary chart reporting the results of a final multiple regression analysis covering fifteen service characteristics[50] plus the eleven client characteristics analyzed earlier. The length of each bar again represents the relative power[51] of each service characteristic to predict the change scores. The overpowering influence of the counselor-client relationship was again startling. It had more than double the predictive power of the second highest factor—counselor-client disagreement—and exceeded any client characteristic shown in chart 83. By comparison, the influence of number of interviews and number of different services was relatively minor.

In general, the findings already reported on the relation of the various service factors to outcomes were confirmed.[52] Also evident is a stronger association of service characteristics with counselors' than with clients' scores. What accounts for this pattern is not clear. Perhaps the following factors contributed: (1) more careful ratings by counselors, (2) professional expectations and biases, and (3) a relation between the type of service provided and the amount of feedback on outcomes that reaches the counselor.

Judging by the multiple correlation findings, all these factors combined account together for only 38 percent of the variance in counselors' scores and only 21 percent of the variance in clients' scores.[53] Would inclusion in the analysis of some of the more intangible aspects of clients' assets and the treatment process have increased these figures? Until answers are provided by further research, the sources of client change will still remain, to some extent, elusive. ■

10
PROFILES OF
SPECIAL
GROUPS:
COUPLES WITH
MARITAL PROBLEMS

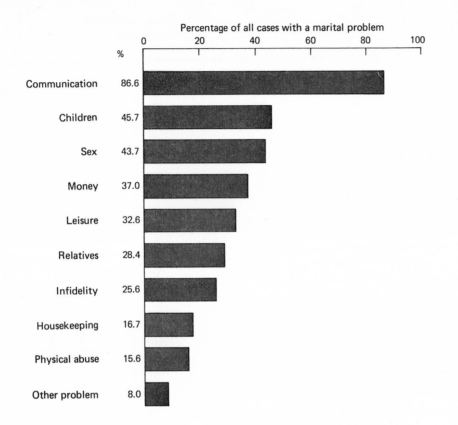

Percentage of all cases with a marital problem

	%	
Communication	86.6	
Children	45.7	
Sex	43.7	
Money	37.0	
Leisure	32.6	
Relatives	28.4	
Infidelity	25.6	
Housekeeping	16.7	
Physical abuse	15.6	
Other problem	8.0	

Chart 98 begins a short series focused on the largest problem group in the sample–couples with marital problems. Among intact families seeking help from family agencies during the sample week, about two-thirds (67 percent) had a marital problem. Communication was by far the most frequent area where this problem was evident.[1] Almost nine out of every ten couples with marital problems were faced with difficulties in communication. As clients put it:[2] "We can't talk to each other"; "I can't reach him"; "She doesn't understand me"; or, "Every time we talk to each other, it ends in an argument." Yet, without communication how can one know what the problem is, much less resolve it?

Conflicts over children were the next highest in frequency. Such conflicts tend to center on discipline and child-rearing practices.[3] Sexual difficulties were almost as frequent and involved more than four couples in ten. Conflicts over money and leisure time were reported for about one couple in three; infidelity for about one in four; and housekeeping and physical abuse each for about one in six. Alcoholism was the largest identifiable subgroup under "other,"[4] but nonsupport, personal habits, problems over religion or culture, drugs, gambling, and crime were also reported in this category.

In comparison with those who had separated, couples who were still living together had more frequent difficulties with communication, sex, housekeeping, use of leisure time, and handling of children; those who had already separated reported more frequent difficulties with infidelity, physical abuse, and arguments over money and relatives.

Patterns by socioeconomic status are shown in chart 99. At all levels, communication was the most frequent and probably the most basic difficulty affecting the marital relationship. Problems in other areas varied less by socioeconomic status than might have been predicted. Conflicts or differences between the partners over sex, use of leisure time, and the handling of children were somewhat more frequent at the upper than at the lower status levels; those involving money, physical abuse, and such "other" serious problems as alcoholism and nonsupport were more prevalent at the lower levels. Differences over relatives, housekeeping, and infidelity showed no clear socioeconomic pattern. The variations that were found by socioeconomic status were more marked for nonwhite than for white clients, but there was little overall difference by race in the total number of areas involved in the marital problem.

Five items showed a puzzling upswing at the upper middle socioeconomic level. Perhaps this traditionally relatively conservative group tends to be more sensitive to differences related to sex, leisure, infidelity, children, and relatives than either their more affluent or their less affluent counterparts who may be accustomed to more permissive and accepting life-styles.

A question suggests itself: To what extent do these areas of conflict or difficulty fluctuate throughout the marital life cycle? While this study does not provide direct longitudinal data, some clues can be obtained by comparing intact marriages that have lasted for less than twelve years with those that have continued for twelve years or more. Such comparisons showed difficulties with relatives (parents, in-laws, and so on) to be more common in the younger than in the older marriages (32 versus 24 percent) and difficulties with their own children more common in marriages that had persisted to twelve years or beyond (40 versus 59 percent).[5] These figures suggest that for younger couples the problem of independence from their families of origin looms large, whereas the more mature couples have to cope with the emancipation efforts of their own adolescent children. Most other conflict areas were slightly less frequent in the more mature marriages: Sexual problems stood at 44 instead of 46 percent; money problems, at 35 instead of 39 percent; infidelity, at 21 instead of 25 percent; housekeeping conflicts, at 17 instead of 19 percent; and physical abuse, at 13 instead of 15 percent.[6] For couples who have had twelve or more years to cope with and solve their conflicts, these are amazingly small declines.

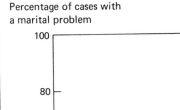

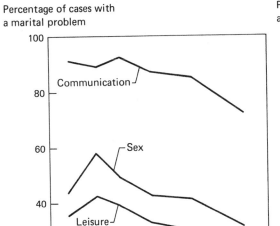

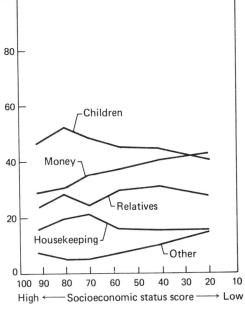

Even these figures make no allowance for the fact that the worst marriages usually do not survive to the twelfth year. On an overall basis, there was little difference between the two groups. Those married less than twelve years averaged 3.5 areas involved in the conflict or difficulty; those married twelve years or over, 3.4 areas.

Viewed as a whole, the marital problems brought to family agencies clearly pervade not one but many areas of the marriage, tend to be serious rather than mild (see chart 20), and are widely prevalent regardless of socioeconomic status, race, or duration of marriage. Counseling for such couples is an essential community service that deserves considerably more adequate public and private support than it is now receiving. ∎

Profiles of special groups: couples with marital problems

MARITAL AND CHILDREN'S PROBLEMS BY YEARS MARRIED

Chart 100

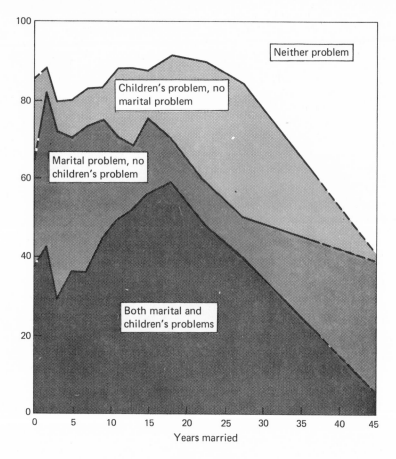

Percentage of cases [a]

Neither problem

Children's problem, no marital problem

Marital problem, no children's problem

Both marital and children's problems

Years married

[a] Percentages at lower and upper extremes of years married represent projections of trends prevailing at midpoints of top and bottom categories.

these types decline gradually, but only to be replaced by others less easily remedied (see chart 23).

These extremely high problem levels clearly reflect the situation for families in trouble. Proportions for the general population tend to be much lower.[7] Nevertheless, the intensification of marital and children's problems shown here in the middle period of marriage has its counterpart in general research findings of decreasing marital satisfaction during the children's school years, with some evidence of a rise in marital satisfaction after the children are launched on their own lives.[8] Boyd C. Rollins and Harold Feldman, for example, after noting a "substantial decrease in general marital satisfaction . . . during the childbearing and childrearing phases," commented: "These data suggest that the experiences of childbearing and childrearing have a rather profound and negative effect on marital satisfaction for wives."[9]

This convergence of findings highlights the need for family agency leadership in a community-wide preventive and developmental approach designed to help normal families cope more effectively with these predictable family life cycle changes. Assisting normal families to cope has been one function of agency family life education programs and various innovative group approaches to helping young couples. These programs should be more widely available and should be incorporated in a national family support system. ■

Marital and children's problems vary markedly according to the number of years a couple has been married. As chart 100 indicates, after a brief initial peak followed by a small decline,

marital and children's problems in combination gradually rise to involve over 90 percent of agency families at the point when their children are usually teenagers. Thereafter, problems of

About one couple in five who applies to a family agency is attempting to cope with a marriage of two persons of clearly diverging backgrounds. As chart 101 indicates, the difference most frequently was one of religion, followed by education, country of birth, and race. Another common type of difference, that of age, is not shown. Since corresponding data for the country as a whole are not available except for race and age differences,[10] it is not possible to know whether agencies serve more or less than a proportionate number of these mixed marriages in general.

The duration of these marriages at the time the couples sought agency service varied widely. Marriages involving mixed educational background or differences in country of birth were typically of long standing, averaging 15.8 and 16.6 years, respectively. Some marriages were of more than thirty years duration, probably reflecting the earlier period of high immigration. Marriages across religious or racial lines tended to be more recent. Interracial marriages averaged 7.6 years and interreligious marriages, 9.7 years.

Do couples in these mixed marriages encounter more marital problems than do other couples? The answer is that, among agency applicants, they report marital problems only slightly more frequently. Seventy percent of the mixed background group had a marital problem as compared with 66 percent of the nonmixed group. Their marital problem was also more likely to be the principal problem. This was especially true if the couple was of mixed religious background. The areas involved in marital conflict or difficulty also differed somewhat between the mixed and the nonmixed group. In particular, conflict over

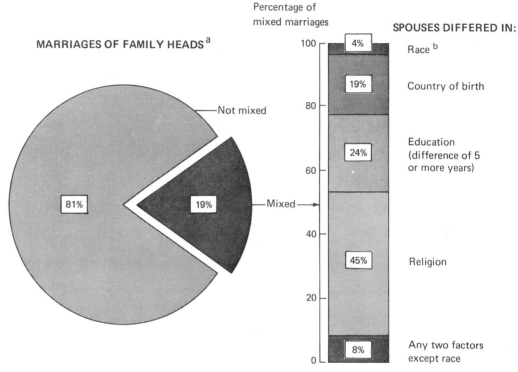

MARRIAGES OF FAMILY HEADS[a]

81% — Not mixed

19% — Mixed

Percentage of mixed marriages

SPOUSES DIFFERED IN:

4%   Race [b]

19%   Country of birth

24%   Education (difference of 5 or more years)

45%   Religion

8%   Any two factors except race

[a] Includes separated couples where information was available.

[b] Includes marriages mixed on other factors in addition to race.

the children, relatives, and physical abuse tended to be slightly higher for the mixed marriage group.

These mixed-marriage couples were also a little more likely to have a children's problem (71 versus 68 percent). Their total problem count was only minimally higher (4.5 versus 4.3 problems),[11] but their total problem situation was more often rated severe (53 versus 46 percent). While none of these individual differences was large, in combination they do suggest that agency applicants with marriages in which the partners diverge in some major aspect of their backgrounds face, on the average, somewhat more complex problem situations than do other clients. ∎

DIRECTION OF MOVEMENT OF MARRIAGE AND IN WHOSE INTEREST[a]

Chart 102

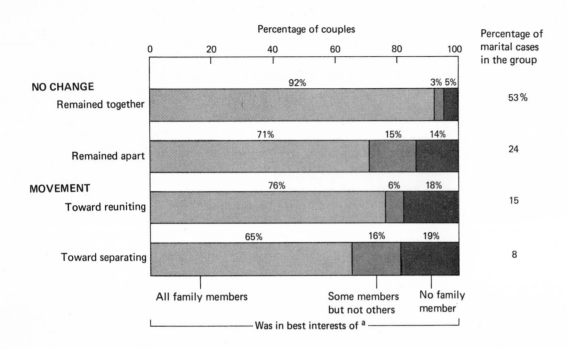

Percentage of couples

Percentage of marital cases in the group

NO CHANGE
Remained together — 92% 3% 5% — 53%

Remained apart — 71% 15% 14% — 24

MOVEMENT
Toward reuniting — 76% 6% 18% — 15

Toward separating — 65% 16% 19% — 8

All family members | Some members but not others | No family member

—— Was in best interests of [a] ——

[a] Based on ratings by counselor.

Chart 102 deals with the question: Does counseling have any effect on whether a marriage moves toward divorce?[12] The answer is far from dramatic. About three couples in four who came with a marital problem made no change in their position on this issue during the period of counseling. More than half were planning to remain married when they came and planned no change in this respect when they terminated. How many of these might have moved toward separation without professional help with their problems is not known. Another one in four was separated at intake and planned to remain so at termination. About 15 percent who were separated when they first applied shifted toward reuniting during treatment. A smaller group—8 percent—moved in the course of treatment from staying together toward separating. The proportion who made any legal change in their marriage during the treatment period was even smaller—7 percent. About one in seven of these moved toward remarriage; the other six, in the direction of separation or divorce.

In whose best interest were these changes? Moving toward staying together or reuniting were both more often reported in the interests of all family members than were separating or remaining apart. Nevertheless, even moving toward separation was seen as in the best interests of all family members for 65 percent of those who chose this way out. When the interests of different family members were separately assessed, counselors reported remaining together or reuniting as most often in the interests of the husband, next most often in the interests of the children, and least often in the interests of the wife. Conversely, separating or remaining apart, which was infrequent, was most often reported as in the best interests of the wife, next most often in the interests of the children, and least often in the interests of the husband.[13] Fortunately, the interests of the various family members were seldom in conflict. For 83 percent, the direction of movement at closing was in the best interests of all concerned. In only 10 percent was it not in the interests of any family member.

From these findings, it is obvious that the success of marital counseling can not be judged by whether a marriage is "saved."[14] Breakup may not be in question, may be unavoidable, or may be in the best interests of all concerned. To measure outcomes in terms of prevention of breakup would put pressure on counselors to violate two basic professional principles: the client's right to autonomy and the counselor's obligation to work solely in the best interests of his client. ∎

Apparently it is more difficult to achieve improvement in marital problems when the marriage is of long standing. According to counselors' reports, as shown in chart 103, 48 percent of couples married less than twelve years showed improvement in their marital problem during treatment, as contrasted with the significantly lower figure of 37 percent of those married twelve years or more. In addition, the proportion of the long-standing marriages receiving no counseling on their marital problem at all was twice that of the shorter marriages—perhaps because they took their marital problems for granted and asked for help instead with newly emerging problems.

This decline in improvement for couples whose marriage was of long duration was more pronounced for husbands than for wives, as the following figures indicate:

| | Percentage reported improved[a] | |
	Married under 12 years	Married 12 years or more
Counselors' ratings:		
Husband better	49.7	38.9[b]
Wife better	69.3	61.2
Clients' ratings:		
Husband better	63.8	54.2[b]
Wife better	73.1	61.7[b]

[a]Data limited to couples living together, whose most important problem was a marital one, and who submitted a follow-up report.
[b]Difference in the percentage improving between the under- and over-12-year groups was statistically significant.

This finding is similar to that of Brenda Wattie, who also reported that improvement was less frequent in husbands than in wives as the duration of the marriage increased.[15]

IMPROVEMENT IN MARITAL PROBLEM BY YEARS MARRIED[a]

Chart 103

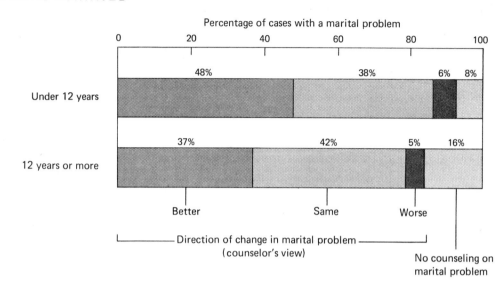

[a] Only married family heads included.

Change scores for these same types of couples[16] further confirmed the difficulty of achieving progress when marriages were of long standing. Counselors' scores averaged + 4.9 for couples married less than twelve years but only + 4.0 for those married twelve years or more. Contrasts in a similar direction were evident for clients' scores for these same two groups (+5.2 versus +4.4). Both differences were statistically significant.[17]

These consistent patterns lead one to hypothesize an increase over time in role inflexibility, hostile and ineffective communication patterns, repetitive rationalizations and denials, valuation of secondary gains, and a general level of disenchantment and resignation—an attitude of "What can you do?" For maximum effectiveness and for the sake of the children, it is clear that young couples must be reached early in their marital careers or even in the courtship stage. Agency experimentation with early prevention through a group approach to marriage enrichment is increasing. However, marriages of many years' duration can also be helped, as these data indicate. ∎

Further description of marital problem cases and comparisons with children's problems

A marital problem was the most important problem for 45 percent of all intact families in the sample.[18] These couples were in the main a severely troubled group. At intake, 66 percent presented an adult personality adjustment problem; 35 percent, a money-management problem; 34 percent, a parent-child relationship problem; 34 percent, a problem in social contacts or use of leisure time; 24 percent, a problem related to child-rearing or child care; 16 percent, a home management problem; and 15 percent, an alcoholism problem.[19] For another 38 percent of intact families, a children's problem was primary. To what extent do these two major groups differ in their response to service?

In contrast to the group with a focus on children's problems, the group with marital problems tended to apply earlier in their marriage, to be involved in a more serious total problem situation, and to terminate with fewer interviews. (The accompanying table gives details.) They were also more likely to terminate on an unplanned basis before service was completed. In six cases in ten, one partner or both simply decided not to continue.

The outcomes achieved also were consistently less favorable for the group with marital problems.[20] They were also less positive than for families for whom the marital problem was secondary or absent. Moreover, if the application for help with a marital problem was delayed until after the conflict had escalated to the point of separation, both the number of interviews and the progress achieved were even less.[21]

On the other hand, the group with marital problems had one important asset–the husband was more likely to become involved in treatment when a marital problem was the most important one than when the primary focus was on a children's problem.[22] When both partners were seen, counselors reported significantly more progress than when only one spouse was involved.[23]

These findings indicate that if couples with marital problems are to be given maximum help, they should be reached early in the conflict process and, if feasible, both partners should be involved in treatment.

	Most important problem[a]	
	Marital	Children's
	Median age of family head[b]	34.2	42.5
Average years married	10.1	15.4
Average number of interviews	7.3	9.2[c]

	Percentage of cases	
Severe problem situation[c]	59%	39%
Locus of problem[c] (as seen by client)		
Self	8	8
Relationship with others	73	31
Other family members	14	51
Situational	4	5
Involvement of husband in treatment		
Husband phoned for appointment[c,e]	23	9
Husband seen in first interview	60	47
Husband seen at some time during treatment	71	62
Both husband and wife seen	67	60
Husband seen most often	26[c]	10

	Most important problem[a]	
	Marital	Children's
	Percentage of cases	
Primary treatment modality		
Husband-wife interviews	36	19
Family interviews	3	14
A child under 18 seen	—[d]	75[c]
Termination		
Planned	47%	54%[c]
Decision mutual	44	47[c]
Reason		
Service completed	22	28
Family decided not to continue	59	49
Main reason for change (client's view)		
Change in self	34	25
Change in another person	6	10
Change in relationship within family	22	16
Outcomes		
Counselors' ratings[c,f]		
Husband improved	41%	30%
Wife improved	63	58
Clients' ratings[c,f]		
Husband improved	61	49
Wife improved	68	63
Total problem situation improved		
Counselors' ratings	67	72[c]
Clients' ratings	66	72[c]

	Average change scores	
Counselors' scores	+4.6	+4.8
Clients' scores	+4.9	+5.2

[a] Seen as most important by either counselor or client at any point in treatment. Limited to married couples living together except as noted.
[b] Medians limited to cases with change scores from both counselors and clients.
[c] Includes separated couples.
[d] Not computed.
[e] Data from phone study.
[f] Not limited to same cases for counselors and clients.

■

11
PROFILES OF SPECIAL GROUPS:
CLIENTS SIXTY-FIVE
AND OVER

SERVICE REQUEST FOR

PERSONS 65 AND OVER

PERSONS UNDER 65

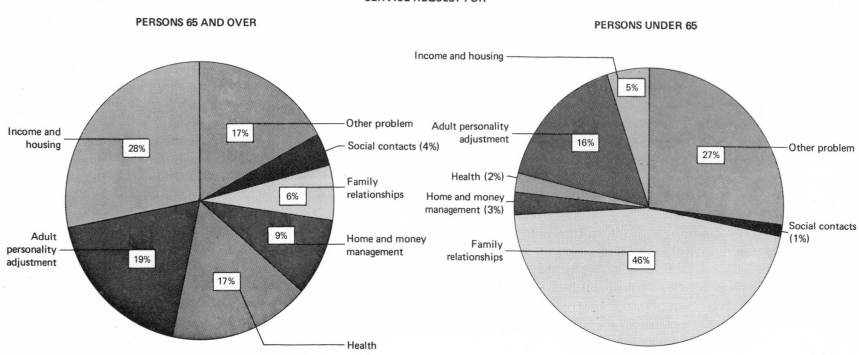

Although few persons beyond sixty-five are served by family agencies,[1] those who do apply provide a stark profile of the needs of this group. Clients in this age range were more likely than applicants at younger age levels to be subsisting below the poverty level, to live in metropolitan areas, and to be white. Nearly half were from the lowest socioeconomic group. Half either lived alone or with one or more other elderly relatives only.

In comparison with younger applicants, service to those sixty-five and over[2] focused more than eight times as often on health problems; five times as often on income or housing problems; four times as often on a problem of social contacts; three times as often on money management; and slightly more often on personality adjustment problems.[3]

In contrast, a focus on family relationship problems was only one-seventh as frequent as with younger applicants. Obviously, expansion of service to this needy and neglected group would require a reduced focus on family relationship problems and increased programming in a wide variety of practical services.   ■

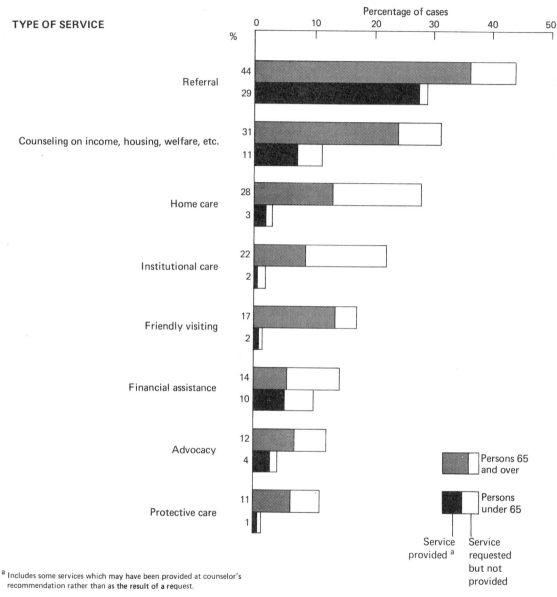

TYPE OF SERVICE

Percentage of cases

Referral — 44, 29

Counseling on income, housing, welfare, etc. — 31, 11

Home care — 28, 3

Institutional care — 22, 2

Friendly visiting — 17, 2

Financial assistance — 14, 10

Advocacy — 12, 4

Protective care — 11, 1

Persons 65 and over

Persons under 65

Service provided [a]   Service requested but not provided

[a] Includes some services which may have been provided at counselor's recommendation rather than as the result of a request.

Profiles of special groups: clients sixty-five and over

Reports on the services provided to older clients and on their unmet service requests again mirror the plight of those in their later years. Judged in these terms, need for home care and institutional care were both more than nine times as frequent when those concerned were sixty-five or over as when they were younger. The need for friendly visiting and escort service was eight times as high; for protective services, seven times as high; for help with advocacy or with problems related to income, housing, or welfare, three times as high; and those for referral, half again as high as when the request related to the needs of a younger person. Only about five in ten of the needs of this senior group as identified at intake resulted in the provision of the type of service needed, as compared with about six in ten of those of younger applicants.

Likewise, at follow-up, at least one client in five from the older group reported unmet needs as contrasted with only one in twelve among those under sixty-five. Older respondents also identified certain needs not reported by counselors, such as the need for legal services or for money for basic maintenance.

Many unmet needs of older clients were of a costly or time-consuming nature or involved services agencies were not in a position to provide. In fact, the total package of service supports needed to enable the older person to cope with the escalation of practical problems in the final decades of life greatly exceeds what local family agencies alone can undertake. Cooperative action on a broader scale at the community, state, and national level is the only feasible answer. ■

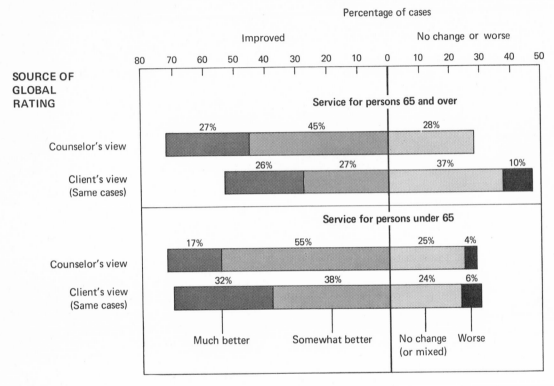

Percentage of cases

Improved / No change or worse

Service for persons 65 and over

Counselor's view: 27% | 45% | 28%

Client's view (Same cases): 26% | 27% | 37% | 10%

Service for persons under 65

Counselor's view: 17% | 55% | 25% | 4%

Client's view (Same cases): 32% | 38% | 24% | 6%

SOURCE OF GLOBAL RATING

Much better | Somewhat better | No change (or mixed) | Worse

In the perspective of the 1960s, the major gain in service for clients sixty-five and over has been an increase in the intensity of service. In 1960, cases with a principal problem related to aging received an average of only 1.3 interviews, including interviews with other family members and collaterals. By 1970, the same agencies reported 6.0 interviews for cases applying for help for an aged person only—more than a fourfold increase. Even this higher level falls below the volume of service actually needed by this group as is

evident from the findings of FSAA's special project, Social Work Teams with Aging Family Service Clients. This project reported an average over two years of service of twenty-one interviews per client, aged sixty and over.[4]

How clients sixty-five and over evaluated their period of service with the agency is reported in chart 106. The most striking feature is the contrast between counselors' views and those of clients in the higher age range. Counselors reported improvement in more than seven cases in ten among those

sixty-five and over. No client was reported worse. In contrast, only a little over five in ten of the clients themselves reported improvement, four in ten reported no change, and one in ten claimed the situation was worse. The differences are statistically significant in spite of the relatively small sample. Those at younger age levels took a more positive view of outcomes and also agreed more closely with their counselors. There were also differences in the type of service reported as having the most positive influence: Direct service was the most positive in the case of clients sixty-five and over and counseling in the case of younger clients.

Why were there these marked differences between the counselors' and the clients' views of the same service? Probably the clients' awareness of the aging process and their frequent reaction of depression contributes to their relatively low ratings. Since the client does not feel better, perhaps he does not see the changes as improvements. Moreover, he has to cope with his disappointment over the agency's frequent inability to meet his increased need for specialized direct services. The counselor, recalling the client's previous situation and knowing what the alternatives might have been, may see the client as distinctly better off than he would have been without service; hence he reports improvement. This is one more dramatic illustration of counselor-client differences in perspective that have been a salient finding throughout the study. Increased alertness to these differences can improve the counselor-client relationship and in some cases also the effectiveness of service for all age groups. ∎

APPENDIX

Study plan, data collection process, and follow-up experience

Sample selection and bias

All voluntary agencies with membership in FSAA in 1970 were invited to participate in the study. Eighty-one percent, or 273 agencies, elected to do so. Because proportionately more of the larger agencies participated, the contributing agencies represented 87 percent of all family service clientele. Participation by agencies that held membership in both the Child Welfare League of America and in FSAA was somewhat greater than their proportion in the total membership. Sectarian agencies were not represented in proportion to their numbers since one-fourth did not participate. Regionally, the participation ranged from 76 percent of the agencies in the Southeast to 89 percent in the Southwest. Seven out of eight Canadian agencies participated.

To parallel the U.S. census, the sample was drawn from one week of intake in the spring of 1970. The week of April 29 to May 5 was suggested and about three-quarters of the participating agencies did select that week. The rest chose an alternate week as close in time as possible to those dates. To the extent that there are seasonal variations in intake, the sample reflects the late spring period.

Each agency was asked to report all applicants or reapplicants whose first in-person contact with the agency's social work staff occurred during the sample week.[1] All programs or departments serving identified clients were to be included, such as family and children's services, homemaker service, Travelers Aid, legal aid, placement and adoption, services for the aged, mental health services, family life education, and outreach projects.

Omission of some eligible programs and cases was acknowledged by a few agencies. A few programs in which agencies were under contract to business corporations to provide services to their employees were omitted at the request of the corporations. A few innovative programs with teenagers were omitted because of agency concern over confidentiality. Some programs that were located in outlying areas or that were not seen as part of the agency's usual services were omitted because of administrative uncertainties or problems. Among these were the services of two agencies to Spanish-speaking residents. Services in two primarily black communities were omitted because some local staff members were concerned that there might be an adverse reaction in view of the communities' earlier unfortunate experiences with research surveys. The overall effect of the known omissions in the sample was some underrepresentation of lower socioeconomic, nonwhite, and Spanish-speaking clients and of newer, nontraditional service programs of a group work or outreach nature.

Agency services that did not serve identified clients directly were omitted by design. Among these were consultation to other agencies, organizations, or community groups, advocacy efforts on behalf of groups of persons, social work training and supervision, and the full range of agency administration, research, interpretation of community needs, and program planning.

Size of sample

The 273 participating agencies submitted intake reports on 3,746 cases. This report is based on 3,596 of these cases which were submitted by the 266 U.S. agencies participating in the census. The 150 cases submitted by the Canadian agencies were not included in this report because sections of the report involve comparisons with population data for the United States and with data from the 1960 FSAA census analysis, which did not include Canada.[2] Closing reports were submitted by the counselors on 94 percent of the U.S. sample.[3] Follow-up reports were received on 53 percent of the sample, or 1,906 clients.

In addition, about fourteen hundred self-report questionnaires completed by persons attending family life education meetings during the census week were submitted by forty-three U.S. agencies having program sessions of this type during the sample week. An optional part of the census participation was the completion of brief reports on telephone intake and telephone inquiries during the census week. Reports of 2,806 phone calls were submitted by 134 agencies. These two special service areas—family life education and service by phone only—were not included in the basic sample for this report but are reported on briefly in charts 28 and 32.[4]

Client follow-up procedures

According to plan, all cases in the basic census sample were to be followed up as soon as possible after case closing (or at the end of two years if the case was still open). Since it was not feasible to obtain and analyze responses from more than one family member, the person who had had the most service contacts was to be selected as the respondent whenever possible. Two methods of follow-up were available to agencies—personal interview and mail questionnaire. Separate forms were designed for each because of necessary changes in wording, but the differences were slight and the forms were considered equivalent. (The mail questionnaire is reproduced on pages 170 through 173.) At the outset, agencies were asked to choose one of these two methods as their primary approach. The interview approach was recommended because it was thought that it would secure a higher response rate.

The only firm requirement of the interview method was that the interviewer not be the person who had provided service on the case.[5] With this exception, the interviewers could be other staff members, students, board members, or volunteers. If the mail questionnaire was used, it was required, in addition, that the intended respondent have at least an eighth-grade education and be able to speak English; otherwise it was expected that the client be interviewed.

Both types of follow-up were to take place as soon as possible after closing. Agencies were asked to send out the mail questionnaires with a cover letter from the agency executive and a stamped return envelope addressed to the national FSAA office.[6] Two attempts, two weeks apart, were to be made to secure a mail questionnaire response. If none was received by the national office within a designated period, the agency was asked to interview those who had not replied.

Actual follow-up returns

Fifty-three percent of the intake sample were successfully followed up. About three-fourths of the follow-up responses were obtained by interview and one-fourth, by mail questionnaire.[7] Approximately 80 percent of the agencies selected the interview as their primary method of follow-up.[8] The average time lag between the date of the last interview and follow-up was between two and three months for the interview approach and about a month longer for the mail questionnaire response. About 87 percent of the follow-up reports reflected the views of the person who had been seen most often.

Relative effectiveness of the interview and mail questionnaire

The relative success of the two follow-up methods is of major concern for future studies. The details are, however, difficult to reconstruct because of gaps in the reporting of cases not successfully followed up. Agencies were asked: Was any follow-up attempted on the case? If a follow-up was attempted, why was it not successful? Did the family reject the follow-up, or could they not be located? For cases in which the client was located at the time of follow-up, the best estimate available is that the interview approach yielded a 72 percent return and the mail questionnaire, a 56 percent return. (These two percentages are both higher than the overall follow-up return of 53 percent for the total sample because in this instance cases for which no follow-up was attempted or the client could not be located were dropped from the base.) For discussion of the reasons for unsuccessful follow-up attempts, see pages 106 and 107.

A second aspect of effectiveness is the relative completeness of the information obtained. As was anticipated, the interview method again was more successful. On the interview schedules, an average of 90 percent of the evaluations needed for the change score were completed; on the mail questionnaires, 77 percent. Also, 22 percent of the mail questionnaires but only 9 percent of the interviews were unusable in the change score analysis because returns were incomplete.[9]

A third element in effectiveness, the quality of the response received, was more difficult to assess. Chart 73 reveals that lower client change scores were derived on the average from the mail questionnaires than from the interview schedules; this difference was not, however, statistically significant. When the actual change scores were compared with the predicted scores for the same cases, the client change scores computed from mail questionnaires were significantly below expectations, while those based on interviews were approximately at the expected level. The frankness of clients' write-in comments suggests that clients may feel freer to give negative responses on a mail questionnaire than when being interviewed by someone identified with the agency. For additional information on this last point, see footnote 27, section 7.

Response of local agencies to their follow-up experience

In general, the agencies that used the personal interview form of follow-up were pleased with that approach[10] and felt it to be the better method. They reported that the clients were cooperative and seemed appreciative of the agency's interest in their feelings about the service they had received. Few clients expressed any feeling that the interview was intrusive or a breach of confidentiality. Setting up the interview appointment was sometimes difficult and in many cases a telephone interview was substituted for a visit to the home. Final counts indicated that about half the interviews took place in the home; 30 percent on the phone; and 20 percent at the agency.

Agencies were divided in their opinion of the relative merits of trained versus untrained interviewers. They noted that trained interviewers, such as caseworkers, had the skills to obtain the needed information in a responsible way, but that their time was expensive. Untrained interviewers, on the other hand, required training and supervision but often compensated with enthusiasm for their lack of experience. Several agencies were particularly pleased with the use of board members as follow-up interviewers. They felt it was educational for the board members and increased their involvement with the agency. There were occasional complaints from agency staff about the length and detail of the follow-up schedules. Clients who came to the agency for a very specific direct service sometimes felt that certain parts of the schedule were not pertinent to their situation, but there were no complaints received from clients about detail or length. Perhaps complaints of this nature were expressed by not completing the questionnaire or the interview. There was little feedback from either agencies or clients specifically on the mail questionnaire form of follow-up—probably because this method involved agency staff to a much lesser extent and the reactions of the clients would not be known unless clients deliberately made them known, which seldom happened. There were differences of opinion among the agencies as to which form of follow-up was easier to administer.

In summary, the interview method proved to be more efficient than the mail questionnaire in terms of response rate and completeness of returns. The mail questionnaire, on the other hand, often yielded a greater feeling of vitality and directness than did the interview schedules. An agency planning its own client follow-up would have to weigh the relative merits of these several factors and determine which method was best for its own use.

In general, few problems or negative reactions were expressed by agencies with regard to the client follow-up portion of the census. On the contrary, many agencies reported that the experience had been a positive, informative one for them and had spurred them to initiate their own client follow-up for purposes of local evaluation. The findings appear to support the effectiveness and value of going directly to the client for evaluations of agency service.

Technical explanation of methods of analysis

Basically, the analysis of the census returns followed accepted procedures for descriptive statistics. In sections 8 and 9, certain additional procedures were introduced involving the use of multiple regression equations for computing predicted scores. These processes are described separately on page 120. Basic specifications applicable throughout the report are as follows:

Chart format

The chart format was chosen to provide the reader with a quick overview of the major findings. Because of the prohibitive cost, it was not feasible to publish in addition a full set of supporting tables. For this reason, key percentage figures have been given in the charts whenever feasible. Because of the large sample, actual case counts can usually be disregarded. In those occasional instances when the base used for percentages drops below fifty, the reader is alerted. Readers desiring further information on sample size can secure good approximations by referring to the counts released in the U.S.-Canada comparisons.[11]

Area and programs covered

All charts and tables, unless otherwise noted, cover the total U.S. sample, including cases served by specialized programs or departments. However, the reader should visualize the data as reflecting mainly the programs of family service departments and the regular programs of nondepartmentalized agencies since about 85 percent of the total sample consisted of such cases. Local agencies wishing to undertake comparisons with national data are cautioned that if a substantial proportion of clients in their samples were served through special programs, these cases should be omitted before comparisons are made with national figures.

Trend data

Since this study is to some extent a replication of an earlier census conducted in the spring of 1960,[12] ten-year trends have been computed whenever feasible. To assure comparability, these trend figures, except as otherwise noted, have been based on special analyses that eliminated for both years reports from any agency that did not participate in both studies. In addition, these trend comparisons omit adoption cases from the 1970 counts since cases of this type were not included in the 1960 study. As a result, the trend figures never agree exactly either with those for the total 1970 sample or with those published in 1960. These same-agency comparisons are based on a total of 485 cases in 1960 and a total of 2,832 cases in 1970. Because of the relatively small sample for 1960, trends quoted in percentage terms have usually been tested for statistical significance, using chi-square procedures. They can be considered not statistically significant unless so reported.[13]

Comparisons with the general population

The comparisons with the general population that are presented are believed justifiable because (1) participating agencies were widely distributed and included all regions; (2) almost all major metropolitan areas were represented; and (3) the bias in regional representation probably had little influence on the findings since regional differences themselves usually proved to be minor.[14] To improve comparability with figures for the general population, comparisons were confined to metropolitan areas when this was feasible. In a few instances, U.S. figures were also adjusted to the age composition of the agency sample (by the use of agency data as weights). In many situations, these refinements were not feasible because the necessary details for the general population were not available at that time.[15] Sources of all U.S. data are cited in the Notes.

Percentages and missing information

With minor exceptions, percentages have been based on the number of cases for which the specific item was reported. For maximum accuracy, percentages have not been artificially rounded to total 100 percent except when this was required for charting purposes.

Counts for any particular subject normally exclude cases for which that particular item of information was lacking. Usually these omissions represented less than 5 percent and almost always less than 10 percent of the total cases for which the appropriate schedule was available.

Significance tests

Tests of significance were applied selectively in relation to what was needed for the types of inferences being drawn. Normally, they were omitted in straight descriptive accounts and in comparisons with the total U.S. population. They were used more extensively when conclusions about trends or the relationship of one factor to another were in question.

Certain abbreviated methods of reporting have been adopted. For example, the word *significant* has been reserved throughout solely for its statistical meaning. Wherever this word is used, it can be taken to mean statistically significant at least at the .05 level or beyond on a two-tailed test. When the difference is reported as "highly significant," the significance level was at or below the .01 level. In most such instances, because of the very large sample, it was below the .001 level. In order not to unnecessarily complicate the text and footnotes, exact significance levels are seldom cited. In addition, when the level was of secondary importance only, the word *highly* was sometimes omitted even though this level of significance was reached. Therefore, some significance levels are understated. Except in sections 8 and 9, which are separately discussed, the procedures used were commonly t-tests or chi-square tests, usually with a correction for continuity. When the issue was whether the percentage of agreement was significantly above zero, Light's modified chi-square test (A_p) was used.[16]

Special scores

Six special scores were developed or adapted for this study: socioeconomic status index, change score, index of client involvement in seeking help, disagreement index, merged relationship ratings, and predicted score.[17] Only two of these scores require supporting information on sources and procedures beyond that given when they were first introduced—the socioeconomic status scores and the predicted scores. These explanations follow.

Socioeconomic status scores

A general description of these scores is given on page 31, together with a table illustrating the types of families representative of each category. The following supplementary details indicate more precisely the sources and procedures utilized.

As previously indicated, the socioeconomic status scores for each case were computed by adding the percentile rankings for the case, as measured in relation to the general population, on three correlates of socioeconomic status and then dividing by three.[18] The three correlates used were: education of the family head, total family income in 1969, and occupation of the chief breadwinner. The percentile scores used in these ratings were obtained as follows:

1. Educational scores were provided in unpublished form by Herman P. Miller, director, Population Division of the United States Bureau of the Census. They were based on the findings of the March 1970 sample population survey regarding the number of years of school completed by adults twenty-five and over.

2. Income scores were also provided in unpublished form by Miller and were derived from the same source.

3. Occupational scores were provided by Paul M. Siegel and Robert W. Hodge, also in unpublished form.[19] These scores were based on the findings of sample surveys they conducted, along with Peter H. Rossi, for the National Opinion Research Center in 1964 and 1965. Siegel and Hodge converted their findings in these two studies into occupational prestige scores for each of the occupational titles used by the U.S. Bureau of the Census in 1960. Using these same scores, they also ranked these occupations in deciles of roughly equal size, taking into account the number of employed persons in each occupation. For purposes of the present project, these deciles were converted into percentile ratings using the same methods and the same prestige scores and occupational frequencies as used by Siegel and Hodge. In addition, appropriate prestige scores were estimated for the new occupational titles added to the federal census procedures in 1970, using the Siegel-Hodge scores for related occupations as a guide. These percentile scores were then applied to the cases in the sample after they had first been coded according to the standard occupational coding procedures of the U.S. Bureau of the Census.[20]

The procedure used in the present study for scoring socioeconomic status was an adaptation of that used by the U.S. Bureau of the Census in its analysis of the 1960 population.[21] Staff were guided in this process by telephone consultation with Larry Sutter of the U.S. Bureau of the Census. Other than the updating of the percentile scores, the major change made was the substitution of occupational prestige scores based on the independent research of Hodge and Siegel for ratings of occupation based on the income and education findings for each occupation in the decennial census. This shift was considered advisable in order to provide independent ratings for occupation to replace the earlier ratings that were dependent on the other two components of the score. Since occupational status tends to be stable and to be closely associated with income and education, the substitution probably had only a minor effect on the final ratings.

A further problem concerned the naming of the categories, an undertaking approached reluctantly to facilitate the reader's interpretation of the charts. The labels were intended to parallel approximately those used in the 1960 FSAA census,[22] which in turn were patterned, insofar as feasible, on the boundaries designated in Hollingshead's two-factor index for Classes I through V.[23] In 1960 and again in 1970 the Class V category was subdivided into two parts—"upper lower" and "lower lower." Boundaries for all categories were estimated as follows: The FSAA census returns for 1960 had already been coded by two different processes—a modified version of Hollingshead's two-factor index and an approximation of the procedures used by the U.S. Bureau of the Census in 1960 for their socioeconomic status score. These two scores were cross-tabulated so that it could be determined what scores of the latter type were roughly equivalent to the categories in Hollingshead's system. Boundaries were then selected to reflect the central tendencies of each of these categories in terms of the alternate scoring procedure. No claim is made that the current categories are in any sense closely equivalent to those of Hollingshead since the necessary adaptations and translations resulted both in unknown changes and in some minor upgrading of selected cases.

Predicted change scores
In addition to the actual change scores (described on page 101), section 9 utilizes predicted change scores. While these were also described earlier in nontechnical terms (see page 120), an expanded and more

technical version of these procedures is provided here.

As was explained earlier, these scores were designed, insofar as feasible, to control statistically for the influence of client characteristics and other selected factors on the change scores so that the reader would be able to assess, without interference from these factors, the effects on outcomes of the various service inputs. These scores were designed as a statistical substitute for random assignment of cases to various treatment procedures and types of counselors since it was not feasible in a nationwide study to ask local agencies to assign cases on the basis of national research requirements. The alternate procedure used in this project to study the impact of service copes with the problem by letting the case take its natural course, noting the client and service characteristics, and then assessing the results for that case against a computed score that reflects normal expectations for this case based on what is known about the association between the characteristics of that case and outcome scores in general.

The procedures adopted involved the use of multiple regression prediction equations. The resulting predictions represent the most probable value for the two types of change scores, taking into account the average experience of the follow-up group for all cases having the same characteristics on specified dimensions as the case for which the prediction was made. It is recognized that adoption of this approach to prediction involved acceptance of certain statistical compromises because many of the variables available were not based on an equal-interval measurement scale with a zero point. For support for the

use of ordinal and nominal variables in multiple regression analyses, the reader is referred to the writing of Jacob Cohen[24] and Sanford Labovitz.[25]

The steps through which the actual predictions were secured were as follows:

1. Selected client and service characteristics were first reviewed for their suitability for correlational analysis. Some were already inherently measurement data (e.g., age of family head). Most others presented a natural ordinal or rank order (e.g., severity, level of improvement predicted, socioeconomic status scores, and the like). The difficulty of the problem selected as the principal focus of service was rank-ordered on the basis of the relative proportion of cases which counselors reported improved on that specific problem. Nominal data, such as whether or not counseling was provided, were coded according to the approach suggested by Cohen.[26]

2. Since the statistical procedures utilized involve an underlying linearity assumption, the variables used in the predictions were next tested for linearity. All except four out of the fifteen utilized proved to be significantly linear at the .05 level or below for both the dependent variables—change scores based on counselors' ratings and change scores based on clients' ratings. The other four variables were significantly linear (at the .05 level or below) for one of the dependent variables but not for the other.[27] To maintain comparable prediction procedures for scores derived from counselors' and clients' judgments, no transformations were attempted. It is recognized that the linearity constraint involved in the method makes for imperfect predictions whenever there are patterned departures from linearity, such as occurred with age of family head and

size of family. Because such variables were in the minority and were utilized simultaneously with many others in computing procedures and because the deviations from linearity were primarily at the upper extreme, the predicted scores are not believed to have been seriously affected by the linearity constraint.

3. The next step involved two multiple regression analyses, each involving eleven client characteristics as independent variables and one of the two change scores as the dependent variable.[28] All analyses were limited to the 1,606 cases for which both change scores were available. The standardized regression coefficients resulting from this first step are cited in chart 83. The predicted scores, residuals, and standardized residuals that also resulted were preserved and entered as data on one of the computer tapes for the project. These residuals, representing the difference between actual and predicted scores, can be thought of as new change scores controlled for the eleven client characteristics.

4. The next step was to analyze the relationship of those residuals to the number of interviews (chart 84).

5. The process described in steps 3 and 4 above was then repeated adding number of interviews to the list of independent variables used in the prediction process. Again the predicted scores and the residuals were preserved for use as data for examining the relation of the change scores to the number of different services, the counselor-client relationship, and disagreement, with client characteristics controlled.

6. The process was then repeated a third time with these three additional variables added in as independent variables. The third set of predicted scores[29] and the residuals

that resulted were again saved on the tape and used to examine the relation of other service inputs to change scores.

7. To secure averages that could be shown graphically and to permit further refinements in the analysis and additional significance tests, the residuals obtained from these regression analyses were used as data[30] to examine the influence of various aspects of treatment. The methodology involved one-way analysis of variance, t-tests, and matched-t-tests as outlined for computer use in the *Data-Text Primer,*[31] using in each instance *not* the actual scores but the residuals as the basic data. In addition, two- and three-way analysis of variance procedures were used to take into account simultaneously the change scores from the two types of respondents and other important dimensions. This analysis utilized the repeated measure design as outlined in the *Data-Text Primer* for nonorthogonal factorial designs, using the method of unweighted means.[32] Because of the approximations involved, use of this method was limited, with very minor exceptions, to situations where case counts in individual cells exceeded fifty. Analyses of this repeat-measure type were based on the standardized residuals in order to reduce to comparable units the two types of residuals based on different raters and having different means and standard deviations.

8. The results of these various analyses are portrayed in the charts in section 9, not in terms of residuals, but in terms of actual and predicted mean scores. The predicted and actual scores were charted rather than the residuals because they were considered more easily understood by the reader unaccustomed to statistics. This method of charting has the additional advantage of enabling the

reader to examine within the same chart both the original findings for each service characteristic and the fluctuations from group to group in the levels of the predicted lines which indicate variations in the expected levels for the types of cases involved. Those desiring mean residual figures can compute them simply by subtracting the predicted from the actual means cited at the bottom of each chart.

9. The final step was to extend the regression analysis to include all twenty-six of the client and treatment variables simultaneously. The standardized regression coefficients resulting from this process are reported in chart 97 insofar as they involve treatment variables. In general, they confirmed the findings of the analysis of variance applied to the residuals. The zero-order correlations of all twenty-six independent variables with the two change score measures are given in Appendix table 1.

The procedures outlined in steps one through nine were adopted initially because of the special circumstances and constraints inherent in a large, nationally administered study. Nevertheless, the use of predicted scores and residuals as data for further analysis proved to have distinct advantages. It made it possible (1) to assess outcomes with available client characteristics controlled in spite of nonrandom initial case assignments; (2) to accommodate to a heterogenous sample by subclassification into more homogeneous subgroups, for each of which separate norms could be computed; and (3) to draw conclusions about the contributions of service by examining the deviations from predicted outcomes for several minimum service comparison groups that emerged naturally from available data (see charts 84, 85, 86, and 96).

In addition, it introduced a useful element of flexibility into the analysis in that the method made it possible to delay final selection of the predictors of the dependent variables (from among those for which data were available) until their relative predictive power could be tested and to examine in relation to outcomes certain additional service factors for which data were collected but which were not initially seen as warranting close study in this context.

This approach would seem to have potential utility in other research projects. For example, it would make it possible to compare outcomes with various treatment procedures and client groups without the need to introduce research constraints that might interfere with normal service patterns and with individualized practice decisions intended to maximize treatment effectiveness. It is recognized, however, that the approach is probably more appropriate when large samples are to be analyzed with the assistance of advanced computer facilities. It is also recognized that it requires a sensitive outcome measure, a broad-based sample for the computation of norms, and the advance identification, recording, and reporting of all factors that are to be considered for use in the computation of the predicted scores.

See pages 168 and 169 for tables 1 and 2.

Table 1. Correlations between selected client and service characteristics and number of interviews, relationship ratings, and change scores

Client characteristics	Zero-order correlations[a]				Service characteristics	Zero-order correlations[a]			
	Number of interviews	Counselor-client relationship	Change scores from Counselors' reports	Clients' reports		Number of interviews	Counselor-client relationship	Change scores from Counselors' reports	Clients' reports
Counselor's initial prediction of outcome	.11***	.16***	.21***	.11***	Counselor-client relationship	.17***	1.00	.49***	.30***
Degree of client involvement in seeking service	.08***	.04	.15***	.15***	Extent of counselor-client disagreement	−.08***	−.42***	−.35***	−.25***
Difficulty of type of problem receiving most service	.03	.11***	.10***	.07**	Number of family members seen	.30***	.01	.16***	.05
Severity of total problem situation	.01	−.13***	−.13***	−.13**	Whether fees were charged	.07**	−.01	.17***	.10***
Influence of factors other than agency service	b	−.03	.04	.21***	Total number of interviews	1.00	.15***	.27***	.15***
Race of client	.04	−.03	.08***	.04	Whether any counseling was provided	.09***	−.04	.11***	.08***
Size of family	.07**	.01	−.05	−.03	Number of different services provided	.31***	.11***	.17***	.04
Number of neighborhood or community problems	.03	−.03	−.07**	−.11***	Whether counselor and principal client were of same sex	.02	.06*	.07**	.03
Number of problems presented at intake	.09***	−.07**	−.05	−.07**	Whether assignment was to planned short-term service	−.07**	.02	.05*	.05
Socioeconomic status	b	−.04	.05*	.07**	Whether more than one counselor was involved	.22***	−.05*	.06*	.05
Age of family head	−.03	.05	−.04	−.09***	Whether on waiting list and for how long	.09***	−.07**	−.02	−.02

[a]All correlations based only on cases with change scores from both counselors' and clients' reports. The asterisks accompanying the correlations indicate the level of statistical significance as follows: *** = significant at the .001 level; ** = significant at the .01 level; * = significant at the .05 level; no asterisk indicates that the correlation is not statistically significant.
[b]Slight negative correlation below .005.

Table 2. Component change scores by number of interviews and type of service provided[a]

	Number of interviews					Type of service provided		
Change score component	One	Two to five	Six to nine	Ten to nineteen	Twenty or more	Direct service only	Counseling plus direct service	Counseling only
	(N=447)	(N=571)	(N=246)	(N=175)	(N=167)	(N=61)	(N=460)	(N=1,085)
Counselors' evaluations:[b]								
Specific problems	3.8	5.3	6.5	7.5	7.9	5.5	5.5	5.6
Problem coping	3.9	5.7	6.8	7.8	8.3	3.6	6.3	5.8
Family relationships	1.9	3.6	5.2	5.8	6.6	0.8	3.9	4.2
Change in family members	2.6	3.8	4.8	5.0	5.4	1.7	4.0	4.0
Clients' evaluations:[b]								
Specific problems	4.4	4.8	5.6	6.1	6.5	4.5	4.5	5.4
Problem coping	5.2	5.7	6.1	7.0	7.6	4.7	5.8	6.2
Family relationships	4.1	4.2	4.8	5.5	6.6	2.4	4.4	4.9
Change in family members	3.9	4.2	4.8	5.6	5.8	2.6	4.1	4.8

[a]These component scores were computed in the same manner as were the overall change scores described on page 101. Basically, within each component area, the "worse" evaluations were subtracted from the "better" evaluations and the result was divided by the total number of items evaluated and multiplied by ten. The range of possible scores for each component area, as for the overall change scores, is −10 to +10. The overall change score for the counselor and for the client is not the average of the four component change scores, but is a computation based on all of the individual evaluations.
[b]The counselors' and clients' scores are based on the same cases. There is some variation in the number of cases on which each component score is based, because component scores could be computed only when the section was answered. The N's cited refer to the cases on which the score for specific problems was based. Problem coping and change in family members were based on slightly fewer cases. The family relationship component lost more cases, but still was generally within 5 to 10 percent of the number of cases shown. The only severe loss was for the family relationship score for the cases receiving direct service only, which was based on twenty-three cases or about 38 percent of the N cited.

FAMILY SERVICE STUDY

Since you recently have been to a family service agency, we are eager to know whether the service you received from this agency was helpful or not. Your opinions are important to us. Please answer all questions even if you have to give your best guess. If either you or your family have been to this same agency before this last contact, please tell us only about your most recent period of service.

1. Did you or your family have problems you wanted the agency to help you with? _____ Yes _____ No

   If YES, what was the most important problem you wanted their help with?

   _____

   If NO, what was the purpose of your contact with the agency?

   _____

HOW DID THE AGENCY TRY TO HELP YOU? FOR EXAMPLE--

2. Did they counsel you or talk with you about any problems?

   _____ Yes _____ No

   If YES, was this helpful?

   Yes→ ⌐ Very helpful?
        └ Somewhat helpful?
   _____ No
   _____ Don't know

3. Did the agency try to help you in any other way, such as giving you emergency money, helping you find better housing, helping you place or adopt a child, providing homemaker service, special care for a member of your family, tutoring, legal help, educational meetings, etc.?

   _____ Yes _____ No

   If YES, what was the service?

   _____

4. Did they suggest some other place where you might go for help?

   _____ Yes _____ No

   If YES, where?

   _____

   Did you go?

   Yes→ ⌐ Very helpful?
        └ Somewhat helpful?
   _____ No
   _____ Don't know

   Was it helpful?

   Yes→ _____ Did it help? _____ Yes _____ Don't know yet
   _____ No
   _____ Not yet, but still planning to go

5. Was there any kind of service or help you expected from the agency that you didn't get?

   _____ Yes _____ No

   If YES, what was it?

   _____

6. In addition to anything you have already mentioned, was there any other kind of help you needed that the agency did not provide or help you arrange?

   _____ Yes _____ No

   If YES, what was it?

   _____

7. In general, how satisfied were you with the way you and your counselor got along with each other?

   _____ Very satisfied
   _____ Satisfied
   _____ No particular feelings one way or the other
   _____ Not satisfied
   *

   *If you were not satisfied, what was the difficulty?

   _____

8. Was there anything about the agency or its program or policies that made problems for you or your family, such as fees, having to wait, distance to agency, appointment hours, change to new counselor, etc.?

   _____ Yes _____ No

   If YES, what was it?

   _____

9. Why did you stop going to the agency?

   _____

10. Would you consider going back to this agency again if you needed help in the future?

   _____ Yes _____ No

   If NO, why not?

   _____

The questions on this page ask about problems that you and your family had when you came to the agency and whether these problems are now BETTER, the SAME, or WORSE. If you do not live with your family, there may be some items that won't apply to you, perhaps "Problems between husband and wife" or "Raising children...," etc. Just skip those.

11. When you first came to the agency did you or any other members of your family have any of the following problems? (Read list and check all that were a problem for anyone in your family.)

12. For each problem you checked in Question 11, please put a check mark in one of the three columns below to indicate whether that problem is now BETTER, the SAME, or WORSE compared with when you first came to the agency. The change could be either in the problem itself, or in the way you or your family handle it now, or in how easy or hard it is to live with.

TYPE OF PROBLEM	BETTER	SAME	WORSE
Problems between husband and wife	—	—	—
Problems between parents and children (child under 21)	—	—	—
Problems between other family members . . . . (Who?			
Raising children, taking care of their needs, training, discipline, etc. . . .			
Taking care of house, meals, or family health matters.	—	—	—
Managing money, budgeting, or credit.	—	—	—
Problems in social contacts or use of leisure time	—	—	—
Not enough money for basic family needs . . .			
Being unemployed or in a poor job	—	—	—
Housing problems.	—	—	—
Unwed parenthood.	—	—	—
Legal problems (such as divorce, custody, rent, bills, etc., not involving crime).	—	—	—
Doing poorly at work or having trouble holding a job.			
Doing poorly or misbehaving in school	—	—	—
Drinking too much	—	—	—
Taking drugs.	—	—	—
Getting in trouble with the law	—	—	—
Trouble getting along with others	—	—	—
Trouble handling emotions or behavior	—	—	—
Health problems, physical illness, or handicap.	—	—	—
Need for physical care (for aged, child, sick, etc.).	—	—	—
Need for protective services (for aged, child, etc.).	—	—	—
Mental illness.	—	—	—
Mental retardation.	—	—	—
Other problem . . . . (What?	—	—	—

☐ NO PROBLEMS

CONTINUE TO QUESTION 12 ON RIGHT SIDE OF THIS SAME PAGE. ➜

3

13. In addition to the kinds of help we have been asking about, family agencies are also concerned with neighborhood and community conditions which cause problems for families. For this reason we would like to know whether any of the following were a serious problem for you or your family when you came to the agency. (Check all that were a problem.)

___ Poor job opportunities
___ Poor or no job training opportunities
___ Poor schools
___ Rundown neighborhood
___ Unsafe neighborhood
___ Heavy drug use in area

___ Poor police protection
___ Unfair credit practices
___ Poor health resources
___ No day care centers for children
___ No home care services for aged or sick
___ Inadequate legal help
___ Discrimination (racial, ethnic, religious, etc.)
___ Poor recreational opportunities
___ Poor or costly transportation
___ Other conditions (What? _____)

[ ] NO COMMUNITY SITUATIONS WERE A SERIOUS PROBLEM FOR OUR FAMILY (Skip to Question 14.)

Do you know of any way the agency tried to help with any of these problems? ___ Yes ___ No

If YES: How?

Was what they did helpful to you and your family? ___ Yes ___ No ___ Don't know

14. People who have been to family agencies sometimes find that, regardless of what they came about, there are changes in how the members of the family get along together. Would you say that since you started at the agency there has been any change for the better or for the worse in the way the members of your family-- (Check one column for each item.)

| If you have no family nearby, answer in terms of your other relationships. |

	BETTER	SAME	WORSE	NOT A PROBLEM
Talk over problems, listen to each other, share feelings. . .	___	___	___	___
Handle arguments and work out differences	___	___	___	___
Accept and help each other, pay attention to each other's needs.	___	___	___	___
Feel toward each other (how close and comfortable, how you enjoy each other).	___	___	___	___
How husband and wife get along sexually (Answer only if you are the husband or wife.). . .	___	___	___	___
Get along in other ways . . . . . . (How? _____)	___	___	___	___

15. When people work on their problems at a family agency, they sometimes find that there is a change in how they feel about those problems and the way they handle them. If you have discussed any problems with the agency, would you say that you personally have noticed since then any change for the better or worse in--

	BETTER	SAME	WORSE
The way you feel about your problems (how worried, overwhelmed, angry, confused, guilty, etc.).	___	___	___
The way you understand your problems (what they are and who or what contributes to them)	___	___	___
The kinds of ideas you have on what to do about your problems (what should or should not be tried).	___	___	___
The way you work with others in handling problems (talking things over instead of fighting or avoiding, etc.).	___	___	___

Since coming to the agency, have you actually--

Made any decisions on what to do about your problems? ___ Yes ___ No

Taken any specific action on your problems? * ___ Yes ___ No

*If you have taken some action, did this turn out to--

___ help with your problem
___ make no difference
___ make things worse
___ can't tell yet

16. Which members of your family (including yourself) have changed for the better (even slightly) in behavior, attitudes, feelings, or ability to handle problems since you first went to the agency? (Consider all members of your family, whether they were seen at the agency or not.)

List all those who have changed for the better. Do not use their names. Instead write "myself," "husband," "son," "daughter," "mother-in-law," etc.

1. _____
2. _____
3. _____
4. _____

☐ NO ONE CHANGED FOR THE BETTER

Which changed for the worse in behavior, attitudes, feelings, or ability to handle problems?

1. _____
2. _____
3. _____
4. _____

☐ NO ONE CHANGED FOR THE WORSE

17. Considering all members of your family and all problems you discussed with your counselor, how would you say things are now compared with when you first went to the agency?

____ Much better
____ Somewhat better
____ Unchanged
* ____ Somewhat worse
* ____ Much worse
* ____ Better in some ways but worse in others

*If things got worse, please describe what happened:
_____
_____
_____
_____

☐ NO PROBLEMS DISCUSSED

Do you think your husband or wife (if any) or others in your family would agree with your report of how things have changed or not changed?

____ Yes
* ____ No
* ____ Some would, some wouldn't
____ Don't know
____ Live alone

*If anyone would NOT agree, what would the disagreement be about?
_____
_____

18. If you feel there have been any changes in any members of your family or in any problem situations since you first went to the agency, what do you think was the main reason for the changes you reported?
_____
_____
_____

19. How do you feel the service provided by the agency influenced the changes you have reported?

____ Helped a great deal
____ Helped some
____ Made no difference
____ Made things worse

20. Did anything not related to the agency influence the changes you have reported?

____ Yes ____ No

If YES, what was it? _____
_____

Did this make things better or worse for you and your family?

____ Better ____ Worse

21. Who filled out this questionnaire?

____ Husband or father
____ Wife or mother
____ Other (Who? _____)

Thank you very much for your help. Your answers will be studied carefully along with many others in order to continue to improve services to families and individuals.

Please make sure you have answered all the questions and mail questionnaire in the stamped, self-addressed envelope that came with it. (If you have misplaced this envelope, mail to: Research Department, Family Service Association of America, 44 East 23rd Street, New York, N. Y. 10010.)

FORM NO. 3400-22

NOTES

Notes to Introduction: the findings in perspective

1. For a discussion of some of the issues facing the field at that time, see Scott Briar, "The Casework Predicament," *Social Work,* 13 (January 1968): 5-11; also Scott Briar, "The Current Crisis in Social Casework," in *Social Work Practice, 1967,* Selected Papers, 94th Annual Forum, National Conference of Social Welfare, Dallas, Texas, May 25-26, 1967 (New York: Columbia University Press, 1967), pp. 19-33.

2. Three listings of special local agency projects have been issued by the library staff of the Family Service Association of America. See "A Catalog of Selected Special Service Projects of FSAA Member Agencies," issues for 1970, 1972, and 1973, plus the Supplement issued in 1971 (mimeographed). The full range of these special projects is not reflected in the census findings because many projects involved activities not covered in the present study and others involved types of contact too brief to qualify for inclusion as cases.

3. Dorothy Fahs Beck, *Patterns in Use of Family Agency Service* (New York: Family Service Association of America, 1962).

4. "FSAA 1970 Census Statistics for Canada with Comparative Data for United States," mimeographed (New York: Family Service Association of America, 1972).

5. Richard A. Cloward, "Social Class and Private Social Agencies," in *Education for Social Work,* Proceedings of the Eleventh Annual Program Meeting, Council on Social Work Education, Boston, Massachusetts, January 23-26, 1963 (New York: Council on Social Work Education, 1963), pp. 123, 126.

6. Herman Levin, "The Future of Voluntary Family and Children's Social Work: A Historical View," *Social Service Review,* 38 (June 1964): 172-73.

7. Only 0.3 percent of the family heads in the 1970 census sample were reported as living together as married although not legally married. Although this status was undoubtedly underreported, there is little reason to doubt that this group is underrepresented in agency caseloads. Probably, in most cases, it is the parents of the young people following these life-styles who apply to family agencies, not their children.

8. See Richard A. Cloward and Irwin Epstein, "Private Social Welfare's Disengagement from the Poor: The Case of Family Adjustment Agencies," in Mayer N. Zald, *Social Welfare Institutions: A Sociological Reader* (New York: John Wiley & Sons, 1965), pp. 623-44.

9. For an explanation of the recommended approach of family agencies to advocacy services, see *Family Advocacy: A Manual for Action,* ed. Ellen Manser (New York: Family Service Association of America, 1973).

10. Helen Harris Perlman's definition of casework reflects the concept of casework that was basic to the change score. She wrote: "This help, casework, is a process focused on the person's felt need and is guided by assessments of his motivations, capacities, and resources. Its purpose is to enable a person (or family) suffering from a general social problem or a uniquely personal one to suffer less, to cope better, and, as a result, to feel able to deal with his tasks and relationships with increased confidence, steadiness, and satisfaction." Helen Harris Perlman, "Once More, With Feeling," in Edward F. Mullen, James R. Dumpson, and Associates, *Evaluation of Social Intervention* (San Francisco: Jossey-Bass Inc., 1972), p. 196.

11. The nature of these changes was traced in detail in a small project that preceded the present study. See Joel G. Sacks, Panke M. Bradley, and Dorothy Fahs Beck, *Clients' Progress within Five Interviews: An Exploratory Study Comparing Workers' and Clients' Views* (New York: Family Service Association of America, 1970).

12. The correlation between the two measures was +.74 for counselors' reports and +.70 for clients' reports.

13. The relevant charts are numbered 84, 85, 86, 89, 90, and 96.

14. See page 120 and the Appendix for a further explanation of the predicted scores.

15. Some might argue that another possible factor is a placebo effect, simply from receiving some attention from the agency, similar to the improvement reported in medical experiments from inert medication; however, it is unlikely that this effect would be correlated with the amount of service.

16. Geismar is one of the few social work researchers who has examined the effect of the counselor on outcomes. In reporting his findings, he concluded: "In a detailed analysis of service input, the social worker emerges as a more important outcome variable than the substantial number of treatment resources and intervention patterns examined. The relatively more successful worker was found to have been supportive rather than directive, to have shown accelerated efforts toward providing information and coordinated community services, and to have elicited greater client participation in treatment." Ludwig L. Geismar, Bruce Lagay, Isabel Wolock, Ursula C. Gerhart, and Harriet Fink, *Early Supports for Family Life: A Social Work Experiment* (Metuchen, N. J.: Scarecrow Press Inc., 1972), p. 170. For a more general discussion of the role of the counselor in outcomes, see Charles B. Truax and Robert R. Carkhuff, *Toward Effective Counseling and Psychotherapy: Training and Practice* (Chicago: Aldine Publishing Company, 1967).

17. See page 105 for a discussion of the sources of difference in outcome ratings as identified from the data for the present study.

18. The most conspicuous differences were found for treatment modality, planned short-term treatment, and payment of fees.

19. What is suggested here is, first, independent reporting by counselor and client on the same set of questions, followed—with the consent of both parties—by a face-to-face discussion between them to ascertain the reason for the differences evident and which were real and which simply a matter of definition or lack of information.

20. To a certain extent this process has already begun. Brenda J. S. Wattie, of the Family Service Centre of Ottawa, Canada, utilized in her study of planned, short-term service both the family relationship items in the FSAA client follow-up questionnaire and also an independent before-and-after Q-sort test of family concepts. She found a statistically significant correlation between total scores from her follow-up questionnaire and the Q-sort ratings (personal correspondence with the author).

21. The problem is how, without denying service, to find a group with equivalent motivation and crisis status that also has problems of a type and severity similar to those of regular clients. Probably the best possibility is to look for a situation in which an agency is forced to close intake for a period for reasons beyond its control. If, given such a situation, a list could be kept of persons telephoning for appointments, these persons could be followed-up when service was resumed and queried at that time about what had happened in the interim.

22. Steven Paul Segal, "Research on the Outcome of Social Work Therapeutic Interventions: A Review of the Literature," *Journal of Health and Social Behavior,* 13 (March 1972): 3-17.

23. Ibid., p. 8.

24. Among the studies that have included a follow-up assessment by clients themselves are: Geismar et al., *Early Supports for Family Life;* Robert G. Ballard and Emily H. Mudd, "Some Sources of Difference between Client and Agency Evaluation of Effectiveness of Counseling," *Social Casework,* 39 (January 1958): 30-35; Leonard S. Kogan, *A Study of Short-Term Cases at the Community Service Society of New York* (New York: Community Service Society, 1957); Leonard S. Kogan, J. McVicker Hunt, and Phyllis F. Bartelme, *A Follow-Up Study of the Results of Social Casework* (New York: Family Service Association of America, 1953); William J. Reid and Ann W. Shyne, *Brief and*

Extended Casework (New York: Columbia University Press, 1969); Ann W. Shyne, *A Study of the Youth Bureau of the Community Service Society* (New York: Community Service Society, 1959); Elizabeth Most, "Measuring Change in Marital Satisfaction," *Social Work,* 9 (July 1964): 64-70; Natalie Siegel, "A Follow-Up Study of Former Clients: An Example of Practitioner-Directed Research," *Social Casework,* 46 (June 1965): 345-51; and Sacks, Bradley, and Beck, *Clients' Progress within Five Interviews.*

25. Geismar et al., *Early Supports for Family Life,* pp. 222-23.

26. Segal, "Research on the Outcome of Social Work Therapeutic Interventions," p. 7. For the original Eysenck reference, see Hans J. Eysenck, "The Effects of Psychotherapy: An Evaluation," *Journal of Consulting Psychology,* 16 (October 1952): 319-24. Eysenck used as base line figures the discharge rate for institutionalized neurotics and the rate of termination of disability claims from policyholders treated by general practitioners for inability to work because of psychoneurosis. Both measures seem far removed from casework practice.

27. Julian Meltzoff and Melvin Kornreich, *Research in Psychotherapy* (New York: Atherton Press, 1970), p. 71.

28. Ibid., p. 174.

29. Ibid., p. 177.

30. A number of summaries of these controlled studies have appeared. See Alan L. Grey and Helen E. Dermody, "Reports of Casework Failure," *Social Casework,* 53 (November 1972): 534-43; Joel Fischer, "Is Casework Effective? A Review," *Social Work,* 18 (January 1973): 5-20; Geismar, *Early Supports for Family Life,* pp. 170-90; and Edward J. Mullen and James R. Dumpson, "Is Social Work on the Wrong Track?" and Ludwig L. Geismar, "Thirteen Evaluative Studies," both in Edward J. Mullen, James R. Dumpson, and Associates, *Evaluation of Social Intervention,* pp. 1-14, 15-38. For a commentary in this same area, see Scott Briar, "Effective Social Work Intervention in Direct Practice: Implications for Education," in Scott Briar, William B. Cannon, Leon H. Ginsberg, Stephen Horn, and Rosemary C. Sarri, *Facing the Challenge,* Plenary Session Papers from the 19th Annual Program Meeting of the Council on Social Work Education (New York: Council on Social Work Education, 1973), pp. 17-30.

31. Fischer, "Is Casework Effective? A Review," pp. 14-18.

32. See charts 79, 80, 81, and 83 and accompanying comment.

33. See chart 77 and accompanying comment.

34. An illustration of this problem is also available from the present study. Community leaders tend to see "saving the marriage" as a possible "hard data" measure for marital counseling. However, when this measure was tested in the present study against the counselors' judgments about who would benefit, it was found that for more than one-fourth of the marital cases, this goal would have been against the best interests of all family members. For additional cases it would have been against the interests of some but not all family members. For most of the rest, no breakup was planned when they came to the agency.

35. Geismar, *Early Supports for Family Life,* p. 186.

36. Ibid., pp. 54-55, 224. In commenting on the difference between the high proportion of improvement reports received from clients through his follow-up questionnaire and the much lesser change reported on his family functioning Profile, Geismar states: "The reader's attention is called to the fact that fairly substantial changes would have had to occur for a rating of a Profile to be lowered or raised, whereas relatively minor alterations in the functioning of the family might have resulted in the client or worker responding 'better' or 'worse,' as the case may be. Furthermore, it was not possible, using the Profile mode of measurement, for a client rated as adequate throughout the study to show positive movement, yet adequacy is not equated to functioning which is completely problem-free." (p. 224)

37. On the Movement Scale developed by the Community Service Society and used in some of these studies, the average change is less than one point. See J. McV. Hunt, Margaret Blenkner, and Leonard S. Kogan, *Testing Results in Social Casework: A Field Test of the Movement Scale* (New York: Family Service Association of America, 1950). On the Geismar scale used in many of the studies, the average change in the ratings of component areas is less than half a point. See Ludwig L. Geismar and Beverly Ayres, *Patterns of Change in Problem Families: A Study of the Social Functioning and Movement of 150 Families Served by the Family Centered Project* (St. Paul: Family Centered Project, Greater St. Paul Community Chest and Councils, 1959). Geismar's definitions of the different levels of family functioning by subareas are given in Ludwig L. Geismar, *Family and Community Functioning: A Manual of Measurement for Social Work Practice and Policy* Metuchin, N.J.: Scarecrow Press, Inc., 1971). For an explanation of the Movement Scale and definitions of the different levels of movement, see J. McV. Hunt and Leonard S. Kogan, *Measuring Results in Social Casework: A Manual on Judging Movement,* rev. ed. (New York: Family Service Association of America, 1952).

38. Because of the heavy influence of intervening developments, some investigators have questioned the use of long-term follow-ups for evaluation. For example, Philip R. A. May and his associates have concluded that "controlled studies are doomed to depreciate progressively with the passage of time from the end of the controlled treatment period with much of their discriminating power being eroded by contamination. . . . It is inevitable that the longer the follow-up, the more all treatments approximate the same end result. . . . On the other hand, short-term, immediate outcome, now viewed somewhat as second best, would seem to be a legitimate field of interest, susceptible to study with a reasonable degree of accuracy." See Philip R. A. May, A. Hussain Tuma, and Wesley Kraude, "Community Follow-Up of Treatment of Schizophrenia—Issues and Problems," *American Journal of Orthopsychiatry,* 35 (July 1965): 762. Follow-up in the present study followed the short-term model. The average duration of treatment was 2.8 months and the average interval before follow-up contact was an additional three months.

39. This is the approach used by Fischer in "Is Casework Effective? A Review," p. 6.

40. For example, two studies with control groups known to the authors that showed favorable results were not included in any of these reviews: Elizabeth Most, "Measuring Change in Marital Satisfaction," *Social Work,* 9 (July 1964): 64-70, and Brenda J. S. Wattie, "A Search for Criteria for the Use of Planned Short-Term Treatment with Family Service Agency Clients—An Exercise in Service Evaluation," mimeographed (Ottawa, Canada: Family Service Centre of Ottawa, 1972). Presumably, they were not included either because they were not known to the authors or because the control groups utilized were not considered adequate. These stringent criteria were set up without due recognition either of feasibility problems or of the bias in sample selection inherent in this requirement. After a review of psychotherapy research, Hans H. Strupp and Allen E. Bergin concluded that "it now seems clear that a true no-therapy control group is essentially impossible to set up and implement except in a carefully restricted institutional setting." See Hans H. Strupp and Allen E. Bergin, "Some Empirical and Conceptual Bases for Coordinated Research in Psychotherapy: A Critical Review of Issues, Trends, and Evidence," *International Journal of Psychiatry,* 7 (February 1969): 18-90.

41. Fischer, "Is Casework Effective? A Review," p. 14. Segal, in "Research on the Outcome of Social Work Therapeutic Interventions: A Review of the Literature," also concludes: "The evidence with respect to the effectiveness of social work therapeutic intervention remains equivocal. The trends in the data, however, point strongly in the negative direction." (p. 13).

Notes to section 1

1. U.S. figures for chart 1 from U.S. Bureau of the Census, *Current Population Reports,* Series P-20, No. 218, "Household and Family Characteristics: March 1970" (Washington, D.C.: U.S. Government Printing Office, 1971), pp. 46, 73.

2. 1960 U.S. figure from U.S. Bureau of the Census, *Current Population Reports,* Series P-20, No. 106, "Household and Family Characteristics: March 1960" (Washington, D.C.: U.S. Government Printing Office, 1961), p. 14. 1970 U.S. figure from same source as footnote 1. 1960 FSAA figures from "What Kinds of Families Come to Family Service Agencies?" *Family Service Highlights,* 22 (April 1961): 94. Agency figures here are not limited to agencies participating in both the 1960 and 1970 census.

3. The figures cited here are based on the same sources as those charted but differ for both the U.S. population and agencies because these figures include families headed by a person sixty-five or over with one child still living in the same household. In the chart, those families are included in the figures by age of oldest child at home. Agency figures are not limited to agencies participating in both the 1960 and 1970 census.

4. Souces for U.S. data in table as follows: Family size and percentage of doubled-up families (called subfamilies in U.S. census, defined as families related to, but not containing, the head of the household, such as a son and daughter-in-law) from U.S. Bureau of the Census, *Census of Population: 1970,* "General Social and Economic Characteristics," Final Report PC(1)-C1, United States Summary, (Washington, D.C.: U.S. Government Printing Office, 1972), pp. 1-400, 1-388. U.S. data for number of own children and percentage of families with children from U.S. Bureau of the Census, *Census of Population: 1970,* "General Population Characteristics," Final Report PC(1)-B1, United States Summary, (Washington, D.C.: U.S. Government Printing Office, 1972), p. 1-278. Another perspective on the opportunities for prevention is provided by the discrepancy between agency clients and the U.S. population in the average number of children under six per 1,000 women of childbearing age (fifteen–forty-four): 515 children for agency clients and 315 for U.S. population. (Sources for U.S. data for children from Bureau of the Census, *Census of Population: 1970,* "General Social and Economic Characteristics," p. 1-263; U.S. data for women from "General Population Characteristics," p. 1-278.)

5. U.S. figures for this chart from Bureau of the Census, *Census of Population: 1970,* "General Population Characteristics," p. 1-278.

6. 1960 U.S. figures from U.S. Bureau of the Census, *U.S. Census of Population: 1960,* "Detailed Characteristics. United States Summary," Final Report PC(1)-1D (Washington, D.C.: U.S. Government Printing Office, 1963), p. 1-463. 1960 and 1970 agency figures from Dorothy Fahs Beck and Mary Ann Jones, *Family Agency Clients: Who Are They? What Do They Want? What Do They Get? A Visual and Verbal Interim Report on the Early Findings of the 1970 FSAA Census* (New York: Family Service Association of America, 1972), chart 1. Agency figures are limited to agencies participating in both the 1960 and 1970 census.

7. 1970 U.S. figures from Bureau of the Census, *Census of Population: 1970,* "General Social and Economic Characteristics," p. 411. 1960 U.S. figures from Bureau of the Census, *U.S. Census of Population: 1960,* "Detailed Characteristics. United States Summary," p. 459. If the 1960–70 comparison had been confined to the same agencies in both years, the actual percentage of applicants not living in families would have been 14 percent for 1970 and 12 percent for 1960.

8. The phrase, *due to marital conflict,* can be used since the U.S. census counts spouses temporarily absent for other reasons in another category. U.S. data are from U.S. Bureau of the Census, *Current Population Reports,* Series P-20, No. 225, "Marital Status and Living Arrangements: March 1971" (Washington, D.C.: U.S. Government Printing Office, 1971), p. 24. Sample data for 1971 were used because full census data were not yet published. The U.S. percentages are based on figures adjusted to the same proportion of family heads under forty-five as were found in the agency sample. Without this adjustment, the contrasts would have been considerably greater owing to the higher proportion of older persons in the general population.

9. Bureau of the Census, *Census of Population: 1970,* "General Population Characteristics," p. 1-278. In the agency sample, 6.0 percent of all persons fourteen or over were separated, in the U.S. population, 1.9 percent; 4.4 percent were divorced in the agency sample, 3.4 percent in the U.S.; widowed were 3.9 percent of the agency sample, 7.8 percent in the U.S.; 56.3 were married in the agency sample, 61.5 percent in the U.S. These figures could not be age-adjusted because the necessary details by age groups were not available when the manuscript was prepared.

10. The percentage distribution by marital status of heads of agency families (from agencies participating in both the 1960 and 1970 census) shifted between 1960 and 1970 as follows: married, from 82.4 to 72.8; separated, from 10.0 to 11.6; divorced, from 2.7 to 8.0; widowed, from 3.7 to 4.8; and single, from 1.2 to 2.9. The percentage distribution by marital status of heads of U.S. families shifted in this same decade as follows: married, from 88.9 to 87.0; separated, from 1.5 to 2.4; divorced, from 1.9 to 3.0; widowed, from 5.6 to 5.3; and single, from 2.1 to 2.2. 1960 U.S. figures are from Bureau of the Census, *U.S. Census of Population: 1960,* "Detailed Characteristics. U.S. Summary," p. 1-459. 1970 U.S. figures are from same source used for chart, but figures here are not age-adjusted and therefore do not correspond with charted figures. 1970 agency figures do not agree with those charted because the latter were based on agencies that participated in both the 1960 and 1970 census.

11. U.S. Bureau of the Census, *Current Population Reports,* Series P-20, No. 212, "Marital Status and Family Status: March 1970" (Washington, D.C.: U.S. Government Printing Office, 1971), p. 19.

12. U.S. figures for this chart from Bureau of the Census, *Census of Population: 1970,* "General Population Characteristics," p. 1-261, and *Census of Population: 1970,* "General Social and Economic Characteristics," p. 1-359. A metropolitan area is, in general, a county (or group of contiguous counties) which contains at least one city of 50,000 inhabitants or more. If the rural residents living in metropolitan areas are included in the metropolitan figures, 95 percent of agency clients and 65 percent of the general population reside within a metropolitan area.

13. U.S. Bureau of the Census, *U.S. Census of Population: 1970,* "Number of Inhabitants. United States Summary," Final Report PC(1)-A1 (Washington, D.C.: U.S. Government Printing Office, 1971), p. 1-45. It was not feasible to collect separate information on city size for suburban residents served by city agencies. This limitation probably results in a slight overstatement of the extent of the concentration of the clientele of agencies in larger cities. The actual distribution of the persons in the agency sample by the size of city for the main office was: cities of less than 25,000, 8.5 percent; 25,000 to 50,000, 9.8 percent; 50,000 to 100,000, 19.0 percent; 100,000 to 250,000, 18.5 percent; 250,000 to 500,000, 18.5 pecent; 500,000 to 1,000,000, 18.9 percent; 1,000,000 or over, 11.9 percent.

14. "FSAA 1970 Census Statistics for Canada with Comparative Data for United States," mimeographed (New York: Family Service Association of America, 1972), p. 4.

15. Beck and Jones, *Family Agency Clients,* chart 3.

16. U.S. figures for this chart and accompanying table

from Bureau of the Census, *Census of Population: 1970,* "General Population Characteristics," p. 1-263.

17. Ibid., p. 1-262. If the figures are adjusted to cover only metropolitan areas where the black population is concentrated, the contrast remains, but at a slightly lower level (21.7 percent for agency clients versus 12.0 percent for the U.S. population).

18. Bureau of the Census, *Census of Population: 1970,* "General Social and Economic Characteristics," p. 1-439. If the figures are adjusted to cover only metropolitan areas, the contrast is increased to 5.5 percent for U.S. and 2.3 percent for agencies.

19. U.S. Bureau of the Census, *Current Population Reports,* Series P-20, No. 213, "Persons of Spanish Origin in the United States: November 1969" (Washington, D.C.: U.S. Government Printing Office, 1971), p. 4. Agency figures in chart 7, unlike those in chart 6, are not limited to agencies participating in both the 1960 and 1970 census.

20. Revision of the data to apply only to metropolitan areas reverses slightly the direction of the difference for American Indians (0.2 percent for U.S. and 0.3 percent for agencies), but increases the contrast for the "other" group (principally Oriental). For the latter, the U.S. figure becomes 1.3 percent as compared with 0.3 percent for agencies. These metropolitan comparisons do not control for agencies participating in both the 1960 and 1970 census.

21. Bureau of the Census, *Census of Population: 1970,* "General Social and Economic Characteristics," p. 1-361.

22. U.S. figures for this chart from Bureau of the Census, *Census of Population: 1970,* "General Population Characteristics," p. 1-293. Data on Spanish origin for the general population by these regional divisions are not available.

23. For actual figures, see FSAA memorandum of May 10, 1972, from Dorothy Fahs Beck and Mary Ann Jones to Regional Vice Presidents and Regional Representatives, "Selected Characteristics of Clients by FSAA Regions as Revealed in the 1970 FSAA Census," table 3.

24. U.S. figures for this chart from *Religion in America, 1971* (Princeton, N.J.: Gallup International, Inc., 1971), p. 70. Comparisons of agency and U.S. figures on religion are approximate since there are no U.S. census figures on religion.

25. Trend figures for agencies are based on counts for all persons fourteen years of age and over rather than on family heads. The count for Protestants dropped from 72.3 percent to 66.1 percent; Roman Catholics increased from 18.1 percent to 25.4 percent; Jewish applicants dropped from 4.0 to 1.9 percent; those

of other faiths dropped from 1.4 to 0.8; and those with no religious preference increased from 4.1 to 5.8. Since comparisons were limited to agencies participating in the census in both 1960 and 1970, they can not be attributed to changes in agency membership.

26. U.S. figures for this chart from Bureau of the Census, *Current Population Reports,* "Household and Family Characteristics: March 1970," p. 69.

27. 1960 U.S figures from Bureau of the Census, *U.S Census of Population: 1960,* "Detailed Characteristics. U.S. Summary," p. 1-470. Agency trends from 1960 to 1970 are from Beck and Jones, *Family Agency Clients,* chart 6. Age adjustments were not feasible in these trend figures because the necessary details were not available for 1960.

28. 1970 U.S. figures for this chart from U.S. Bureau of the Census, *Current Population Reports,* Series P-60, No. 80, "Income in 1970 of Families and Persons in the United States" (Washington, D.C.: U.S. Government Printing Office, 1971), p. 26. Figures for chart were recomputed to exclude farmers.

29. For agency and U.S. trends from 1960 to 1970, see Beck and Jones, *Family Agency Clients,* chart 7. The agency figures in that chart are limited to agencies participating in both the 1960 and 1970 census. The 1960 U.S. figures are from Bureau of the Census, *U.S. Census of Population: 1960,* "Detailed Characteristics. U.S. Summary," p. 1-475. The U.S. figures marked 1970 were actually from a 1969 sample. The U.S. figures in chart 11 in this report are more accurate.

30. 1960 U.S. figures for this chart from U.S. Bureau of the Census, *Current Population Reports,* Series P-60, No. 35, "Income of Families and Persons in the United States: 1959" (Washington, D.C.: U.S. Government Printing Office, 1961), p. 23. 1970 U.S. figures for this chart from Bureau of the Census, *Census of Population: 1970,* "General Social and Economic Characteristics," p. 1-422. 1960 agency figures from Beck and Jones, *Family Agency Clients,* chart 11.

31. Based on figures from the consumer cost of living index of the Bureau of Labor Statistics. The index was 87.3 for 1959 and 109.8 for 1969 with 1967 as the base year. These indices are for the entire U.S. rather than for metropolitan areas. The real income figures cited are therefore probably slightly overstated.

32. U.S. figures for this chart from Bureau of the Census, *Census of Population: 1970,* "General Social and Economic Characteristics," p. 1-377, 1-400. Specifications of U.S. definition of poverty from U.S. Bureau of the Census, *Current Population Reports,* Series P-60, No. 76, "24 Million Americans—Poverty in the United States: 1969" (Washington, D.C.: U.S. Government Printing Office, 1970), p. 18.

33. U.S. figures for this chart from *Welfare in Review,* 8 (November-December 1970): 28. Base figure used from Bureau of the Census, *Census of Population: 1970,* "General Population Characteristics," p. 1-263.

34. 1960 U.S. figure from correspondence from Ida C. Merriam, then director, Division of Program Research, Department of HEW, to Dorothy Fahs Beck, April 30, 1962.

35. See sources cited for chart 13.

36. The percentage distribution on this basis was: upper, 8.9 percent; upper middle, 7.7 percent; middle middle, 11.1 percent; lower middle, 22.7 percent; upper lower, 30.0 percent; and lower lower, 19.7 percent.

37. Some socioeconomic data on family life education attendees were collected. They are reported in chart 32. It was not feasible to include these data in the remaining charts.

38. Age-adjusted figures for this chart were computed from U.S. Bureau of the Census, *Current Population Reports,* Series P-23, No. 12, "Socioeconomic Characteristics of the Population: 1960" (Washington, D.C.: U.S. Government Printing Office, 1964), p. 19. In contrast to chart 15, data for this chart exclude persons not living in families.

39. The comparability of the data for agency clients in 1960 and 1970 is subject to the qualification that the scoring of occupational data was based on major occupational group only in 1960 but on full occupational detail in 1970. In addition, the method of rating the status of occupations was improved. (See Appendix for explanation of socioeconomic scoring procedures.) Since the results of the two rating procedures are known to correlate very closely, the effect on the trends shown is believed to be inconsequential. This is further confirmed in chart 17 in which the less refined procedures used in 1960 were applied to both 1960 and 1970 with essentially no change in the amount or direction of the trend.

40. 1960 U.S. figure for education from Bureau of the Census, *U.S. Census of Population: 1960,* "Detailed Characteristics. U.S. Summary," p. 1-470. 1970 U.S. figure for education from Bureau of the Census, *Current Population Reports,* "Household and Family Characteristics: March 1970," p. 69. 1960 and 1970 U.S. figures for occupation from Bureau of the Census, *Current Population Reports,* "Income in 1970 of Families and Persons in the United States," p. 26. 1960 and 1970 U.S. figures for income from Bureau of the Census, *Census of Population: 1970,* "General Social and Economic Characteristics," p. 1-377. The scoring procedures used followed those developed for the 1960 U.S. census analysis of socioeconomic status. They are described in *Methodology and Scores of Socioeconomic Status,* Bureau of the Census

Working Paper No. 15 (Washington, D.C.: U.S. Government Printing Office, 1963). In general, the scores assigned to each case reflect the relative percentile position of that case in relation to the general population on the characteristic being rated. Actual scores are based on the midpoint of each interval in a cumulative percentage distribution of that characteristic in the general population beginning at the low end of a ranked series. Scores had to be slightly modified from those reported in Working Paper 15 because it was necessary to accommodate to the specifications for data available for families at two points in time. In order to restrict the ratings to families, actual scores for education and income were newly computed for both years, using the same procedures as described in Working Paper 15. Occupational ratings for both years were taken directly from those reported in Working Paper 15. They reflect the relative position of each occupation when judged by the education and income of those in that occupation. It was not feasible to apply retrospectively to 1960 the more precise procedures utilized in rating occupations in 1970 in the two preceding charts. In contrast to certain earlier charts, this chart includes all occupations, including farmers, and rural as well as urban residents. Unattached individuals are excluded from all figures. Lack of the refinements possible in earlier charts on these same topics reduces the differences between agencies and the general population for income and occupation but increases the contrasts for education.

41. Actual figures for U.S. and agency data are: for education, 50.0 for U.S. compared with 58.7 for agencies in 1960, 49.9 for U.S. compared with 54.0 for agencies in 1970; for occupation, 57.1 for U.S. compared with 57.4 for agencies in 1960, 60.1 for U.S. compared with 61.4 for agencies in 1970; for income, 50.0 for U.S. compared with 45.9 for agencies in 1960, 49.8 for U.S. compared with 41.9 for agencies in 1970. When the three indicators are combined, the figures are 52.4 for U.S. compared with 54.0 in 1960, and 53.3 for U.S. compared with 52.4 for agencies in 1970.

Notes to section 2

1. Agreement between clients' views of their problems at follow-up and counselors' diagnostic assessments at intake was 38 percent, or approximately the same as when counselors attempted to estimate clients' views.

2. Of the white cases, 45.6 percent had a severe problem situation as compared with 42.9 percent of the nonwhite cases; 44.7 percent of the white cases were rated moderate as compared with 41.8 percent of the nonwhite cases; and 9.7 percent of the white cases were rated mild compared with 15.3 percent of the nonwhite cases.

3. Figures refer throughout to clients' views of their problems as reported by the intake counselor. All trends cited apply to agencies that participated in both the 1960 and 1970 census.

4. Even the slight increase in applications related to the personality adjustment problems of adults could be related in part to the impact on parents of increased intergenerational conflicts.

5. Children's problems included problems related to parent-child relationships, school achievement and behavior, and child and adolescent adjustment.

6. Data on how long families remain in various stages and the definitions of the family stages were derived from Evelyn Mills Duvall, *Family Development,* 4th ed. (Philadelphia: J. B. Lippincott Co., 1971), p. 121. Duvall based her data on length of time in each stage on U.S. government sources.

7. Not shown are problems related to work (work performance and unemployment). These continue at a fairly steady level until retirement, when they fade out. Other miscellaneous problems (including other family relationships and legal problems), also not shown, peak after retirement.

8. Inadequate income, housing, and unemployment problems appear in both the family problem and the environmental problem charts. Because the information in these three areas came from the family problem question, the base counts for these percentages differ slightly from those for the remaining problems listed.

9. These figures understate the actual number of environmental problems clients must cope with since they were not asked to report all their external problems but simply those that presented a serious problem for them when they came to the agency.

10. Statements are based on a correlation analysis. Only significant associations are mentioned.

11. Clients served through legal aid departments averaged 7.3 problems per case, those on special projects, 4.0 problems, and those on Travelers Aid programs, 2.1. These compare with an averge of 1.7 problems for those served through family service departments.

Notes to section 3

1. These figures exclude reapplications except those that were initiated by reason of a new referral. However, only 20 percent of all cases were reapplications.

2. The largest increase during this period was in referrals from schools (from 9.8 to 12.8 percent), probably again a reflection of the increased use of agencies for adolescent problems. With the expansion of public welfare, public social agency referrals also increased (from 4.4 to 6.5 percent). There was only a minor increase in referrals from occupational sources, in spite of national efforts to encourage use of family agency service by labor unions and blue-collar workers. All these comparisons are limited to the same agencies participating in the 1960 and 1970 census. None of these increases was statistically significant.

3. These counts include 129 reports from five Canadian agencies participating in the census. The rest of the figures cited here are based only on the 2,806 reports from the 134 U.S. agencies that took part in the phone study. These latter reports have been extensively analyzed by Professor Edmund Sherman and twelve of his students at the School of Social Work of Hunter College, New York City. A report of their findings has been submitted to the library of the Family Service Association of America.

4. When these callers who made appointments and did not keep them were added to those who made no appointment, the percentage receiving information about the agency became 51 percent; information about service arrangements, 45 percent; referral elsewhere, 39 percent; counseling by phone, 36 percent; information about community resources, 22 percent; and other services, 7 percent.

5. Of the requests included in these counts, 3.3 percent were made on behalf of persons not living in the household. Persons included here were mainly husbands, wives, children, and parents living apart from those making the application.

6. For white-nonwhite differences computed in this manner, see "FSAA 1970 Statistics for Canada with Comparative Data for United States," mimeographed (New York: Family Service Association of America, 1972), p. 10.

7. For methodology on supplementary study of family life education, see Appendix for an explanation of data collection procedures. The authors are indebted to Charlotte Tileston for the analysis of the socioeconomic status of family life education attendees presented here. Other aspects of the family life education findings have been analyzed by Ms. Tileston under the direction of Professor William Warren E. Gordon at the George Warren Brown School of Social Work, Washington University, St. Louis, Missouri. A report of the findings has been submitted to the library of the Family Service Association of America.

8. It is not clear whether family life education programs appeal selectively to well-educated parents or whether this finding is the fortuitous result of the particular groups that happened to be sampled that week. Each family life education meeting in the sample provided a substantial number of attendees whose characteristics were related to the theme of the meeting. For this reason, the types of meetings that happened to have been held in the sample week had more influence on the results than any one case in an ordinary sample would have had. Four meetings of upper-status groups happened to occur during the census week—a meeting of a law class, a meeting of a women's civic group, a session of Plays for Living, and a meeting at a boys' private school.

9. For one-interview closings, terminations because service was completed were more frequent for nonwhite than for white clients. Terminations because either the counselor or the client was unwilling to continue showed a reverse pattern with such closings being more frequent with white clients. At follow-up, these one-interview nonwhite clients gave as their reason for closing more often than white clients their belief that they could handle their situation on their own. No nonwhite client in this group was reported terminating because of dissatisfaction with the counselor or the service. The proportion who reported that the service was of no help was 8 percent for the nonwhite group and 9 percent for the white group.

10. Unpublished preliminary data from the FSAA Department of Systems and Statistics, based on 1972 yearly report questionnaires, indicate that more than twice the proportion of agencies in cities of 500,000 and over had waiting lists as was true of agencies in cities of less than 100,000. For data on the concentration of nonwhite clients in the large cities, see discussion of chart 4.

11. Robert B. Hill, *The Strengths of Black Families* (New York: National Urban League, 1971), pp. 11-12, 44-46

12. Dorothy Fahs Beck and Mary Ann Jones, *Family Agency Clients: Who Are They? What Do They Want? What Do They Get? A Visual and Verbal Interim Report of the Early Findings of the 1970 FSAA Census* (New York: Family Service Association of America, 1972). Text related to chart 20.

13. In 1960, 13 percent failed to return when they were kept waiting for four weeks or less, 38 percent when they waited for five to eight weeks, and 45 percent when they waited nine weeks or more. In 1970, 15 percent failed to return when they were kept waiting four weeks or less, 23 percent when they waited for five to eight weeks, and 41 percent when they waited nine weeks or more. The 1970 figures are based on 343 cases placed on the waiting list and hence are less subject to chance fluctuations than the 1960 figures which were based on only 58 cases.

14. In 1970, agencies without waiting lists reported the principal reason for termination as service completed for 33.0 percent of their closings and the client's decision not to continue for 42.7 percent. Agencies with waiting lists reported 29.5 percent of their terminations as a result of completion of service and 46.3 percent as a result of the client's decision not to continue. These differences are both statistically significant. Similar differentials were also found in 1960. See Dorothy Fahs Beck, *Patterns in Use of Family Agency Service* (New York: Family Service Association of America, 1962), p. 25.

15. These are net figures that reflect the balance between two conflicting trends. Only 47 percent of the clients in the 1970 sample were served by agencies maintaining waiting lists as contrasted with 68 percent in 1960. This reduction was counterbalanced by an increase from 18 to 24 percent in the proportion of applicants asked to wait for service in agencies that did have such lists.

16. Beck, *Patterns in Use of Family Agency Service*, p. 32.

Notes to section 4

1. For details on these referrals, see page 67.
2. The figure for family life eduation excludes persons served only through family life education programs.
3. In these percents each separate area of counseling or other service shown in chart 35 was counted as a separate service.
4. Interview counts also varied by the principal problem seen by the counselor at intake. In descending order, average interview counts on this basis were as follows: personality adjustment of a child under thirteen, 12.1; need for physical care or protective service for a child or adolescent, 10.5; child-rearing or child-care practices, 10.0; unwed parenthood, 10.0; parent-child relationships, 9.0; management of home or family health, 8.8; health problems, physical illness, or handicap, 8.5; poor school performance or behavior, 8.5; personality adjustment of an adolescent or youth, 7.9; personality adjustment of an adult, 7.6; marital problems, 7.2; mental illness, 7.2; other family relationships, 6.8; drug abuse or criminal or delinquent behavior, 6.0; need for physical care or protective service for aged person, 6.0; social contacts or use of leisure time, 5.9; management of money, budgeting, etc., 5.4; other problem, 5.4; housing, 4.5; alcoholism, 4.4; personality adjustment of an aged person, 3.7; legal problems, 2.7; inadequate income for basic needs, 2.7; unemployment or unsuitable job, 2.6; and need for physical care or protective service for an adult, 2.2.

5. Alan L. Grey and Helen E. Dermody, "Reports of Casework Failure," *Social Casework*, 53 (November 1972): 534-43; Joel Fischer, "Is Casework Effective? A Review," *Social Work*, 18 (January 1973): 5-20; and Edward J. Mullen, James R. Dumpson, and associates, *Evaluation of Social Intervention* (London: Jossey-Bass, Inc., 1972).

6. The averages charted include all interviews with family members and collaterals within two years. For comparative purposes they necessarily utilize the 1960 problem categories and include only agencies participating in both the 1960 and 1970 census. Comparisons with averages for all cases in 1970 indicate that this latter restriction does not result in major distortions of general patterns.

7. This category merges problems in parent-child relationships with the personality adjustment problems of a child or adolescent.

8. The actual changes in the average number of interviews (including collateral interviews) were as follows: Averages for problems of physical illness or handicap increased from 5.4 in 1960 to 8.8 in 1970; economic or employment problems increased from 1.8 to 3.1; marital problems, from 6.5 to 7.3; and personality adjustment problems, from 6.8 to 7.6. Some 1960 averages are based on very small samples and are therefore only suggestive.

9. To maximize the representation of the newer modalities, the modality involving the greatest number of family members was coded whenever there was a tie between two treatment modalities. If the tie was between husband-wife interviews and other joint interviews, the husband-wife interview count was coded. If the tie was between group treatment and other service contacts, the group treatment modality was counted as primary.

10. These observations must be considered suggestive since only ninety-five advocacy requests and 111 advocacy services were reported for the entire sample.

11. The percentage of clients referred for various kinds of help were as follows: mental health, 20.9; financial assistance, 15.9; legal services, 9.6; general caretaking services, 8.2; medical or dental care, 8.2; family counseling, 7.8; vocational services, 7.8; housing, 4.3; special education, 3.6; financial counseling, 2.2; and alcoholism, 2.0. Fewer than 2 percent of the clients were referred for maternity care, family planning, or recreational activities. Referrals for adoption, foster care, child placement, and drug abuse were each made for less than one percent of the clients. (Counts include both referral and steering.)

12. This difference between the upper and lower group on failure to follow through was not statistically significant.

13. Evaluation of referral services was complicated by

the large group who did not follow through on the suggested referrals.

14. Evaluations of intervention services related to neighborhood and community conditions were not charted because the data were based on small samples (153 reports from counselors and 123 reports from clients). Services referred to here do not include counseling in regard to environmental problems.

15. See "FSAA 1970 Statistics for Canada with Comparative Data for United States," mimeographed (New York: Family Service Association of America, 1972), p. 12.

Notes to section 5

1. Classifications throughout are based on the characteristics of the counselor closing the case.

2. Livia Lowy, *Characteristics of the Professional Staff of FSAA Member Agencies, January 1, 1967*, "Part I, General Summary and Ten-Year Trends" (New York: Family Service Association of America, 1968), p. 4.

3. *Family Service Statistics*, "Facts and Trends of FSAA Member Agencies: 1970" (New York: Family Service Association of America, October 1971), p. 7.

4. "Racial Composition of Staff and Board in 261 FSAA Member Agencies: January 1, 1970 and June 1, 1971," mimeographed (New York: Family Service Association of America, 1971). In this report, Canadian and Jewish agencies were omitted. The white and black counts include staff of Spanish origin.

5. This difference was also statistically significant.

6. In 32 percent of the husband-wife cases treated by trained male counselors, husband-wife interviews were the primary modality as compared with only 26 percent of cases of this type treated by trained women counselors. This difference is statistically significant. Male counselors also used group treatment more frequently (in 5 percent of their husband-wife families as compared with 2 percent for women counselors).

7. Lowy, *Characteristics of the Professional Staff of FSAA Member Agencies*, p. 5.

8. The scale was computed by adding the counselors' and clients' ratings. Ratings ranged from "unsatisfactory," which was assigned a value of one, to "very satisfactory," which was assigned a value of five.

9. None of the correlations cited for this discussion have been controlled for other factors. The actual figures for the correlations referred to in this summary appear in the Appendix, table 1. All are limited to cases with a follow-up report. Significance levels tended to be high even for low correlations because of the large sample.

10. Ranking was based on the principal focus of treatment, using categories ordered according to the percentage of cases reported improved when the problem received attention.

11. The transfer group also included a few cases treated by two counselors simultaneously.

12. Agreement in relationship and global outcomes reflect agreement in direction not degree. For example, agreement was counted as having occurred if both client and counselor gave a "satisfied" rating regardless of whether one was "very satisfied" and the other "partly satisfied." However, in an earlier report, agreement on these items was counted only when counselor and client agreed in degree as well as direction; hence, the lower agreement figures. For these latter figures, see Dorothy Fahs Beck and Mary Ann Jones, *Family Agency Clients: Who Are They? What Do They Want? What Do They Get? A Visual and Verbal Interim Report on the Early Findings of the 1970 FSAA Census* (New York: Family Service Association of America, 1972), chart 31. The percentages for presence of specific problems were based on the proportion of problems seen by either counselor or client which were seen by both. In this instance the percentage of agreement was separately computed for each case and the results pooled.

13. The significance of the disagreement on the counselor-client relationship very nearly reached the .05 level. "Presence of specific problems" did not lend itself to testing since more than one problem per case was included in the base.

14. Seven items were based on a direct comparison of the counselors' and clients' reports: what the problems were, the most important problem at intake and follow-up, how satisfactory the counselor-client relationship was, the primary reason for termination, who decided to terminate, global improvement rating, and the closeness of the change scores based on the report of each respondent. Four additional items were based only on the counselors' reports: the counselor's perception of disagreement on problems at intake, the most important problem at intake, service decisions, and whether termination was a mutual decision. Seven of the items in the index were simple yes-no possibilities, but the other four involved scales of agreement.

15. To the unknown extent that the responses were unreliable, this would also have tended to increase the disagreement index.

16. The correlation of socioeconomic status and the disagreement index was r = −.08 which, because of the large sample size, was significant at the .001 level.

Notes to section 6

1 The text and chart are limited to the primary reason for closing as reported by the counselor. If all reasons had been included, the percentages would have been as follows: family decided not to continue, 51 percent; service completed, 37 percent; situational factors, 13 percent; needed service unavailable at the agency, 11 percent; counselor felt it unwise to continue, 7 percent; insufficient staff, one percent; eligibility requirements, one percent; and other reasons, 3 percent. Because more than one reason was often reported, the total exceeds 100 percent.

2. This trend is consistent with the substantial and statistically significant drop in initial requests from clients for referral or steering reported on page 57. Changes in the wording of the item may also have been a factor. In 1960 the checklist for primary reason for closing included the item, "referred elsewhere." In 1970, this item was rephrased to "service needed unavailable at agency," which was then subdivided by cross-tabulation by whether referral service was or was not given. Other changes in primary reason for termination between 1960 and 1970 (same agencies) were as follows: Closed because service was completed increased from 25.3 to 31.5 percent; closed because client decided not to continue increased from 39.5 to 43.7 percent. The former is statistically significant but may be the result of the rephrasing and reordering of the list. The latter is not statistically significant. No other reasons for closing lend themselves to comparison.

3. Compliments about the agency or service averaged 1.3 per case for this group as compared with a general average of 0.9.

4. A few reported that they were still continuing or planning to return. A small percentage of cases were not closed at the end of two years.

5. Complaints for this group averaged 2.6 per case as compared with a general average of 1.0.

6. Clients' reason for termination was given on the average about three months after the counselors rated the relationship.

7. Counselors' and clients' relationship ratings correlate with each other only at the level of r = +.24. While this is highly significant statistically, only 6 percent of the variation in one type of rating is accounted for by variations in the other.

8. This conclusion can not be proved conclusively from the present study because relationship ratings were obtained at the same time as the outcome evaluations. To make certain that the good relationship actually contributed to a good outcome and was not simply a reflection of the outcome, relationship ratings would have to

be collected prior to the time when the outcomes were known.

9. For white clients at the upper and middle-status levels, the proportion of negative reasons for closing was 35 percent as compared with 34 percent for the lower; corresponding figures for nonwhite clients were 47 and 29 percent respectively.

10. See discussion of waiting lists related to chart 34. This group was particularly low in complaints about the relationship with the counselor.

11. Dorothy Fahs Beck, *Patterns in Use of Family Agency Service* (New York: Family Service Association of America, 1962), p. 35.

12. For details on differences in services see chart 36.

13. Interview counts showed a substantial difference by who made the termination decision. When both parties agreed that it was the client's decision, interviews averaged only 5.4. They were even lower (4.3) when termination was dictated by other family members. When both parties agreed that the decision was mutual, the average number of interviews increased to 9.1. If both thought it was the counselor's decision, the average was 10.0. Clearly, counselors were making more than an average investment in service to clients before they decided on their own initiative to terminate the case.

14. The fact that the questions were not put in parallel form to the two parties would increase the difference. Therefore no great weight should be placed on the fact that in only 47 percent of the cases with data for both parties was there agreement on responsibility for termination.

15. Beck, *Patterns in Use of Family Agency Service*, p. 34.

16. This reason for termination has often been referred to as "client unwilling to continue" or "did not continue despite plan."

17. Of all cases, 16.5 percent withdrew before the second interview; 13.3 percent withdrew between the second and fifth interviews; 12.5 percent withdrew after the fifth interview.

18. See also charts 33 and 81.

19. These averages are based only on cases where the closing counselor was a caseworker rather than a social work assistant or a student.

20. For differences in outcomes see charts 93 and 94.

Notes to section 7

1. The figures given here differ from those published in *Highlights of FSAA News,* 2 (October 1972). All cases with a follow-up report were included in the earlier report regardless of whether a closing report was available; the figures here are limited to cases with a global rating from both counselor and client.

2. The chances were less than .001 that either level of agreement would have occurred on a chance basis. The correlation between the two global ratings was low (r = +.24), but it was nevertheless significant at the .001 level.

3. It was not feasible in this study to secure separate ratings from each adult family member. Therefore, whenever possible (in about 87 percent of the follow-ups), the family member that the counselor saw most often was selected as the follow-up respondent.

4. When major crises reported by the counselor, the client, or both were consolidated, there were nine deaths (including one murder), one suicide, five attempted suicides, five runaways, and five criminal or delinquent acts (two drug-related), and one drug overdose.

5. The first two items have already been discussed (see charts 46, 60, and 61). For information on the influence of external factors, see chart 80.

6. The level of agreement was significant below the .001 level. The test used both here and for number of interviews was the modified chi-square test (A_p) suggested by Richard Light in "Measures of Response Agreement for Qualitative Data: Some Generalizations and ALternatives," *Psychological Bulletin,* 76 (1971): 365-77.

7. The next three highest reports of "worse" were for income, housing, and unemployment (10 percent), school performance (10 percent), and money management (9 percent).

8. See Joel G. Sacks, Panke M. Bradley, and Dorothy Fahs Beck, *Clients' Progress within Five Interviews: An Exploratory Study Comparing Workers' and Clients' Views.* (New York: Family Service Association of America, 1970).

9. Negative changes were more frequent in the feeling aspect than in any other, a finding that again fits with practical experience. Often, the opening of problem areas for discussion results in increased anxiety, which provides the energy and impetus for change. At other times, increased anxiety is encouraged by practitioners to counter a defense of denial and to promote increased motivation for work on the problem.

10. The five items selected for the assessment of changes in family interaction reflect the findings of two earlier FSAA studies: an exploratory and conceptual study of the treatment of marital problems and a developmental study on evaluation techniques conducted in New London. Two reports of the former include: Dorothy Fahs Beck, "Marital Conflict: Its Course and Treatment as Seen by Caseworkers," *Social Casework,* 47 (April 1966): 211-21, and Elsbeth Herzstein Couch, *Joint*

and Family Interviews in the Treatment of Marital Problems (New York: Family Service Association of America, 1969). A final report is in process. The latter study is reported in Sacks et al., *Clients' Progress within Five Interviews.*

11. The five items shown in chart 68 were also used by Brenda J. S. Wattie in a study of changes in intact families served by the Family Service Centre of Ottawa, Canada. Before-and-after Q-sort tests of family concepts were also administered to clients in that study. Her data indicated that scores based mainly on client responses to these five family relationship items agreed more closely with the findings of this independent family concept test than did either counselors' ratings or the ratings of case records by trained readers. See Brenda J. S. Wattie, "A Search for Criteria for the Use of Planned Short-Term Treatment with Family Service Agency Clients—An Exercise in Service Evaluation," mimeographed (Ottawa, Canada: Family Service Centre of Ottawa, 1972).

12. This procedure is based on the assumption that both clients and counselors can usually perceive correctly the direction of change but can not evaluate reliably the amount of change without extensive directions and close supervision. It further assumes that a summation of indicators of changes in many areas can substitute for a formal assessment of the total amount of change in all areas (because of the tendency of changes in one area or person to spread to other areas and other family members).

13. Double weight was assigned to changes in either direction in the principal problem, to taking action on a problem, and to changes in persons twenty-one or over (or under twenty-one but married). All other items received a weight of one. The summation procedure is based on the assumption that, given a large and comprehensive sampling of indicators, no gross distortion results from adding or subtracting component indicators *as if* they were equal, or from substracting deterioration ratings from improvement ratings *as if* one canceled the other.

14. The change score was not computed if no service or only adoption service was provided, if no problems were evaluated, if more than half of the possible evaluations were missing, or if the sections on problem-coping, family relationships, and family members changing had all been skipped by the respondent.

15. It was not deemed feasible in this study to ask either counselors or clients to fill out the questionnaires twice; likewise (for reasons of length), no equivalent items were included in the questionnaires themselves; hence no estimate of reliability could be made.

16. The standard deviation for the counselors' change scores was 3.3; for clients' change scores, 3.6 (when limited to cases with both scores).

17. Major summaries include: Alan L. Grey and Helen

E. Dermody, "Reports of Casework Failure," *Social Casework,* 53 (November 1972): 545-43; Joel Fischer, "Is Casework Effective? A Review," *Social Work,* 18 (January 1973): 5-20; Edward J. Mullen, James R. Dumpson and associates, *Evaluation of Social Intervention* (London: Jossey-Bass, Inc., 1972), pp. 1-38: and Ludwig L. Geismar, Bruce Lagay, Isabel Wolock, Ursula C.Gerhart, and Harriet Fink, *Early Supports for Family Life: A Social Work Experiment* (Metuchen, N. J.: Scarecrow Press, Inc., 1972), pp. 169-90.

18. Geismar et al., *Early Supports for Family Life,* pp. 68-69.

19. Statements of significance throughout this discussion of change score differences are based on analysis of variance F tests and correlation procedures. Unless otherwise specified, the sign of the difference was retained. This means that what was tested was the significance of the association between the factors in question and the differences in scores, taking account both of the amount and the direction of the difference. Usually the patterns noted were statistically significant whether or not the sign was retained.

20. The disagreement index was more highly associated with the difference between the two scores when the sign was dropped than when it was retained; however, the pattern was statistically significant on either basis.

21. This correlation was highly significant statistically only when the direction of the difference was taken into account.

22. Examples of differences have already been identified—perceptual changes related to problem-coping (see chart 67), and changes in income, housing, and unemployment (see chart 66).

23. The statistical significance of this increase was canceled out when the sign of the difference was retained because changes following closing tended to be in both favorable and unfavorable directions.

24. A multiple regression analysis of the association between twenty-one factors and the signed difference between counselors' and clients' change scores yielded a multiple correlation coefficient of $r = +.69$, indicating that these twenty-one factors together accounted in a statistical sense for 48 percent of the variance in these differences. Of these twenty-one factors, all those significantly related to these differences without control of other factors have been mentioned in the text for this chart. Two additional factors that were statistically significant for the unsigned differences but not for the signed differences (time lag and severity) have also been mentioned.

25. Follow-up reports were obtained for 53 percent of the sample, but some lacked full outcome details. In other instances, there was no closing report or the closing report lacked the details needed for the change score. In

addition, no change score was computed for adoption cases.

26. A prediction procedure explained on page 120, which takes into account client characteristics, number of interviews, and the counselor-client relationship, produced a predicted counselor change score average of $+4.7$ for the interview group and $+5.1$ for the mail questionnaire group. Corresponding predictions for client scores were $+5.0$ and $+5.2$, respectively. The actual scores for the interview group did not differ significantly from the predicted, but the actual scores for the mail questionnaire group did differ from the predicted, the counselors' scores being significantly above expected and the clients', below.

27. This pattern appears to be part of a general tendency for the client change scores to be lower as the distance increases between the client and the agency in the follow-up method employed. Further support for this hypothesis is provided by the average client change scores for three forms of interviews. From the least to the greatest distance between agency and client, the scores were: interviewed in the office (19 percent), $+5.3$; interviewed at home (48 percent), $+5.0$; and interviewed by phone (31 percent), $+4.8$. Since other factors that may be associated with the place of interview and may also affect the change score have not yet been examined, the conclusions must be considered tentative only.

28. Reassurance that these four components actually reflect a consistent picture of change is provided by the fact that each correlates with the total change score at least at the $+.78$ level. Some correlations reached levels as high as $+.89$. Each also correlated at a level between $+.52$ and $+.65$ with the separate global evaluations provided by the same respondents, a fact that validates their compatibility with the overall concept of progress that these judgments represent. All these correlations were also highly significant statistically.

Notes to section 8

1. Both counselors' and clients' change scores likewise diverged markedly from the average change scores when "no change" or "deterioration" was the actual global evaluation at closing. On that basis, scores for "no change" were $+0.8$ and $+1.0$ for counselors' and clients' reports respectively, instead of the levels shown in chart 75—$+2.6$ and $+3.9$. When the global rating was "deterioration," the scores averaged -0.2 and -0.9 respectively, instead of $+3.1$ and $+5.0$ as shown.

2. This pattern of greater improvement when the pre-

diction was for "deterioration" rather than "no change" was also present in clients' global evaluations, but not in those for counselors.

3. Counselors' change scores for all cases were $+4.8$ for mild cases, $+4.7$ for moderately severe cases, and $+3.9$ for severe cases.

4. The following negative indicators were utilized in this index: Initiative in seeking help came from a third party, not from a family member; referral was from an authoritative source (police, probation officer, and so on); client dropped in without appointment for the first interview; client saw no problem; client saw problem as entirely outside himself; client made no request for service; and counselor's prediction was for termination after one interview. The following positive indicators were also used: Application was self-initiated; client made appointment for first interview; both spouses came in for the first interview; client described problem at follow-up as involving himself or a relationship in which he was involved; and counselor predicted client would continue for six or more interviews. At least five indicators had to be present before the index was computed on a case. The resulting index is considered to be an indication of the client's involvement in seeking help as revealed through his activities, requests, and presentation of his problems. The index may not accurately reflect the client's actual emotional involvement. It is recognized that many of the items included are to some extent associated with socioeconomic status or type of problem.

5. Counselors' change scores for all cases were as follows: low involvement, $+3.5$; neutral (or mixed), $+3.7$; moderate, $+4.3$; high, $+4.7$. This association was statistically highly significant.

6. For recent systematic summaries of casework outcome studies, see Alan L. Grey and Helen E. Dermody, "Reports of Casework Failure," *Social Casework,* 53 (November 1972):534-43; Joel Fischer, "Is Casework Effective? A Review," *Social Work,* 18 (January 1973): 5-20; Edward J. Mullen, James R. Dumpson, and associates, *Evaluation of Social Intervention* (London: Jossey-Bass, Inc., 1972), pp. 1-38; Ludwig L. Geismar, Bruce Lagay, Isabel Wolock, Ursula C. Gerhart, and Harriet Fink, *Early Supports for Family Life: A Social Work Experiment* (Metuchen, N.J.: Scarecrow Press, Inc., 1972), pp.169-92; Steven Paul Segal, "Research on the Outcome of Social Work Therapeutic Interventions: A Review of the Literature,"*Journal of Health and Social Behavior,* 13 (March 1972):3-17; and Scott Briar, "Family Services and Casework," *Research in the Social Services: A Five-Year Review,* ed. Henry S. Maas (New York: National Association of Social Workers, 1971), pp. 114-20.

7. See Fischer, "Is Casework Effective? A Review."
8. The client's view of where the problem lay was ob-

tained by coding an open-ended question on the follow-up schedule: What was the most important problem you wanted [the agency's] help with?" Assignment to the problem groups was based on whether either client or counselor reported one of these three problems as the most important problem at any time. A few cases where counselors and clients disagreed about the most important problem appear in two categories.

9. See Geismar et al., *Early Supports for Family Life,* pp. 69-72, 100-102, and 184-85, plus the other studies cited by Geismar on page 184 of that volume. In the present study the "family and home management" category included child-rearing, home and money management, and social contacts and use of leisure time.

10. See summaries of controlled evaluation studies in casework cited in footnote 6, section 8.

11. Classifications in chart 79 are based on the problem given most agency service, whereas most controlled studies have based their samples on target groups defined at the outset without regard to the focus of later service. When all cases in the present sample, including those without a follow-up, were classified according to whether or not any problem related to crime or delinquency was present at intake, counselors' change scores for all cases with such problems at intake (234 cases) averaged +3.4; those without such problems, +4.3. The difference was highly significant statistically. Counselors' change scores for the total sample also showed a significant negative association with the total number of problems seen at intake.

12. Ratings of external factors used in chart 80 were based on clients' reports at follow-up when available and otherwise on counselors' reports. Sometimes clients cited as external factors influences that might well have been related to treatment, such as changes in self or changes in family relationships. These were not counted as external factors in this analysis.

13. For cases with both a counselor and client change score, counselors reported 11 percent of the cases as having some external factor that influenced changes during the course of agency service; 32 percent of the clients reported such a factor. For both counselors and clients, only about one out of ten of the external factors reported was thought to have a negative influence.

14. For data on helpfulness of agency service as a whole, see chart 46.

15. Merging all white and nonwhite cases with a counselor change score, the range in scores by socioeconomic status was from +4.8 for the highest status group to +3.8 for the lowest. This was statistically significant at the .001 level. However, when socioeconomic status was examined with race separately controlled, socioeconomic status was not statistically sig-

nificant for either counselors' or clients' scores. The global ratings of counselors and clients for the same cases also did not vary significantly by socioeconomic status.

16. Client involvement in seeking service was positively correlated at a highly significant level with the socioeconomic score ($r = +.32$). The total number of problems at intake, relative difficulty of principal problem, and number of environmental problems were all negatively correlated at a highly significant level with socioeconomic score. See especially chart 25.

17. These findings are based on comparisons by race with socioeconomic status controlled. The findings were essentially similar without socioeconomic status controlled.

18. Geismar et al., *Early Supports for Family Life,* p. 76. See also pages 72-77 of that volume for further discussion and page 108 for documentation from other studies. It is significant that Geismar's own findings using a broader spectrum of services also did not support the view that casework is less effective with lower-status clients than with upper.

19. This factor was explored by Brenda J. S. Wattie in "A Search for Criteria for the Use of Planned Short-Term Treatment with Family Service Agency Clients—An Execise in Service Evaluation," mimeographed (Ottawa, Canada: Family Service Centre of Ottawa, July 1972). For a summary of the relation of age to outcomes in psychiatric studies, see Julian Meltzoff and Melvin Kornreich, *Research in Psychotherapy* (New York: Atherton Press, 1970), pp. 231-33.

20. For further confirming evidence of decline in positive outcomes with advancing age, see chart 103, which reports outcomes by duration of marriage, and chart 106, which reports outcomes for the group sixty-five and over.

21. The figures shown represent the power of the factor to predict the change score *with the influence of all other factors removed.* Use of this type of rating makes it possible to evaluate a factor without the interpretation being affected by the intercorrelations of one factor with another. The figures are based on the standardized partial regression coefficients reported in the final step in a stepwise regression analysis and are not dependent on the order in which the independent variables are entered. For an explanation and justification of this procedure, see Robert P. O'Reilly, "Major Studies of Racial and Social Class Isolation in the Schools," *Racial and Social Class Isolation in the Schools,* ed. Robert P. O'Reilly (New York: Praeger Publishers, 1970), p. 169. For data on the correlations of each of these factors with change score data without other factors controlled, see Appendix table 1.

22. This is evident from chart 25 and from the discussion of chart 80.

23. Size of family was examined partly to ascertain whether the change score was inherently negatively correlated with family size, the hypothesis being that the larger the family the more difficult it might be to achieve change. However, there proved to be no relation between the change score and family size.

24. See summaries of controlled evaluation studies in the casework area cited in footnote 6, section 8.

25. For counselors' scores, R(the multiple correlation) = +.29; for clients' scores R = +.32.

Notes to section 9

1. Throughout section 9, three types of questions are addressed: The first is whether a given service factor as a whole is significantly related to the change scores. In chart 84, for example, the issue is whether number of interviews affects the change score; elsewhere the factor may be treatment modality, counselor-client relationship, or the like. Tests on this issue utilize analysis of variance techniques that take into account simultaneously the total pattern of variations *in all categories.* Tests of this type are usually applied separately to counselors' and clients' scores, as is the case here. Occasionally such tests include simultaneously both counselors' and clients' ratings, using an analysis of variance repeat measure procedure.

The second issue is whether each specific change score average differs significantly from the average predicted *for this same category* on the basis of client (and possibly other) characteristics. The answers are given by asterisks placed at the bottom of each bar, indicating the level of significance whenever the difference between the predicted and actual scores reaches a statistically significant level. For example, in chart 84, the three asterisks beside the average one-interview scores for both counselors' and clients' reports indicate that the amounts by which the actual scores fell below the predicted scores for the same category were highly significant statistically.

The third issue is whether the results of one specific category of service are significantly better or worse than those of another category shown in the same chart. These issues are addressed with t-tests that *compare figures for one specific category with those for another.* For example, footnote 2 of this section reports the results of comparisons of this type between the one-interview category and the two-to-five interview category, the six-to-nine interview category, and so on for counselors' and clients' scores separately.

With minor exceptions, all these types of tests were applied routinely to the differences between actual and predicted scores (the residuals) rather than to the actual scores (see Appendix explanations of predicted scores). In order not to unnecessarily confuse the reader, this qualification usually is not noted in the text for each specific test reference.

2. For counselors' scores, the difference between the one-interview residuals and those for further interviews began to be statistically significant by the second category of two-to-five interviews; for clients' scores, it became statistically significant by the fourth category of ten-to-nineteen interviews.

3. When data are examined without grouping for number of interviews, the crossover point is at four interviews.

4. Beyond twenty interviews, counselors' change scores by number of interviews were as follows: 20-24, +6.6; 25-29, +6.9; 30-39, +7.3; 40-59, +7.5; 60 and over, +6.9. In these same ranges, clients' average scores were as follows: +6.2, +5.9, +7.4, +6.4, and +6.8.

5. Since the components used in computing the change score do not provide for rating amount of improvement for each item, the improvement resulting from extended service may not always be apparent in the change score averages.

6. Among cases for which both counselors' and clients' change scores were available, there were sixty-one that received no counseling; 460 that received counseling plus other service; and 1,085 that received counseling only.

7. Predictions for this chart took account of many factors in addition to client characteristics. Among these was number of interviews. (See Appendix explanation.)

8. Tests referred to were F tests of actual component scores for the three groups shown in the chart. All were statistically significant, most highly so, except counselors' scores for changes in specific problems receiving attention.

9. The unmarried parenthood group was an exception to this pattern since this group tended to have relatively high change scores. However, this group was a relatively small component of the total.

10. Joel Fischer, "Is Casework Effective? A Review," *Social Work,* 18 (January 1973): 5-20.

11. It is suggested that investigators in future studies secure their ratings of relationship at a point in time well before outcomes are rated.

12. These findings held in spite of the fact that counselors' and clients' ratings of relationship were correlated only at the level of $r = +.24$ and their change scores only at the $r = +.34$ level. Similar independence of the source of the ratings was found when the counselor-client relationship was analyzed in relation to clients' reasons for terminating (see chart 54). In both areas, the association was less marked when relatively independent sources for the ratings were utilized than when ratings were from the same source. This fact would suggest that outcomes probably did influence clients' relationship ratings to some extent. Nevertheless, in both instances, the association remained marked and highly significant statistically regardless of who did the rating.

13. Charles B. Truax and Robert R. Carkhuff, *Toward Effective Counseling and Psychotherapy: Training and Practice* (Chicago: Aldine Publishing Company, 1967). For a summary of the research evidence, see pages 176-89 of that volume.

14. For a further description of this index, see footnote 14 for section 5.

15. John E. Mayer and Noel Timms, "Clash in Perspective Between Worker and Client," *Social Casework,* 50(January 1969):32-40; and John E. Mayer and Noel Timms, *The Client Speaks: Working Class Impressions of Casework* (New York: Atherton Press, 1970).

16. About 9 percent of the cases in chart 89 were persons living apart from all other family members. In almost one-third of those cases, however, more than one family member was seen. If chart 89 had been limited to cases with more than one family member living in the same household, the actual change scores, going from one to three or more persons seen, would have been: +4.0, +4.8, and +5.7 for the counselors and +4.7, +5.1, and +5.3 for the clients. In both instances, contrasts from low to high would have been increased.

17. These findings are also consistent with charts 69 and 70 which showed that persons who were seen were more likely to improve than those not seen. Comparisons in these earlier charts were based on the percentage of persons reported improved. The change score is a family change measure that takes into account changes in multiple areas and all family members. From the findings in chart 89, it would appear that not only the individual but the total family benefits from the inclusion of additional family members in the direct agency contact.

18. The F test for clients' change scores related to number of family members showed a significance level of .16; that for clients' global ratings, a level of .06; a t-test of one person seen versus three persons seen, a level of .18. However, when both counselors' and clients' ratings were used in a combined analysis of variance test, the significance level for number of family members seen rose to .001, but there was also a highly significant interaction with the rater.

19. See pages 104-105 for a further discussion of sources of difference between counselors' and clients' change scores.

20. This conviction is evident in the responses received from practitioners in the FSAA marital project. See Elsbeth Herzstein Couch, *Joint and Family Interviews in the Treatment of Marital Problems* (New York: Family Service Association of America, 1969).

21. The influence on change scores of who was seen was also highly significant statistically when analyzed as a total pattern. This was true both for the F test applied to counselors' ratings only and for an analysis of variance test applied simultaneously to the two types of ratings. It was also true for counselors' scores when the nonfollow-up group was added in. The association of who was seen with the global ratings did not reach the .05 level of significance for either clients' or counselors' ratings, but in both instances it was below the .10 level.

22. This finding might seem to suggest that if only one spouse is to be seen, the choice should perhaps be the wife; however, this difference between cases in which husbands and wives are seen alone was not statistically significant.

23. This conviction is documented in Couch, *Joint and Family Interviews.*

24. Since the predictions are based on the experience of the total group with two change scores and this chart is limited to families receiving three or more interviews, actual scores tend to be consistently above predicted. Since the same limitation applies to all categories, the comparisons between modalities are not invalidated.

25. The F test applied to variations in change score residuals by modality indicated a significance level of .004 for counselors' reports for families receiving three or more interviews. The same level of significance was found for husband-wife families similarly analyzed.

26. In several instances the more favorable counselors' scores for family interviews over other modalities were statistically significant. For instance, with both the family relationship and family members changing component scores, family interviews yielded significantly better results than did individual interviews.

27. Group treatment cases involved considerably more interviews—an average of 26.9 for cases with both change scores—but these were group interviews that did not require as much staff time per case.

28. Reading from top to bottom and left to right,

the number of cases on which these percentages were based were as follows: 647, 299, 43, 72, 61; 649, 300, 42, 72, 59; 406, 186, 24, 47, 33; and 406, 189, 24, 47, 34.

29. These tests were based on planned short-term treatment versus continued service cases classified by number of interviews.

30. These interview counts apply only to the cases shown in chart 92 which is limited to three-or-more-interview cases. For the total sample, planned short-term cases averaged five interviews and continued service, nine interviews.

31. Counselors reported 67 percent of the wives showed improvement with short-term service and 71 percent with continued service. The reverse was reported for husbands improving (47 versus 45 percent). Neither difference was statistically significant. When the sample was confined to intact families receiving counseling, clients' reports again showed these same patterns; however, in this case counselors reported that more wives improved with planned short-term service than with continued service (68 versus 62 percent).

32. Brenda J. S. Wattie, "A Search for Criteria for the Use of Planned Short-Term Treatment with Family Service Agency Clients—An Exercise in Service Evaluation," mimeographed (Ottawa, Canada: Family Service Centre of Ottawa, July 1972).

33. For further details on planned short-term treatment, see pages 59 and 62.

34. William J. Reid and Ann W. Shyne, *Brief and Extended Casework* (New York: Columbia University Press, 1969). For a basic discussion of the approach, see also William J. Reid and Laura J. Epstein, *Task Centered Casework* (New York: Columbia University Press, 1972).

35. Wattie, "A Search for Criteria for the Use of Planned Short-Term Treatment." Wattie reported that her findings for husbands were influenced by the strong and persistent preference of one worker for continued service. If the cases served by this worker had been omitted, the findings for husbands in this study would have shown a clear superiority for planned, short-term treatment.

36. Wattie's study reported an average of 8.2 interviews for continued service and 5.9 interviews for planned short-term service (page 38); Reid and Shyne's study, 26.0 interviews for continued service and 7.0 interviews for planned short-term service (page 58).

37. The difference between male clients treated by male and female counselors was also not statistically significant—probably because of the small sample of male clients being treated by male counselors (seventy-seven cases).

38. Chart 97 shows the standardized regression coefficient for sex-matching to be statistically significant. This finding probably was strengthened by two circumstances: Women as principal clients showed, in general, better change scores than did men as principal clients; and female clients were more likely to have a counselor of the same sex than were male clients.

39. Cases treated by Spanish counselors, students, case aides, and social work assistants were excluded from this analysis.

40. In forty cases, both counselor and client were black; in 171 cases, the counselor was white and the client was black.

41. There were only fifty-one cases with both change scores in which a white client was assigned to a black counselor.

42. The statistically significant zero-order correlation of racial matching with counselors' change scores of $r = +.07$ is also not definitive since white clients received higher change scores on the average and also were more frequently assigned to counselors of their own race.

43. This category included those transferred immediately after intake, those transferred later, and those assigned simultaneously to two counselors.

44. These policies are documented in a report from the FSAA Personnel Committee, "Social Work Assistants in Family Service Agencies," mimeographed (New York: Family Service Association of America, 1969). See page 72 of that report for information on extent of use of social work assistants.

45. For explanation of the various categories for reason for termination, see page 80.

46. The difference (stated in terms of residuals) between clients' scores for "service completed" and those for "needed service unavailable, referred" was statistically significant at the .016 level. Other comparisons between clients' scores for this final category and those for various intermediate categories were not statistically significant.

47. Interview counts and global ratings reported on this page relate to the follow-up group. Figures for the total sample would be lower.

48. For detail on reasons given by clients for terminating agency service, see page 81.

49. When deviations of change scores from predicted were analyzed by reason for termination, F was significant for counselors' scores at the .001 level; for clients, at the .04 level.

50. While fifteen service characteristics were included in this multiple regression analysis, only those characteristics where the probability that the association was due to chance was less than .30 were included in this chart. Service factors not meeting this require-

ment included: (1) primary treatment modality involved use of multiple-client interviews, (2) primary treatment modality involved group treatment, (3) counselor and client were matched on race, and (4) social work assistants provided some or all of the service.

51. These scores are based on the standardized partial regression coefficients reported in the final step in two stepwise regression analyses, one for counselors' scores and one for clients' scores. They reflect the relative power of each factor with the influence of all the other factors removed and are not dependent on the order in which the independent variables are entered. For support of this use of the partial standardized regression coefficients, see footnote 21, section 8.

52. The findings already reported were based mainly on an analysis of variance approach and related F tests utilizing as data the differences between actual and predicted scores (the residuals). The standardized coefficients shown here were secured from a multiple regression analysis of twenty-six independent variables related to the change scores as criterion variables.

53. The final multiple correlation coefficient (R) was +.62 for counselors' ratings and +.46 for clients' ratings.

Notes to section 10

1. Reports used as the basis for this chart were provided by counselors at closing. They were not obtained directly from clients.

2. Clients' remarks as reported by Dorothy Fahs Beck and Robert W. Roberts in "Marital Applicants and the Problems They Bring," mimeographed, chap. 1 of the as-yet-unpublished FSAA marital study, *The Treatment of Marital Problems,* Dorothy Fahs Beck, editor. This chapter is one of fifteen which have been completed in draft form and are available on loan from the FSAA library.

3. Statement is based on counselors' reports in Beck and Roberts, "Marital Applicants and the Problems They Bring."

4. More than one applicant in ten telephoning for help on a marital problem mentioned in this initial phone contact that alcoholism was an associated problem.

5. Both of these differences were statistically highly significant.

6. None of these differences was statistically significant.

7. The high level of marital and children's problems shown in this chart differs from that cited in chart 23 because this chart is limited to married couples, whereas the clients covered by chart 23 include single, widowed, and divorced applicants. Note also that the data shown were not obtained by following the same families over their family life cycle. These data differ from general population studies because families in this study have applied for help with current problems; a general population sample includes families with no serious problems. Fifty percent of respondents aged twenty-five to thirty-four in a general population study reported a marital problem. The percentage with a problem declined on both sides of this age group, dropping to as low as 19 percent for those sixty-five and over. See Gerald Gurin, Joseph Veroff, and Sheila Feld, *Americans View Their Mental Health: A Nationwide Interview Survey* (New York: Basic Books, 1960), pp. 102-104.

8. For summaries of research in this area, see Ludwig L. Geismar, Bruce Lagay, Isabel Wolock, Ursula C. Gerhart, and Harriet Fink, *Early Supports for Family Life: A Social Work Experiment* (Metuchen, N.J.: Scarecrow Press, Inc., 1972), pp. 7-15; Mary W. Hicks and Marilyn Platt, "Marital Happiness and Stability: A Review of the Research in the Sixties," *Journal of Marriage and the Family,* 32(November 1970): 564-66; Boyd C. Rollins and Harold Feldman, "Marital Satisfaction Over the Family Life Cycle," *Journal of Marriage and the Family,* 32 (February 1970): 20-28; and Wesley R. Burr, "Satisfaction with Various Aspects of Marriage Over the Life Cycle: A Random Middle Class Sample," *Journal of Marriage and the Family* 32 (February 1970): 29-37.

9. Rollins and Feldman, "Marital Satisfaction Over the Family Life Cycle," pp. 26-27.

10. The proportion of the marriages of agency clients which were interracial was only very slightly greater than in the general population (.75 versus .70 percent). See U.S. Bureau of the Census. *Subject Report Series. Vol. 2,* Series PC(2)-4C, "Marital Status" (Washington, D.C.: U.S. Government Printing Office, 1970), p. 262. Agency couples showed, in general, slightly less age difference than husbands and wives in the general population. In 45 percent of agency marriages, the husband was no more than two years older or one year younger than the wife. The corresponding figure for the general population is 42 percent. See U.S. Bureau of the Census, *Current Population Reports,* Series P-20, No. 212, "Marital Status and Family Status: March 1970" (Washington, D.C.: U.S. Government Printing Office, 1971), p. 38.

11. Marriages in which the husband was more than three years older or two years younger than the wife also averaged slightly more problems than other marriages (4.5 versus 4.0).

12. Chart 102 is limited to couples for whom information was available on both the direction of movement of the marriage during the course of agency service and in whose best interest the movement was. Because of unknowns in one or both of these areas, 57 percent of the marital cases had to be omitted.

13. The discrepancies in the proportions of husbands and wives benefiting from remaining together and in separating were statistically significant at the .01 level.

14. This is sometimes suggested as the criterion for successful marital counseling because of a combination of community concern over divorce and desertion and pressure for "hard data" outcome measures. If the outcomes in the marital cases in this study had been rated on this basis, 28 percent of the sample would have been rated against a criterion that was not considered by the closing counselor to be in the best interest of any member of the family.

15. Brenda J. S. Wattie, "The Planned Short Term Service Study at the Family Service Centre of Ottawa," paper presented in Atlantic City at U.S. National Conference on Social Welfare, May 1973, pp. 6-7.

16. Scores apply to the types of cases cited in footnote *a* of the table.

17. When the sample was not limited to couples whose most important problem was marital, the decline in improvement ratings with increased years of marriage was much less.

18. Among all cases with either a marital or a children's problem, 44 percent had both problems, 27 percent had a marital problem but not a children's problem, and 29 percent had a children's problem but no marital problem. If a marital problem was present, it was more likely to be the primary problem than was a children's problem when a children's problem was present. There was also an interesting difference between nonsectarian and sectarian agencies in the frequency with which clients reported a marital problem at intake. (Forty-three percent of applicants to nonsectarian agencies reported a marital problem as contrasted with only 22 percent of applicants to sectarian agencies. There was a similar though less pronounced contrast in the proportions presenting a parent-child problem—36 versus 26 percent.)

19. Other problems reported by at least one applicant in ten for whom a marital problem was primary included personality adjustment problem of an adolescent, personality adjustment problem of a child under thirteen, inadequate income, health problems or physical illness or handicap, and mental illness.

20. Except for the change scores for persons changing, which were higher by a very small margin for the marital group, all the component area scores were also lower for cases where the primary problem was a marital rather than a children's problem. Change scores by locus of problem for these two major groups also show interesting differences (see chart 78).

21. For separated couples for whom a marital problem was the most important problem, the average number of interviews was 5.9, as compared with 7.3 for couples with a similar focus who had not separated. Counselors' change scores for the couples who had separated averaged +4.4 and clients' change scores, +4.6, as compared with +4.6 and +4.9 respectively for those still living together. For cases in which a children's problem was primary the situation was the reverse: Cases in which the couple was married averaged 9.0 interviews and change scores of +4.8 and +5.2 from the counselors and clients respectively, while cases in which the couple was separated averaged 12.1 interviews and change scores of +5.6 and +5.5.

22. When either a marital or a children's problem was primary, male counselors averaged more interviews than did female counselors. Contrasts were particularly marked when the person seen most was the husband. When there was no marital problem, female counselors averaged more interviews than male counselors. In marital problem cases, male counselors also saw both partners in a significantly higher proportion of cases than did female counselors (75 versus 63 percent).

23. This was true not only for cases whose primary problem was marital but for married couples in general (see chart 90). A similar but not statistically significant pattern was apparent for clients' scores for the marital group.

Notes to section 11

1. For support of this assertion, see charts 1 and 5.

2. The group described here includes all cases in which the only request for service was for help for persons sixty-five and over. The contrast group requested no service for anyone sixty-five or over. Twenty-two cases in which services were requested for both groups were excluded from this analysis, as well as twenty cases in which no service was requested for a person sixty-five or over but some service was provided to someone in that age group.

3. For further data on problems at this age level, see the postretirement stage in chart 23.

4. Interviews with other family members were not included in this figure. Leonore Rivesman, "Social Work Team with Aging Family Service Clients," final report summary submitted to National Institute of Mental Health, 1971, p. 9.

Notes to Appendix

1. The only exception to the first in-person contact requirement was in the case of "groups recruited as groups." If, at the time of the census, an agency group was meeting whose members had not come in through regular intake but had originally been recruited as a group—for example, through a school, housing project, or hospital—a special sampling procedure was to be utilized. This special approach was devised so that the sample could include identified clients who did not enter service through regular intake procedures; however, it was seldom utilized.

2. The Canadian findings and comparisons with the United States have already been published in a mimeographed report, Family Service Association of America, "FSAA 1970 Census Statistics for Canada with Comparative Data for United States," Mimeographed (New York: Family Service Association of America, 1972).

3. Brief interim reports were requested on all cases that were still open at the end of one year (about 6 percent). The returns on this form were not complete enough to warrant a separate analysis of one year of service, but fifty-five of the one-year reports provided service information that was used in the analysis for cases for which no closing report was submitted. Two percent of the cases for which closing reports were received continued beyond two years of service, the cut-off point for the study. These cases were reported according to their status at the end of two years.

4. If the Canadian reports were added in, there would be about 100 additional family life education reports from one Canadian agency and 129 telephone intake cards from five Canadian agencies. See footnotes 3 and 7, section 3, for information regarding separate analyses of the family life education and telephone intake portions of the study.

5. Racial and ethnic matching was recommended where feasible.

6. While questionnaires were unsigned, each was given its own number. This device made it possible to identify who had or had not responded and to match the follow-up with the counselor's reports on the same case.

7. See pages 106 and 107 for discussion of bias in these returns.

8. This was in spite of the fact that FSAA could only reimburse the agencies for their out-of-pocket expenses for conducting interviews with a maximum of three dollars per interview appointment.

9. The requirements for computing the change score were as follows: At least one problem must be evaluated; at least one evaluation must be present in one of the other three components of the change score (problem coping, aspects of family relationships, and changes in individual family members), and at least 50 percent of the potential change items on a given case must be evaluated. In addition, cases in which no services were provided or in which the only service was to adoptive applicants were excluded from the change score analysis.

10. At the conclusion of the study, questionnaires were sent to participating agencies to elicit their experience with the client follow-up. Responses were received from 102 agencies. The remarks on local agency response to client follow-up are drawn from these questionnaires.

11. Family Service Association of America, "FSAA 1970 Census Statistics for Canada with Comparative Data for United States." Since these comparisons were restricted to metropolitan areas, about 5 percent should be added to the U.S. figures cited in this report to obtain the N's for corresponding items in the present report.

12. Dorothy Fahs Beck, *Patterns in Use of Family Agency Service* (New York: Family Service Association of America, 1962).

13. Occasional differences involving averages, such as average number of interviews and average number of family members seen, were not tested because of the excessive cost of the hand counts required for 1960 to secure the necessary standard deviations. In such instances, differences may well be significant even though this is not stated.

14. FSAA memorandum 72/5–343, May 10, 1972, from Dorothy Fahs Beck and Mary Ann Jones to Regional Vice Presidents and Regional Representatives, "Selected Characteristics of Clients by FSAA Regions as Revealed in the 1970 FSAA Census."

15. When the charts for this report were prepared, some of the reports on the 1970 U.S. census of population were not yet published.

16. Richard Light, "Measures of Response Agreement for Qualitative Data: Some Generalizations and Alternatives," *Psychological Bulletin*, 76(1971): 365–77.

17. Details regarding these scores appear in the following locations: socioeconomic status score, page 31; change score, page 101; index of client involvement in seeking help, footnote 4, section 8; disagreement index, footnote 12, section 5; merged relationship rating, page 129; and predicted score, page 120.

18. If data were available for only two of these, the sum of their scores was divided by two. If data were available for only one, the score for this item was used as the total score. Information on all three items was available in more than 90 percent of the cases.

19. These scores were later included in an unpublished Ph.D. dissertation by Paul M. Siegel, "Prestige in the American Occupational Structure," department of sociology, University of Chicago, Chicago, Illinois, 1971.

20. Instructions were provided by the U.S. Bureau of the Census. For occupational classifications, see U.S. Bureau of the Census, *Census of Population: 1970, "Alphabetical Listing of Industries and Occupations."* This document is available from the superintendent of documents, U.S. Government Printing Office, Washington, D.C. 20402. Stock #0301-2283.

21. This method is described in U.S. Bureau of the Census, *Methodology and Scores of Socioeconomic Status,* Working Paper No. 15 (Washington, D.C.: U.S. Government Printing Office, 1963). Census results utilizing this approach were published in U.S. Bureau of the Census, *U.S. Census of Population: 1960, Subject Reports, Socioeconomic Status,* Final Report PC(2)-5C (Washington, D.C.: U.S. Government Printing Office, 1967). See also Charles B. Nam and Mary G. Powers, "Changes in the Relative Status Level of Workers in the United States, 1950-60," *Social Forces,* 47(December 1968):154-57.

22. Beck, *Patterns in Use of Family Agency Service,* p. 34.

23. "Two Factor Index of Social Position" based on occupation and education developed and published by August B. Hollingshead, 1965 Yale Station, New Haven, Connecticut.

24. Jacob Cohen, "Multiple Regression as a General Data-Analytic System, *Psychological Bulletin,* 70(1968): 426-43.

25. Sanford Labovitz, "The Assignment of Numbers to Rank Order Categories," *American Sociological Review,* 35(1970):515-24.

26. Cohen, "Multiple Regression as a General Data-Analytic System," pp. 423-26.

27. The four variables were the difficulty of the problem receiving the most agency attention, the number of problems at intake, the size of the family, and the age of the family head. The first three were significantly linear for the counselors' scores but not for the clients'

190

Notes

scores, though the significance level for the linearity with the clients' scores was under .2 for three of the four. The age of the family head was linear for the clients' scores but not for the counselors', with a significance level of over .5 for the latter.

28. At the outset twelve client characteristics were entered into the regression analysis. However, the factor of whether or not the case was receiving public assistance was found to contribute nothing to the unique variance and was subsequently eliminated from the prediction process. The multiple regression procedures used are described in David J. Armor and Arthur S. Couch, *The Data-Text Primer: An Introduction of Computerized Social Data Analysis* (New York: Free Press, 1972), pp. 100-108.

29. These predicted scores were necessarily approximate only because (1) representation of each independent variable in the mathematical prediction equation was subject to a linearity constraint, and (2) the inclusion of many factors simultaneously in the prediction equation minimized the influence of any one factor on the final predicted score.

30. When used as data, these residuals—one for the counselor's score and one for the client's—can be regarded as new scores for each case stated in terms of the deviation of the actual change score on that case from its corresponding individually computed predicted score.

31. Armor and Couch, *The Data-Text Primer,* pp. 92-99, 109-19.

32. Ibid., pp. 114-19.